C Programming Quiz Book

A Compendium of over 1,100 short questions, with answers and programs

S.R. Subramanya

Exskillence

San Diego, USA

Table of Contents

Preface

The C programming language was a significant milestone in the history of programming languages. It was the first languages to be used in systems programing, such as in the implementation of (significant portions of) operating systems and other system utilities. It also supported portability of programs across different hardware platforms. In addition to systems programming, it also found way in real-world applications in diverse areas. C is a high-level language with support for several low-level (machine-level) operations (ex. bit and address access/manipulation). The basic language is rather small, in terms of operations and features supported (compared to numerous high-level languages). Support for numerous features and operations are provided by a set of library functions. C is the most used language in embedded applications. C has had tremendous influence on several languages such as C++, Java, C#, etc.

For person who is currently taking, or has already taken a course on C programming , there are no comprehensive resources to facilitate a quick assessment/testing of the understanding of the features/facilities of C, and for analyzing and writing C code. This book aims to fill that need. It is intended to be a quick assessment book / quiz book. It has a vast collection of over 1,100 questions, together with answers and programs.

This is a quick assessment book / quiz book. It covers questions on all the major topics of C programming. The topical coverage includes data types, operators, expressions, control structures, pointers, arrays, structures, unions, enumerated types, functions, dynamic storage management, and Inout/Output and library functions.

Unique features of this book.

- Over 1,100 short questions, with answers and programs.
- Question types consist of (a) True/False (b) sentence completion, (c) program (segment) analysis, and (c) developing programs.
- Questions have a wide range of difficulty levels.
- Questions are designed to test a thorough understanding of various aspects of C.
- Questions and programs can help in internship / job interview preparation.

Who could benefit from this book?

- Students who are currently taking a course on C Programming.
- Students who have already completed a course on C Programming, and are preparing to take written exams and/or interviews for industry/companies.
- Professionals trying to make a switch to Computing/IT industry could use it as a source of self–assessment in C.
- Hiring managers, for making a quick assessment of candidates' C language proficiency.

Notes

Basic Arithmetic Operators: +, -, *, /, %

Assignment Operators: =, +=, -=, *=, /=, %=

Auto-increment and Auto-decrement Operators: ++, --

Logical Operators: &&, ||, !

Comparison (relational) operators: ==, !=, >, <, >=, <=

Bitwise Operators: &, |, ^, ~, <<, >>

Ternary Operator(s): ? :

Questions

A. Data Types, Operators, Expressions

True/False Questions

A1   Software maintenance is the most expansive component of the entire software cycle. _____

A2   Inline functions do not do type checking of parameters. _____

A3   Inline functions have the same performance as normal functions. _____

A4   The sizes of the generated binary files (generated by the compiler) increase with the use of Inline functions. _____

A5   The compilation time of a source file decreases with the use of Inline functions. _____

A6   Inline functions cannot return values. _____

A7   Macros can return values. _____

A8   **typedef** can only be used with user-defined types, but not built-in types. _____

A9   A variable declared in the main() function is visible (accessible) anywhere in the program. _____

A10   A global variable and a local variable cannot have the same name. _____

A11   A variable with block scope declared with the keyword **static** is allocated in the same area of memory as a global variable. _____

A12   A 'static' variable is never visible in more than one file. ____

A13   The rules for the linkage of identifiers are not applicable to function names. _____

A14   A variable declared with the 'static' keyword is unique within its source file, and is invisible in other source files. _____

A15   No storage is allocated to an identifier declared with the keyword **extern**. _____

A16   All variables are not automatically initialized to a default values when declared. _____.

A17   C provides garbage collection (implicit/ automatic reclamation of unreferenced storage). _____

A18   C is dynamically typed. _____

A19   All the letters in a C keyword is in lowercase. _____

A20   C keywords may be used as variable names. _____

A21 $amount is a valid identifier. _____

A22 $576 is a valid identifier. _____

A23   **_amt** is a valid identifier. _____

A24   _273 is a valid identifier. _____

A25   **current_sum** is a valid identifier. _____

A26 $6,379 is a valid identifier. _____

A27   **74Points** is a valid identifier. _____

A28   **total-count** is a valid identifier. _____

A29   Floating point arithmetic does not cause overflow. _____

A30   Integer computations do not cause rounding errors. _____

A31   Arithmetic overflow causes a run-time error. _____

A32   Local variables must be initialized before their values are used in an expression. _____

A33   C requires all variables to have a type declared before they can be used in a program. _____

A34   In C, string is a primitive type. _____

A35   A 'double' to 'float' promotion of primitive type is allowed to occur. _____

A36   The operands of an operator are always evaluated from left to right. _____

A37   C allows overloading of operators. _____

A38   Recursion is often more efficient than iteration. _____

A39   C has different variations of integer datatype. _____

A40   An array may contain only primitive types. _____

A41   The sub-expressions are evaluated from left to right. _____

A42   Array index range checks are not done in C. _____

A43   C does not have a preprocessor. _____

A44   The **#include** files cannot be nested. _____

A45   Macros are processed by the compiler. _____

A46   A macro can take variable number of arguments. _____

A47   The Preprocessor has knowledge of C's syntax. _____

A48   The **#define** directive must appear at the beginning of a program. _____

A49   The **#define** directive cannot have arithmetic expressions. _____

A50   No storage is allocated for **MAX_SIZE** using **#define MAX_SIZE 25**. _____

A51   Variables defined using **#define** do not have the scope rules. _____

A52   Local variables are initialized with default values when they are declared. _____

A53   Use of an uninitialized variable in statement gives compilation error. _____

A54   C does not require declaration of variables before use. _____

A55   Variables declarations can be anywhere a statement can be. _____

A56   A variable in a nested block cannot have the same name as a variable in the enclosing block. _____

A57   C does not support multiple-selection statement. _____
[The switch-case supports multiple selection]

A58   Arrays are not initialized at the time of allocation. _____

A59   C does not have the **goto** control structure. _____

A60   In C, the control expression must be Boolean. _____

A61   C has built-in support for exception handling. _____

A62   An expression cannot be an argument to a function. _____

A63   The **++** and **--** operators can be applied to a 'char' variable. _____

A64   The ++ and -- operators are binary operators. _____

A65   The '%' operator is not valid on floating point numbers. _____

A66   Relational operators are (generally) used for primitive types. _____

A67   There is no value of x for which the expression **(x < 10) && (x > 10)** would be true. _____

A68   There is no value of x for which the expression **(x < 10) || (x > 10)** would be false. _____

A69   The value of the expression **(x <= y ^ x >= y)** would always be true. _____

A70   The value of the expression $(x < y \; ^\wedge \; x > y)$ would always be true. _____

A71   The value of the expression $((x\%y \; == \; 0) \; ^\wedge \; (y\%x \; == \; 0))$ would always be true. _____

A72   For integers x and y, the value of the expression $(x/y \; == \; 0 \; ^\wedge \; y/x \; == \; 0)$ would always be true. _____

A73   For integers x and y, the value of the expression $(x/y \; == \; 1 \; ^\wedge \; y/x \; == \; 1)$ could never be false. _____

A74   For integers x and y, the value of the expression $(x/y \; == \; 0 \; ^\wedge \; x/y \; != \; 0)$ is always true. _____

A75   The value of $(x < y \; || \; x > y)$ is always true. _____

A76   The value of $(x <= y \; \&\& \; x >= y)$ is always true. _____
A77   The value of $(x < y \; \&\& \; x > y)$ is always false. _____

A78   The value of $(x \; == \; y \; || \; x \; != \; y)$ is always true. _____

A79   The value of $(x \; == \; y \; \&\& \; x \; != \; y)$ is always false. _____

A80   The value of $(x \; == \; y \; ^\wedge \; x \; != \; y)$ is always true. _____

A81   The value of $(x \; \% \; y \; == \; y \; \% \; x)$ is always false. _____

A82   For integer values of x and y, the expression $(x/y \; == \; y/x)$ would never be true. _____

A83   In C, arithmetic overflow does not result in run-time error. _____

A84   When x ≠ y, it is never the case that $x \; ^\wedge \; y$ is 0. _____

A85   When x < y, it is always the case that $x \; / \; y$ is 0. _____

A86   When x < y and x ≠ 0, it is never the case that $x \; \% \; y$ is 0. _____

A87   For integer values of x and y, when x ≥ y, it is always the case that $x \; / \; y$ is not 0. _____

A88 When x ≠ y, it is never the case that **x % y** and **x / y** are equal. _____

A89 **(x != y)** is equivalent to **!(x == y)**. _____

A90 **!(x < y)** is equivalent to **(x >= y)**. _____

A91 **(x > y || x < y)** is equivalent to **(x == y)**. _____

A92 The value of the expression **(x < y ^ x > y)** would always be true. _____

A93 Integer arithmetic is always gives the correct result. _____

A94 All integer values in the range supported are accurately represented. _____

A95 Floating point arithmetic is always accurate. _____

A96 The output of dividing a nonzero floating-point number by zero causes an error. _____

The output of dividing a nonzero floating-point number by zero is **inf** or **-inf**.

A97 Variables declared with **const** keyword must be initialized during declaration. _____

A98 Variables declared with **const** keyword can be assigned a value after declaration. _____

A99 A variable declared with **const** keyword has no associated storage cell. _____

A100 No storage is allocated for the declaration **extern int i**. _____

A101 The values of global variables are implicitly initialized when declared. _____

A102 The values of local variables are implicitly initialized when declared. _____

A103　All local variables are not initialized when declared. _____

A104　Literals are treated as constants. _____

A105　A variable of type bool takes 1-bit of storage. _____

A106　The '−' (subtraction) operator is right associative. _____

A107　The '=' (assignment) operator is right associative. _____

A108　In C, files containing one or more subprograms can be independently compiled. _____

A109　The '*' operator in C has operation(s) other than multiplication. _____

A110　C allows variable declarations to be anywhere a statement can be. _____

A111　C supports **union** type. _____

A112　C does not support enumeration types. _____

A113　C does not support default parameters. _____

A114　Local variables in the functions, by default, are stack-dynamic. _____

A115　A local variable (auto or static) inside a block cannot have the same name as an 'extern' variable. _____

A116　Two variables with the same name cannot be declared within the same block. _____

A117　C language does not support concurrency. _____

A118　C supports implicit type conversions (coercions). _____

A119　C does not support explicit type conversions (casts). _____

A120　C uses short circuit evaluation of Boolean expressions. _____

A121　In C, control expressions can be arithmetic. _____

A122   C does not allow mixed-mode expressions. _____

A123   C performs type checks at compile time. _____

A124   C supports nested subprogram definitions. _____

A125   C has exponentiation operator. _____

A126   Initialization of global variables is done at compile time. _____

A127   Initialization of variables declared with 'static' keyword is done at runtime. _____

A128   Initialization of global and static variables are done before the **main()** starts execution. _____

A129   A heap–dynamic variable must be explicitly deallocated. _____

A130   Multiple variables of the same name but with different scopes can be used in the same program. _____

A131   A variable can be defined anywhere in the program where a statement can appear. _____

A132   No arithmetic operation at all can be done on a pointer type.
_____

A133   A character string variable can be assigned a string literal at any time using the '=' assignment operator. _____

A134   The **sizeof** operator can only be used on types, but not on actual variables. _____

A135   The bit shift operators (**<<, >>**) cannot be used on floating point variables. _____

A136   The bitwise operators (**|, &, ^**) can be used on integer variables.
_____

A137   The is no logical XOR operator. _____

A138   A variable declared with **static** keyword is visible across files.
_____

A139　An **extern** variable with the same name may be declared in multiple files. _____

A140　An **extern** variable must be defined in only one file. ____

IOIOIOIOIOIOIOIOIOIOIOIOIOIOIOIOIOIOIOIOIOIOIOIOIOIOIOIOI

Fill-in the-blanks Questions

A1　The high-level language code / program written by the programmer is known as _____ code.

A2　The code / program executed by the computer is known as _____ code.

A3　The software which translates high-level language program into machine language program is known as _____

A4　The software which manages various resources and activities in a computer is known as the _____

A5　A(n) _____ provides facilities such as editing, compiling, running, and debugging during program development.

A6　Program that processes the source code before compilation is known as _____

A7　Macros are processed by _____

A8　Inline functions are processed by _____

A9　The Black Box test is also known as _____

A10　In _____ testing, program unit is treated as a 'black box' whose Inner workings are not visible.

A11　The White Box test is also known as _____

A12　In _____ testing, the internal structure of program unit is transparent, and specific parts can be tested.

A13   A program which does not compile is said to have _____ error(s).

A14   A program which compiles without error(s) but terminates abnormally when run is said to have _____ error.

A15   A program which compiles without error(s) but produces incorrect result(s) is said to have _____ error.

A16   A variable declared outside of any function (including main()) is known as _____ variable.

A17   A variable visible (accessible) anywhere in the program is known as _____ variable.

A18   The section of a program where a (variable) name is visible of known as its _____

A19   All C programs must have a function named _____ where the execution starts.

A20   Although _____ is a valid type, no variable can be declared of that type.

A21   An expression containing operands of different data types is known as a _____ expression.

A22   Implicit type conversion which is automatically done by the compiler is known as _____

A23   Explicit type conversions done by the programmer is known as _____

A24   The two ways of representing a string (sequence of characters) are as _____ and as _____

A25   A block is enclosed between _____

A26   The two broad categories of data types of C are _____ and _____

A27   Data types such as int, char, long, double etc. are known as _____ or _____ types.

A28   Data types such as arrays, structures, and unions are known as
       _____ types.

A29   An identifier declared with the keyword _____ refers to an
       entity declared in another file.

A30   A variable declared with the _____ keyword cannot be
       modified.

A31   A variable with block scope declared with no keyword is allocated
       in the _____ area of memory.

A32   A variable with block scope declared with the keyword **static**
       is allocated in the _____ area of memory.

A33   A global variable (declared outside of any function) is allocated in
       the _____ area of memory.

A34   Variables which are allocated once, and stay in the same memory
       location for the duration of a program's execution are known as
       _____ variables.

A35   A(n) _____ variable can have multiple declarations, but only
       one definition.

A36   A sequence of characters contained between quotes (") is known
       as a _____

A37   The datatype of the result of adding an int, a byte, a long, and a
       double, is _____

A38   The contents of the location pointed to by a pointer is accessed
       using the _____ operator.

A39   The ternary (or conditional operator) is _____

A40   The datatype size operator is _____

A41   The keyword required to declare a constant of a primitive type (ex.
       int, double, etc.) is _____

A42   Given **#define SQR(x) x*x**, a = 3, and b = 5, the value
       of **SQR(a+b)** is ____

A43   Given **#define SQR(x) (x)*(x)**, **a = 3**, and **b = 5**, the value of **SQR(a+b)** is _____

A44   Given **#define MOD(x, y) (x % y)**, **a = 19**, and **b = 5**, the value of **MOD(a+b, b)** is _____

A45   Given **#define MOD(x, y) ((x) % (y))**, **a = 19**, and **b = 5**, the value of **MOD(a+b, b)** is _____

Given the declarations **int i, long int l, float f, double d**, (and assuming suitable initializations) what are the types of the following expressions?

A46   **i + 2** is _____

A47   **2.56 - i** is _____

A48   **i / l** is _____

A49   **l + f** is _____

A50   **i/l + f** is _____

A51   **f/2** is _____

A52   **f - d** is _____

A53   **i/(l + d)** is _____

A54   **l + f** is _____

A55   **l * d** is _____

A56   **l/(i*3.7)** is _____

A57   **f/l - d** is _____

A58   What are the values of the following expressions?

        int a = 2, b = 3, c = 5;

        a > b || c > b   _____

```
b < a + 2 && c <= a + b        _____

(b > c - a) || (a < c / b + 1)_____

b == b % c || a + b > c        _____

(b <= c) && (b + c % a == 0)_____
```

A59   The value of 3 / 4 is _____

A60   The value of (double) (3 / 4) is _____

A61   The value of (double) 3 / 4 is _____

A62   The value of 3 / (double) 4 is _____

A63   The value of 3.0 / 4 is _____

A64   The value of 3 / 4.0 is _____

A65   The value of 19 / 5 is _____

A66   The value of 19 / 5.0 is _____

A67   The value of (double)19 / 5 is _____

A68   The value of 5 % 1 is _____

A69   The value of 17 % 3 is _____

A70   The value of 3 % 17 is _____

A71   For **x** % **n** to be 0 for all values of **x**, the value of **n**, should be
       _____

A72   The value of (int)(12.345 * 100) / 100.0 is _____

A73   The value of (int)(12.345 * 100 / 100) is _____

A74   The output of dividing a nonzero floating-point number by zero is
       _____ or _____

A75   The output of dividing zero by zero is _____

A76   The value of x for which the expression **(x <= 10) && (x >= 10)** would be true, is _____

A77   The value of x for which the expression **(x < 10) || (x > 10)** would be false, is _____

A78   Given x = 5, the value of **(x << 5)** would be _____

A79   Given x = 84, the value of **(x >> 3)** would be _____

A80   The value of **(x == y && x != y)** is always _____

A81   The value of **(x == y || x != y)** is always _____

A82   When x ≠ y, the value of the expression **(x <= y && x >= y)** would always be _____

A83   The value of **(x <= y || x >= y)** is always _____

A84   The value of **(x == y || x != y)** is always _____

A85   The value of **(x == y ^ x != y)** is always _____

A86   When x ≠ y, the value of the expression **(x < y ^ x > y)** would always be _____

A87   The value of **(x == y && x != y)** is always _____

A88   The value of **(x <= y && x >= y)** is true only under the condition _____

A89   The value of **(x < y ^ x > y)** is false only under the condition _____

A90   The value of **(x >= 0) || (x < 0)** is always _____

A91   The value of **(x < y && x > y)** is always _____

A92   The value of **(x == y ^ x != y)** is always _____

A93   For integers x and y, the expression **(x/y == y/x)** would be true only under the condition _____

A94 The value of **(x > 0) || (x < 0)** is always false except when x is _____

A95 The value of **(x > 0) && (x < 0)** is always _____

A96 The value of **! (x > 0) && (x > 0)** is always _____

A97 The value of **(x != 0) || (x == 0)** is always _____

A98 The expression to check if the value of **age** is at least 18 is _____

A99 The expression to check if the value of **age** is between 18 and 65 (inclusive) is _____

A100 The expression to check if the value of **x** is at least 3 and at most 10 is _____

A101 The expression to ckeck if **x** is evenly divisible by 3 and 7 is _____

A102 The expression to check if the value of **count** is not in the range 25 to 35 (inclusive) is _____

A103 Given **x = 3**, the value of **~x** is ____

A104 Given **x = 0**, the value of **~x** is ____

A105 The value of **x | x** for any integer **x** is ____

A106 The value of **x & x** for any integer **x** is ____

A107 The value of **x ^ x** for any integer **x** is ____

A108 The value of **x | ~x** for any integer **x** is ____

A109 The value of **x & ~x** for any integer **x** is ____

A110 The value of **x ^ ~x** for any integer **x** is ____

A111 The value of **x | -1** for any integer **x** is ____

A112 The value of **x & -1** for any integer **x** is ____

A113   The value of **x ^ -1** for any integer **x** is _____

A114   The value of **x | 0** for any integer **x** is _____

A115   The value of **x & 0** for any integer **x** is _____

A116   The value of **x ^ 0** for any integer **x** is _____

A117   Given x = 3 and y = 5, the value of **(x = y)** is _____

A118   Given x = 3 and y = 5, the value of **(x = y == y)** is _____

A119   Given x = 3 and y = 5, the value of **(x = y == x)** is _____

A120   Given x = 7 and y = 5, the value of **x-- - --y** is _____

A121   Given x = 7 and y = 5, the value of **--x - --y** is _____

A122   Given x = 7 and y = 5, the value of **++x + ++y** is _____

A123   Given x = 7 and y = 5, the value of **x++ + y++** is _____

A124   Given x = 3 and y = 7, the value of y after evaluating the expression **(x >= 3)   &&   (y-- > 5)**, is _____

A125   Given x = 3 and y = 7, the value of y after evaluating the expression **(x > 3)   &&   (y-- > 5)**, is _____

A126   Given x = 5 and y = 9, the value of y after evaluating the expression **(x > 5) || (y++ >= 12)**, is _____

A127   Given x = 5 and y = 9, the value of y after evaluating the expression **(x >= 5) || (y++ >= 12)**, is _____

A128   Given x = 5 and y = 9, the value of y after evaluating the expression **(x >= 5) | (y++ >= 12)**, is _____

A129   Given x = 3 and y = 7, the value of the expression **(x >= 3)   &&   (y-- <= 6)**, is _____

A130   Given x = 3 and y = 7, the value of the expression **(x >= 3)   &&   (y-- == 6)**, is _____

A131   Given x = 3 and y = 7, the value of the expression **(x >= 3) && (y-- >= 7)**, is _____

A132   Given x = 3 and y = 7, the value of the expression **(x >= 3) && (y-- == 7)**, is _____

A133   Given x = 3 and y = 7, the value of the expression **(x >= 3) && (--y <= 6)**, is _____

A134   Given x = 3 and y = 7, the value of the expression **(x++ == 3) && (y-- == 7)**, is _____

A135   Given x = 3 and y = 7, the value of the expression **(++x >= 4) && (--y == 6)**, is _____

A136   Given x = 3 and y = 7, the value of the expression **(x++ > 3) && (y-- == 7)**, is _____

A137   Given x = 5 and y = 9, the value of the expression **(x > 5) || (y++ > 9)**, is _____

A138   Given x = 5 and y = 9, the value of the expression **(x > 5) || (++y > 9)**, is _____

A139   Given x = 3 and y = 7, the value of the expression **(x > 3) && (--y <= 6)**, is _____

A140   Given **j** is 0, the value of **j++ + j * 5** is ____

A141   Given **j** is 0, the value of **++j + j * 5** is ____

A142   Given **x** is 1, the value of **x++ + x** is ____

A143   Given **x** is 1, the value of **++x + x** is ____

A144   For any values of **a** and **b**, after executing the statements **a = b + a; b = a - b; a = a - b;**, the value of **a** would be ____ and the value of **b** would be ____

A145   The size in bytes of the data type long is **8**, short is **2**, byte is **1**, and int is _____

A146 The declaration of a constant named PI with value 3.14159265358979, is _____

A147 Unary arithmetic operators are _____

A148 Unary logical operator is ____

A149 Unary bitwise operator is ____

A150 The operators which are both unary and binary (although with different semantics) are ___, ___, ___, ____

A151 To assign to x the larger of the values of x and y, in one statement, is _____

A152 The possible range of values returned by **rand() % 10** is between _____ and _____

A153 The short-circuit operators are _____ and _____

A154 The difference between the computed value in a program and the exact mathematical value is known as _____ error.

A155 The number of bytes required to store **'x'** is _____

A156 The number of bytes required to store **"x"** is _____

A157 The output of **putchar(55)** is _____

A158 The output of **putchar('5')** is _____

A159 The output of **putchar('5' + 12)** is _____

A160 The output of **printf("%d",'A')** is _____

A161 The output of **printf("%d",'Z'-'A'+1)** is _____

A162 The output of **putchar('A'+7)** is _____

A163 The output of **putchar('1' + 16)** is _____

A164 Given **string s = "NOT", t = "ABLE"**, the value of **s+t** is _____

A165   Given **string s = "able"**, the value of **'t'+s+'s'** is
_____

A166   Given a sring **s1** to be **"Program"**, the value of **s1.length()** is ____

A167   Given a sring s1 to be **"Inhabit"**, the value of **s1.substr(0)** is _____

A168   Given a sring s1 to be **"Inhabit"**, the value of **s1.substr(2)** is _____

A169   Given a sring s1 to be "Transportation", the statement using **substr** which returns "sport" is _____

A170   The output of **printf("%.2f", 1234.567)** is _____

A171   The output of **printf("%.4e", 1234.56)** is _____

A172   The output of **printf("%3d", 123456)** is _____

A173   The allocation of memory to variables at runtime is known as _____ allocation.

A174   The unary '*' operator in C is used for the _____ operation.

A175   The relational operator ____ is equivalent to logical XOR operation (in the absence of logical XOR operator).

A176   Multiple names bound to the same entity at the same time is known as _____

A177   The value of **sizeof("A")** is ____

A178   The value of **sizeof('Z')** is ____

A179   The value of **sizeof('\0')** is ____

A180   The value of **sizeof(char)** is ____

A181   The value of **sizeof("")** is ____

A182   The value of **sizeof("\0\0\0\0")** is ____

IOIOIOIOIOIOIOIOIOIOIOIOIOIOIOIOIOIOIOIOIOIOIOIOIOIOIOIOIOIOIOI

Essay-type Questions

A1   Give examples of common syntax errors in C.

A2   Give examples of common run-time errors in C.

A3   Give examples of logical errors in C.

A4   What are the four areas of memory of a typical C program and data, and what do they contain?

A5   Give examples of two operators that are not associative.

A6   What is the difference between coercion and cast?

A7   What is short-circuit evaluation?

A8   Write a macro **DIV_10(x)** which tests if an integer argument is evenly divisible by 10. It should be usable in an 'if' statement, as in **if (DIV_10(a))**.

Give declarations for variable of the following types.

A9   **i**   integer
A10 **pf**   pointer to float
A11 **darr**   array of 10 double precision numbers
A12 **names**   array of 5 pointers to char
A13 **ip**   pointer to an array of 5 pointers to int
A14 **pfn1**   pointer to a function returning double
A15 **pfn2**   pointer to a function returning pointer to int
A16 **apfn3**   array of pointers to functions returning float
A17 **pfn1** Function taking a pointer to char as argument, and returning a pointer to an array of floats
A18 **pfn2** Pointer to a function taking a pointer to char as argument, and returning a pointer to an array of ints
A19 **apfn4**   pointer to an array of 2 functions returning float

A20 **ap**   array of 5 integer pointers
A21 **pai**   pointer to an array of 5 integers
A22 **pap**   pointer to array of 5 integer pointers
A23 **fp**   pointer to a function returning a pointer to array of 3 floats
A24 **fpp**   pointer to a function which takes an argument of type 'int', and returns a pointer to a function which takes an argument of type 'double', returning an int

Determine the data types for the following variables.
A25 `int i`
A26 `int *j`
A27 `float g`
A28 `char * t[10]`
A29 `double s[4][7]`
A30 `int (*h)()`

Determine the data types for the following variables.

A31 `int a[5];`
A32 `int *b[5];`
A33 `int (*c)[5];`
A34 `int* (*d)[5];`
A35 `int * (*(*e)[5]);`
A36 `int * (*(f[5]));`

Determine the data types for the following variables.

A37 `int (*fp)(char*)`
A38 `int(*fparr[5])();`
A39 `double (*fp)(double*)`
A40 `double* (*fp)(double*)`
A41 `float* * fp2(int, float)`
A42 `double * f(double)`
A43 `int **fun(float*, char**)`
A44 `int (*fun[3])(char*, int)`
A45 `float* (*fun)(int, float)[]`

A46 `char* pri_colors[] = {"Red", "Green", "Blue"};`

A47 Write a statement using **printf** to print the following:
`String literal is delimited by " character`

A48 Write a statement using `printf` to print the following:
```
'\n' is the newline character
```

A49 Write a statement using `printf` to print the following:
```
The "\" character serves as an escape character
```

A50 What is happening in the following assignment statement (assuming compatible datatypes)?

```
int a = fn(x);
```

A51 What is happening in the following assignment statement (assuming compatible datatypes)?

```
int a = (*pfn)(x, y);
```

A52 What is happening in the following assignment statement (assuming compatible datatypes)?

```
int a = (*apfn[i])(x, y);
```

A50 What is the output of the following code segment?

```
const int i=10;
i=12;
printf("%d\n", i);
```

A53 What are the values of **a** and **n** after the execution of the following statements?
```
a = 2; n = a++; a = n++; n = a++;
```

A54 What are the values of **a** and **n** after the execution of the following statements?
```
a = 2; n = a++; a = ++n; n = a++;
```

A55 What are the values of **a** and **n** after the execution of the following statements?
```
a = 2; n = ++a; a = n++; n = ++a;
```

A56 What are the values of **a** and **n** after the execution of the following statements?
```
a = 2; n = ++a; a = ++n; n = ++a;
```

A57 What is the output of the following code segment?

```
int n = 08;
printf("n = %d", n);
```

A58 What is the output of the following code segment?

```
int n = 027;
printf("n = %d", n);
```

A59 What is the output of the following code segment?
```
int n = 1000 * 1000 * 2000;
printf("n = %d", n);
```

A60 What is the output of the following code segment?
```
int n = 1000 * 1000 * 3000;
printf("n = %d", n);
```

A61 What is the output of the following program?
```
int main( void )
{
  int a = 1;
  int b = 2;
  {
    int b = 3;
    printf ("a = %d b = %d\n", a, b);
  }
  printf ("a = %d b = %d\n", a, b);
}
```

A62 What is the output of the following program?
```
int main()
{
  int i = 3;
  printf ("block0: i = %d\n", i);
  {
    int i = 5;
    printf ("block0: i = %d\n", i);
    {
      int i = 7;
      printf ("block0: i = %d\n", i);
    }
  }
}
```

A63   Write the statements to assign to variables **min2** and **max2** the minimum and maximum of two numbers in variables **n1** and **n2**, using the ternary operator.

A64   Write the statements to assign to variables **min3** and **max3** the minimum and maximum of three numbers in variables **n1**, **n2**, and **n3**, using the ternary operator.

A65   What is the output of the following code segment?

```
int i=5, j;
j = i++;
printf ("j=%d\n", j);
j = ++i;
printf ("j=%d\n", j);
j = i--;
printf ("j=%d\n", j);
j = --i;
printf ("j=%d\n", j);
```

A66   What is the output of the following code?

```
int main() {
  int i;
  for (i = 1; i <= 3; i++) {
    int a = 1;
    static int b = 1;
    printf("a = %d, b = %d\n", a, b);
    a++;
    b++;
  }
  return (0);
}
```

A67   Given **x** is an 'int' variable, and assuming that 'int' takes 4 bytes, what is the value of N such that **x >> N;** results in 0, for any value of **x**?

IOIOIOIOIOIOIOIOIOIOIOIOIOIOIOIOIOIOIOIOIOIOIOIOIOIOIOIOIOI

B. Control Structures

True/False Questions

B1   The **for** loop is more powerful (in terms of controlling the flow of statement executions) than a **while** loop. _____

B2   Any **for** loop can be rewritten as a **while** loop. _____

B3   The **for**, **while**, and **do-while** loops do not have equivalent expressive power. _____

B4   Any of the **for**, **while**, and **do-while** loops can be transformed to the other having the same effect. _____

B5   The **do-while** loop always executes at least once. _____

B6   The **while** loop always executes at least once. _____

B7   The **for** loop always executes at least once. _____

B8   The index variable of a **for** loop cannot be of type double. _____

B9   **for (;   ;);** is equivalent to **for (; true;);** _____

B10   The **for** statement in C can be rewritten as an equivalent **while** loop. _____

B11   The **for**, **while**, and **do-while** loops do not have equivalent expressive power. _____

B12   Any of the **for**, **while**, and **do-while** loops can be transformed to the other having the same effect. _____

B13   The **do-while** loop always executes at least once. _____

B14   The **while** loop always executes at least once. _____

B15   The **for** loop always executes at least once. _____

B16   The **switch** statement cannot be rewritten by using multiple **if-else** statements. _____

B17   The **break** statement inside an inner loop of a nested loop will pass control out of the all the nested loops to the statement outside of the outermost loop. _____

B18   The **break** statement inside a loop of a nested loop will pass control out of the entire loop. _____

B19   Assignment statements always produce side effects. _____

B20   All the three expressions of the **for** statement must be present. _____

B21   The **exp1** in **for (exp1; exp2; exp3)** can be executed more than once. _____

B22   The **exp1** in **for (exp1; exp2; exp3)** cannot consist of multiple statements. _____

B23   The **exp3** in **for (exp1; exp2; exp3)** can consist of multiple statements. _____

B24   Given the loop: **for (exp1; exp2; exp3) {BODY} exp2** and **exp3** are executed exactly the same number of times. _____

B25   Given the loop: **for (exp1; exp2; exp3) {BODY} exp3** is executed before the 'body' of the loop is executed. _____

B26   The **continue** control statement transfers control to the the outermost loop. _____

B27   The **continue** control statement transfers control to the start of the loop, ignoring further statements after the **continue**. _____

B28   Nesting of **switch** statements ('switch' statement(s) inside another 'switch") are not allowed. _____

B29   The **default** must be at the end of the **switch** statement, after all the **case** statements. _____

B30 The expression associate with the **case** in **switch-case** statement cannot be a variable expression. _____

B31 The '**case**'s cannot be combined and share the same code block. _____

IOIOIOIOIOIOIOIOIOIOIOIOIOIOIOIOIOIOIOIOIOIOIOIOIOIOIOIOI

Fill-in the-blanks Questions

B1 Statement that is used to modify the order of execution is known as _____ statement.

B2 A control statement together with its associated block of statements is known as _____

B3 A loop whose number of iterations is determined by the numeric value of a variable is known as _____ loop.

B4 A loop whose number of iterations is determined by the Boolean condition of an expression is known as _____ loop.

B5 In a _____ loop control structure, the loop body is executed at least once.

B6 It is more natural to use the _____ loop when the number of iterations is known *a priori* (before hand).

B7 The statement block in a _____ control structure is executed at least once.

B8 The _____ construct allows the selection of one of a number of statements or statement groups.

B9 _____ causes a (compound) statement to be executed zero or more times.

B10 The _____ control statement transfers control out of the smallest enclosing loop.

B11 The _____ control statement transfers control to the top of the loop.

B12 An optional **else** clause in an **if–then** [**–else**] statement resulting in nested conditionals being ambiguous is known as _____ problem.

B13 The first statement to be executed in **while (cond_exp) {stmt1; ... stmt17;}** is _____

B14 The last statement to be executed in **while (cond_exp) {stmt1; ... stmt17;}** is _____

B15 The first statement to be executed in **do {stmt1; ... stmt17;} while (cond_exp);** is _____

B16 The last statement to be executed in **do {stmt1; ... stmt17;} while (cond_exp);** is _____

B17 The effect of the statement: **for (; ;);** is _____

B18 The numbet of times the **STATEMENT BLOCK** is executed in the following loop is _____

```
for (int i=23; i <= 47; i++)
{
    STATEMENT BLOCK
}
```

B19 The numbet of times the **STATEMENT BLOCK** is executed in the following loop is _____

```
for (int i=51; i > 36; i--)
{
    STATEMENT BLOCK
}
```

B20 The numbet of times the **STATEMENT BLOCK** is executed in the following loop is _____

```
for (int i=1; i <= 25; i++);
{
    STATEMENT BLOCK
```

}

B21 Given the loop: **for (exp1; exp2; exp3) {BODY}** is itrerated 20 times, the number of times **exp1** is evaluated is _____

B22 Given the loop: **for (exp1; exp2; exp3) {BODY}** is itrerated 20 times, the expression to be evaluated last is _____

B23 Given the loop: **for (exp1; exp2; exp3) {BODY}** is itrerated multiple times, the order of execution of the different components of the loop, after the first iteration is _____, _____, and _____

B24 Given the loop: **for (exp1; exp2; exp3) {BODY}** is itrerated multiple times, the components of the loop which are executed exactly the same number of times are _____ and _____

IOIOIOIOIOIOIOIOIOIOIOIOIOIOIOIOIOIOIOIOIOIOIOIOIOIOIOIOIOI

Essay-type Questions

B1 The following loop was intended to compute $1/2 + 2/3 + 3/4 + ... + 99/100$. What is the error and what is a fix?

```
double sum = 0;
for (int i = 1; i <= 99; i++) {
  sum += i / (i + 1);
}
```

B2 Do the following loops result in the same value of sum?

```
for (int i = 1; i <= 10; ++i) {
  sum += i;
}

for (int i = 1; i <= 10; i++) {
  sum += i;
}
```

Here, ++i and i++ are used standalone with no side-effect. So, they are equivalent.

B3   What is the flaw with the 'while' condition in the following code segment? How could it be fixed?

```
double sum = 0;
double n = 0;
while (n != 10.0) {
   n += 0.1;
   sum += n;
}
```

B4   The following code which was intended to print 1, 2, ... 10 has a flaw. What does it print? What is the correction required?

```
int i;
for (i = 1; i <= 10; i++);
    printf("%d ", i);
```

B5   How many times does the **while** loop execute in the following code segment?

```
int x = 0;
while (x < 5)
   x++;
```

B6   How many times does the **while** loop execute in the following code segment?

```
int x = 10;
while (x < 5)
   x++;
```

B7   How many times does the **while** loop execute, and what will be the value of **sum** after the loop has finished?

```
double n = 0, sum = 0;
while (n <= 1.0) {
   n += 0.1;
   sum += n;
}
```

B8   Does the following code segment result in an infinite loop?

```
int x = 0;
while (x >= 0)
```

```
x++;
```

B9   What is the output of the following code segment?

```
int i=0, x = 0;
while (x >= 0){
  x++;
  i++;
}
printf("i=%d x=%d\n", (i-1), x);
```

B10   What is the output of the following code segment? Rewrite the following code segment using a **for** loop with the same effect.

```
int x = 0;
while (x < 5) {
  x++;
  printf("%d ", x);
}
```

B11   Convert the following 'for' loop to 'while' loop.

```
for (int i=low; i <= high; i++){
  /* STATEMENT BLOCK */
}
```

B12   Convert the following 'while' loop to 'do-while' loop, assuming low ≤ high.

```
int i=low;
while (i <= high){
  /* STATEMENT BLOCK */
  i++;
}
```

B13   What is the output of the following code segment?

```
double sum = 0;
while (sum != 10)
  sum += 0.1;
printf("%d\n", sum);
```

B14   What is the output of the following code segment?

```
double sum = 0;
while (sum < 10)
```

```
    sum += 0.1;
    printf ("%d\n", sum);
```

B15   What is the output of the following code segment?

```
int i, j;
for (i=1, j=5; i<=5; ++i, --j)
  printf ("i= %d j= %d\n", i, j);
```

B16   What is the output of the following code segment?

```
int i, j;
for (i=1, j=5; i<=j; ++i, --j)
  printf ("i= %d j= %d\n", i, j);
```

B17   What is the output of the following code segment?

```
double sum = 0, incr = 0.01;
for (int i=1; i<=100; i++)
  sum += incr;
printf ("%.18f", sum);
```

B18   What is the output of the following code segment?

```
double sum = 0, incr = 0;
for (int i=1; i<=100; i++){
  incr += 0.01;
  sum += incr;
}
printf ("%.18f", sum);
```

B19   What is the output of the following code segment?

```
double sum = 0, decr = 1;
for (int i=1; i<=100; i++){
  sum += decr;
  decr -= 0.01;
}
printf ("%.18f\n", sum);
```

B20   What is the output of the following code segment?

```
double sum = 0, incr = 0, decr = 1.0;
for (int i=1; i<=50; i++){
  incr += 0.01;
  sum = sum + incr + decr;
  decr -= 0.01;
```

```
}
printf ("%.18f\n%.18f\n ", incr, sum);
```

B21 What error does the following code segment have?

```
int x;
double d = 1.5;

switch (d) {
  case 1.0: x = 1;
  case 1.5: x = 2;
  case 2.0: x = 3;
}
```

B22 What error does the following code segment have?

```
int x;
double d = 1.5;

switch ((int)d) {
  case (int)1.0: x = 1;
  case (int)1.5: x = 2;
  case (int)2.0: x = 3;
}
```

B23 What error does the following code segment have, if any?

```
int x;
double d = 1.5;

switch ((int)d) {
  case (int)1.5: x = 1;
  case (int)2.5: x = 2;
  case (int)3.5: x = 3;
}
```

B24 What is the output of the following program?

```
int main() {
  int i, j;
  for (i=1; i<=3; i++) {
    for (j=1; j<=3; j++) {
      if ((i+j) % 4 == 0) {
        printf("Iteration (%d, %d) is not done\n", i, j);
        break;
      }
      else
```

```
            printf("Iteration (%d, %d) is done\n", i, j);
      }
   }
}
```

B25   What is the output of the following program?

```
int main() {
  int i, j;
  for (i=1; i<=3; i++) {
    for (j=1; j<=3; j++) {
      if ((i+j) % 4 == 0) {
        printf("\nIteration (%d, %d) is not done\n", i, j);
        continue;
      }
      else
        printf(" (%d, %d) is done ", i, j);
    }
    printf("\n");
  }
}
```

B26   What is the output of the following program?

```
int main() {
  for (int i = 0; i < 10; i++){
    for (int j = 0; j < 10; j++){
      if ((i+j) % 3 == 0)
        break;
      printf(" (%d, %d) ", i, j);
    }
    printf("\n");
  }
}
```

B27   Rewrite the following code segment using multiple-selection (switch-case).

```
if (k == 1 || k == 2) j = 2*k - 1;
if (k == 3 || k == 5) j = 3*k + 1;
if (k == 4) j = 4*k - 1;
if (k == 6 || k == 7 || k == 8) j = k - 2;
```

B28   What is the output of the following code segment?

```
int i=0;
do {
  if (i < 10) {
    i += 2;
    printf ("%d ", i);
    continue;
  }
  else
    printf ("%d\n", ++i);
} while (i < 15);
```

B29   What is the output of the following code segment?

```
for (i=0; i<3; i++) {
  for (j=0; j<3; j++) {
    for (k=0; k<3; k++) {
      printf ("i=%d j=%d k=%d\n", i, j, k);

      if ((i+j+k) % 2 == 0)
        goto label1;
    }
  }
label1: continue;
}
```

B30   What is the output of the following code segment?

```
for (i=0; i<3; i++) {
  for (j=0; j<3; j++) {
    for (k=0; k<3; k++) {
      if ((i+j+k) % 2 == 0)
        break;
      printf ("i=%d j=%d k=%d\n", i, j, k);
    }
  }
}
```

B31   Rewrite the following code segment using a 'for' loop.

```
    k = (j + 10) / 15;
    loop:
        if k > 5 then goto out
        k = k + 1
        i = 3 * k - 1
        goto loop
    out: ...
    }
```

B32 Rewrite the following code segment without using **switch-case**.

```
j = -3;
for (i = 0; i < 3; i++){
  switch (j + 2){
    case 0: j += 2; break;
    case 2:
    case 3: j--; break;
    default: j = 0;
  }
  if (j > 0)
    break;
  else j = 3 - i;
}
```

B33 What is the output of the following code segment?

```
int a, b, c, m;
a= 352; b = 56; c = 173;
if (a < b){
  if (a < c)
    m = a;
  else
    m = c;
}
else if (b < c)
  m = b;
else
  m = c;
}
```

B34 What is the output of the following code segment?

```
int n, p;
n = 1; p = 1;
while (n < 1000){
```

```
    printf("%d ", n);
    p ++;
    n = n * p;
}
```

B35 What is the output of the following code segment?

```
int x = 1, y = 1;
do {
  printf("%d ", x);
  x = x + y;
  y ++;
} while (y < 10);
```

B36 What is the output of the following code segment?

```
int i, num, term, inc;
term = 1; inc = 1;
for (i = 1; i <= 10; i++){
  num = 2 * term;
  inc ++;
  term += inc;
  printf("%d ", num);
}
```

B37 Write a '**while**' loop which prints out the following sequence of numbers. It starts at 10 and the difference between successive numbers increases by 1 (ex. 1 2 3 4)

      10   9   7   4   0

B38 How many times does the following loop execute?

```
int x, y;
x = 10; y;
do {
  x = x - 1;
  y = x / 2;
} while (y <= 3);
```

B39 In the following C program segment, how many times is **<Statement block1>** executed?

```
for (i = 1;  i <= 5; i++) {
  for (j = 1;  j <= 4; j++) {
```

```
       if (i%2 != 0 && j%2 == 0)
          continue;
          <Statement block1>
     }
   }
```

IOIOIOIOIOIOIOIOIOIOIOIOIOIOIOIOIOIOIOIOIOIOIOIOIOIOIOIOIOI

C. Pointers

True/False Questions

C1 The name of an integer array can be assigned to a variable of type `int*` (pointer to integer). _____

C2 Subscripts cannot be used with a pointer variable. _____

C3 A pointer to an object of a certain datatype cannot be cast to point to another object of a different type. _____

C4 The pointers to simple types and pointers to structured types have different sizes. _____

C5 The size of a pointer is guaranteed to be the size of 'int' or 'long. _____

C6 A pointer can be defined for only for non-primitive types. ____

C7 Pointers cannot be used with multidimensional arrays. _____

C8 Function pointers and data pointers may have different representations. _____

C9 A 'void' pointer can hold the address of any data type. _____

C10 A 'void' pointer cannot be cast to point to any data type. _____

C11 A 'void' pointer cannot be dereferenced. _____

C12 Pointer arithmetic can be done on 'void' pointers. _____

C13 A void pointer can be dereferenced after casting it to a data type pointer. _____

C14 Pointer arithmetic can be done on a pointer to a variable of type double. _____

C15 Pointer arithmetic can be done on a function pointer. _____

C16 Pointer arithmetic uses only integer values. _____

C17 Relational operators can be used with pointer variables. _____

C18 A pointer may not be declared with the type qualifier **const**. _____

C19 A pointer must be initialized when declared. _____

C20 A pointer variable always points to a valid memory address. _____

C21 A pointer variable can have a value of NULL. _____

C22 A pointer variable cannot be reassigned. _____

C23 An array of references is not valid. _____

C24 A variable can have more than one pointer. _____

C25 A pointer and variable it is pointing to, share the same address. _____

C26 Pointers can be declared to point to both primitive types as well as to structures and arrays. _____

C27 There is no generic pointer to functions. _____

Given the declaration **char ch1='G', ch2='T', *cp1, *cp2;**

C28 **ch1 = ch2;** is valid. _____

C29 **cp1 = ch1;** is valid. _____

C30 **cp2 = cp1;** is valid. _____

C31 **cp1 = &ch2;** is valid. _____

C32 **ch2 = cp2;** is valid. _____

C33 **ch1 = *cp2;** is valid. _____

C34 **&cp1 = ch2;** is valid. _____

C35 ***cp2 = *cp1;** is valid. _____

C36 ***ch1 = &cp1;** is valid. _____

C37 &cp2 = &cp1; is valid. _____

C38 Given the declaration int* ap, *ap cannot be on the left-hand side of an assignment. _____

C39 Given the declaration int a, &a cannot be on the left-hand side of an assignment. _____

C40 The declaration int*** ap3; is a valid declaration. _____

C41 The declaration int& a; is a valid declaration. _____

C42 The set of declarations: int **ap2; int a = 5; *ap2 = &a; is valid. _____

C43 Given the definition int fn (float x){ } and the declaration int (*pf)(float); the assignment pf = &fn; is valid. _____

C44 Given the definition int fn (float x){ } and the declaration int (*pf)(float); the assignment pf = fn; is not valid. _____

IOIOIOIOIOIOIOIOIOIOIOIOIOIOIOIOIOIOIOIOIOIOIOIOIOIOI

Fill-in the-blanks Questions

C1 Pointer arithmetic is not valid on _____ and _____ pointers.

C2 Given a datatype DT, the declaration DT a, *pa; and the statement pa = &a; pa++ increments pa by _____ bytes.

C3 Given int a = 5, the declaration of a pointer variable 'ap' to point to 'a' is _____

C4 Given 'bp' to be a pointer with the address of a valid integer variable 'b', the statement to assign the contents of 'b' using 'bp' to an integer variable 'c' is _____

C5   Given **double x = 5.3712**, the declaration of a variable 'xp' which is initialized to the address of 'x' is _____

C6   Given **char c = '@'; char* cp = &c;** the statement using **putchar** to print the contents of 'c' using 'cp' is _____

C7   Given **double x = 7.26; double* xp = &x;** the declaration of a variable 'xpp' to contain the address of 'xp' is _____

C8   Given **int a = 5; int* ap = &a; int** app = ≈** the statement to assign the value of 'a' to an integer variable 'c' using 'app' is _____

C9   Given the declaration **int **ap2;** the datatype of **ap2** is _____

C10 Given the set of declarations: **int **ap2; int a = 5; *ap2 = &a;** the content of **ap2** is _____

C11 Given **char* p**, assuming that the size of 'char is 1 byte and pointer to 'char' is 8 bytes, the value of **sizeof(p)** is _____

C12 Assuming that a character takes 1 byte and a pointer takes 8 bytes, given the declaration **char *b[5];** the number of bytes allocated to **b** is _____

C13 Assuming that a character takes 1 byte and a pointer takes 8 bytes, given the declaration **char (*c)[5];** the number of bytes allocated to **c** is _____

C14 Assuming that a character takes 1 byte and a pointer takes 8 bytes, given the declaration **char* (*d)[5];** the number of bytes allocated to **d** is _____

C15 Assuming that a character takes 1 byte and a pointer takes 8 bytes, given the declaration **char* (*(*e)[5]);** the number of bytes allocated to **e** is _____

C16 Assuming that a character takes 1 byte and a pointer takes 8 bytes, given the declaration **char* (*(f[5]));** the number of bytes allocated to **f** is _____

C17 Given **char* str = " INCORPORATION ";** the **puts** statement to output **CORPORATION** using index of **str** is _____

C18 Given **char* str = " INCORPORATION ";** the **puts** statement to output **RATION** using pointer arithmetic on **str** is _____

C19 Given **char* str = " INCORPORATION ";** the statement to assign the character 'P' in **str** to a character variable **ch**, using index of **str** is _____

C20 Given **char* str = " INCORPORATION ";** the statement to assign the character 'T' in **str** to a character variable **ch**, using pointer arithmetic on **str** is _____

C21 Given **char* str = " INCORPORATION ";** the output of **putchar (*str)** is _____

C22 The value of **"HABIT" + 2** is _____

C23 The value of ***("HABIT"+2)** is _____

C24 The value of **"HABIT"[2]** is _____

IOIOIOIOIOIOIOIOIOIOIOIOIOIOIOIOIOIOIOIOIOIOIOIOIOIOIOIOIOI

Essay-type Questions

C1 Given the declaration **char* str = "Test String";** and the size of a character is 1 byte, the size of an address is 4 bytes, how many bytes are allocated to **str**?

C2 What is the output of the following code segment?
```
int a, *b=&a, **c=&b;
a = 5;
**c = 7;
printf ("a = %d\n", a);
```

C3 What is the error in the following code segment?
```
float **fp2, *fp1;
fp1 = &fp2;
```

C4   What is the error in the following code segment?
```
char ch, **fc2, *fc1;
ch = '$';
fc1 = &ch;
**fc2 = *fc1;
```

C5   What is the error in the following code segment?
```
float x = 3.75, **fp2, *fp1;
fp2 = &x;
```

C6   What is the error in the following code segment?

```
int fn (float x){ }
int *p;
pf = &fn;
```

C7   What is the error in the following code segment?

```
int fn (float x){ }
int fn1();
fn1 = &fn;
```

C8   What is the error in the following code segment?

```
int fn (float x){ }
int *fn2();
fn2 = &fn;
```

C9   What is the error in the following code segment? What is the correction required in the declaration of **pfn**?

```
int fn (float x){ }
int (*pfn)();
pfn = &fn;
```

C10 What is the error in the following code segment? What is the correction required in the assignment?

```
int fn (float x){ }
void (*pfn)(float);
pfn = &fn;
```

C11 What is the output of the following code segment?
```
float x = 3.75, *fp1, **fp2;
```

```
fp1 = &x;
fp2 = &fp1;
printf ("%.2f\n", **fp2);
```

C12 Given 'dp1' is a pointer to double, 'dp2' is a pointer to a pointer to double, and 'x' is a double, what are the declarations and assignments required to have **dp2 to have a value 5.12?

C13 What is the output of the following code segment?
```
char *ptr;
char str[] = "pancake";
ptr = str + 3;
printf("%s\n", ptr);
```

C14 What is the output of the following code segment?
```
int a = 5;
int *p = &a;
*p = 7;
printf("a: %d\n", a);
```

C15 What is the output of the following code segment?
```
int x = 10;
int* p = &x;
*p = 20;
printf("x: %d\n", x);
x = 30;
printf(" (*p): %d\n", *p);
```

C16 What is the output of the following code segment? What is the difference between the two declarations?

```
char* p = "Test";
char s[] = "Best";
puts (p);
puts (s);
```

C17 What is the output of the following code segment?

```
double x = 3.678;
double *dp = &x;
printf(" (*dp): %lf, dp: %p\n", *dp, dp);
dp++;
printf(" (*dp): %lf, dp: %p\n", *dp, dp);
```

C18 What is the output of the following code segment?

```
char* p = "Test";
putchar(p[0]); putchar(p[1]);
putchar(p[2]); putchar(p[3]);
```

C19 What is the output of the following code segment?

```
string p = "Test";
string q = p;
q[0] = 'B';
cout << "p: " << p << "   q: " << q;
```

C20 What is the output of the following code segment?

```
char s[] = "Test";
char* q = s;
q[0] = 'B';
printf("s: %s q: %s\n", s, q);
```

C21 What is the output of the following code segment?

```
char* s = "C is fun and useful";
char* p = s;
puts(p);
```

C22 What is the output of the following code segment?

```
char* s = "C is fun and useful";
char* p = &s[0];
puts(p);
```

C23 What is the output of the following code segment?

```
int a = 10;
void *ptr = &a;
printf("%d", *ptr);
```

C24 What is the output of the following code segment?

```
int a = 10;
void *ptr = &a;
printf("%d", *(int *)ptr);
```

C25 What is the output of the following code segment?

```
int a = 3, * p1;
```

```
p1 = &a;
*p1 = 5;
printf("a: %d, (*p1): %d\n", a, *p1);
```

C26 What is the output of the following code segment?

```
int* p1;
*p1 = 5;
printf("p1: %p, (*p1): %d\n", p1, *p1);
```

C27 What is the output of the following code segment?

```
int a = 3, * p1;
p1 = &a;
free (p1);
```

C28 What is the output of the following code segment?

```
char * p1;
p1 = calloc(10, sizeof(char));
p1[0]= 'a'; p1[1]='b';p1[2]='c';p1[3]='\0';
printf("%p\n",  p1);
printf("%s\n",  p1);
```

C29 What is the output of the following code segment?

```
int * p1;
p1 = calloc (10, sizeof(int));
p1[0]= 1; p1[1]=2;p1[2]=3;p1[3]=4;
printf("%p\n", p1);
printf("%d %d %d\n", *p1, * (p1+1), * (p1+2));
```

C30 What is the output of the following code segment?

```
char * p1 = "Test";
puts (p1);
putchar(*p1); putchar(*p1+1);
putchar(*p1+2); putchar(*p1+3);
putchar('\n');
putchar(*p1); putchar(* (p1+1));
putchar(* (p1+2)); putchar(* (p1+3));
```

C31 What is the output of the following code segment?

```
int a[]={2, 3, 5, 7, 11};
int* pi = a+3;

printf("%lu\n", pi - a);
```

```
printf("%lu\n",    ((int   *)pi   -   (int   *)a)   *
(sizeof(int)));
```

C32 What is the output of the following code segment?

```
int* pi = calloc(2, sizeof(int));
double* pd = calloc(2, sizeof(double));
unsigned long a1 = (unsigned long) (pi+1) -
(unsigned long) pi;
unsigned long a2 = (unsigned long) (pd+1) -
(unsigned long) pd;

printf("a1: %lu, a2: %lu\n", a1, a2);
```

C33 What is the output of the following code segment?

```
int a[]={10, 20, 30};
int* pi = a;

printf("pi: %p, a: %p\n", pi, a);
printf("*pi: %d, a: %p\n", *pi, a);
printf("pi: %p, *a: %d\n", pi, *a);
```

C34 What is the output of the following code segment?

```
int a[]={2, 3, 5, 7, 11, 13, 17};
int* pi = a+3;

printf("*pi: %d, a[3]: %d, *(a+3): %d\n", *pi,
a[3], *(a+3));
```

IOIOIOIOIOIOIOIOIOIOIOIOIOIOIOIOIOIOIOIOIOIOIOIOIOIOIOIOIOIOIOIOI

D. Arrays

True/False Questions

D1   When an array of primitive type is declared, the elements have undefined values. _____

D2   An array cannot be passed as argument to a function. _____

D3   An array cannot be returned from a function. _____

D4   The number of elements of an array must be specified at array declaration. _____

D5   The elements of an array are allocated consecutively in memory. _____

D6   When an array is passed as argument to a function, the function receives a copy of the array. _____

D7   Pointers cannot be used with multidimensional arrays. _____

D8   The parameter passing mechanisms of arrays and array elements are the same. _____

D9   When a 2-dimensional array is passed as argument to a function, the row and column sizes must be specified. _____

D10 Arrays cannot be returned from functions. _____

D11 Array elements can be strings. _____

D12 Array sizes are fixed at compile time. _____

D13 The name of an array variable is equivalent to a pointer to the first element of the array. _____

D14 Pointer arithmetic cannot be done on array names. _____

D15 An array subscript can be a valid expression (evaluating to an integer value). _____

D16 The length of a static array known at compile time is also known to the C runtime system. _____

D17 Strings stored as character arrays must be terminated by a '0'. _____

D18 The elements of an array of primitive type can be heterogeneous. _____

D19 When an array is created using the 'calloc' statement, the element values are automatically initialized to 0. _____

D20 The size of an array can be changed after it is created. _____

D21 The datatype of an array must be specified at the time of declaration. _____

D22 An array of a generic type can be declared. _____

D23 The datatype of an array could be changed during run time. _____

D24 There are no operators to perform array operations. _____

D25 The declaration **int arr [3] = {12, 3, 5, 2}** results in error. _____

D26 The declaration **int arr[] = {2, 3, 9, 1, 7}** is valid. _____

D27 Given **int a[5] = {12, 3, 5, 2, 7}**, the values of **&a[2]** and **a+2** are the same. _____

D28 Given **int b, a[] = {12, 3, 5, 2, 7}, b = a** is a valid assignment. _____

D29 Given **int b[5], a[] = {12, 3, 5, 2, 7}, b = a** is a valid assignment. _____

D30 Given **int *b, a[] = {12, 3, 5, 2, 7}, b = a** is a valid assignment. _____

IOIOIOIOIOIOIOIOIOIOIOIOIOIOIOIOIOIOIOIOIOIOIOIOIOIOIOIOIOIOI

Fill-in the-blanks Questions

D1   An array whose size is determined at compile time is known as
_____

D2   When an array needs to be returned from a function, _____ is returned.

D3   When an array is passed to a function, the function receives
_____

D4   When an array is passed as argument to a function, what is actually passed is the _____

D5   The parameter passing mechanism used, when arrays are passed as arguments to functions, is _____

D6   The parameter passing mechanism used, when array elements are passed as arguments to functions, is _____

D7   The parameter passing mechanism used, when primitive types are passed as arguments to functions, is _____

D8   The parameter passing mechanism used, when structs are passed as arguments to functions, is _____

D9   The parameter passing mechanism used, when unions are passed as arguments to functions, is _____

D10 The parameter passing mechanism used, when arrays are passed as arguments to functions, is _____

D11 A locally declared array within a function is allocated in the _____ area of memory.

D12 An array created using the 'calloc' operator is allocated in the _____ area of memory.

D13 Given `int a[] = {2, 9, 5, 4, 7}`, `a[2]` is ____

D14 Given `int a[] = {12, 9, 5, 14, 25}`, element with value 14 is accessed using ____

D15 Given `int a[5] = {12, 3, 5, 2, 7}`, the value of `*&a[2]` is ____

D16 Given `int *ap, a[5] = {12, 3, 5, 2, 7}`, and `ap = a;` the value of `*ap` is ____

D17 Given `int *ap, a[5] = {12, 3, 5, 2, 7}`, and `ap = a;` the value of `*ap++` is ____

D18 Given `int *ap, a[5] = {12, 3, 5, 2, 7}`, and `ap = a;` the value of `*++ap` is ____

D19 Given `int *ap, a[5] = {12, 3, 5, 2, 7}`, in order to replace 2 by 8 in the array `a` using `ap[3] = 8`, the statement to initialize `ap` is _____

D20 Given `int *ap, a[5] = {12, 3, 5, 2, 7}`, in order to access 2 using `*(ap+2)`, the statement to initialize `ap` is _____ or _____

D21 The expression to increment element at index `i` of array `numlist` is _____

D22 The number of bytes allocated for `str` in the declaration `char str[] = "Test"` is ____

D23 Given `int x[][4] = {{1, 2}, {3, 4}, {5, 6}, {7, 8}}`, the value of `*x` is _____

D24 Given `int x[][4] = {{1, 2}, {3, 4}, {5, 6}, {7, 8}}`, the value of `(*x == &x[0][0])` is _____

D25 Given `int x[][4] = {{1, 2}, {3, 4}, {5, 6}, {7, 8}}`, the value of `*x[2]` is _____

D26 Given the declaration `int* i2`, the value of `i2` is _____

D27 Given the following code segment, the number of elements of the array pointed to by x is ____

```
int** x = calloc(3, sizeof(int *));
x[0] = calloc(1, sizeof(int));
x[1] = calloc(2, sizeof(int));
```

```
x[2] = calloc(3, sizeof(int));
```

D28 Given the declaration `int* i3 = calloc(3, sizeof(int))`, the value of **i3** is _____

D29 Given the declaration `int* i3 = calloc(3, sizeof(int))`, the values of the elements of the array of 3 integers referenced by **i3** are _____

IOIOIOIOIOIOIOIOIOIOIOIOIOIOIOIOIOIOIOIOIOIOIOIOIOIOI

Essay-type Questions

D1 Given the following code segment, give the statement to assign to **x**, the array element with value 28 using **ap**.

```
int x, a[] = {2, 17, 25, 4, 16, 28, 6, 12};
int* ap = a;
```

D2 What is the output of the following code segment?

```
int i=3, a[5] = {2, 17, 25, 4, 16};
printf("%d %d\n", *(a-(i-5)), a[i-2]);
```

D3 What is the output of the following code segment?

```
int a[5] = {2, 17, 25, 4, 16};
printf("%d %d\n", *(a-40), a[70]);
```

D4 What is the output of the following code segment?

```
char *ps, str[15] = "Test String";
printf ("%s\n", str);
ps = &str[5];
printf ("%s\n", ps);
```

D5 What is the output of the following code segment?

```
char str[] = "PERUSING";
char *ps = str;
printf("%s\n", str);
printf("%s\n", ps+3);
```

```
printf("%s\n", str + 4);
```

D6   What is the output of the following code segment for inputs (a) contra, (b) contract, and (c) contraction? Explain the outcomes.

```
char a[5], b[5];
scanf("%s", a);
printf("a: %s\n", a);
printf("b: %s\n", b);
```

D7   What is the output of the following code segment?

```
int x[] = {1, 2, 3, 4, 5};
int *y = x;
for (int i = 0; i < 5; i++)
   printf("%d ", y[i]);
```

D8   What is the output of the following code segment?

```
int arr[2][3] = {{10, 15, 20}, {25, 30, 35}};
printf ("arr[0][0]: %d\n", **arr);
printf ("arr[0][2]: %d\n", *(*arr+2));
printf ("arr[1][0]: %d\n", *(*arr+3));
```

D9   What does the following do? What will be the array contents when the input is {2, 9, 6, 4, 5, 1, 11, 3}?

```
void arr_fn1 (int arr[], int size){
  for (int i=1; i<size; i++)
    arr[i] += arr[i-1];
}
```

D10 What is the output of the following program? What will be the output for the input arr: {22, 19, 16, 24, 25, 17, 14, 12, 9, 15, 19}

D11 What is the effect of the following function? What will be the output for the call **print_permutations ("ant", 0)**?

```
#include <string.h>
#define STR_SIZE 80
void print_permutations (char* str, int k){
  char str1[STR_SIZE];

  strcpy (str1, str);
```

```
if (k == strlen (str)-1)
  puts(str1);
else {
  for (int i=k; i<strlen (str); i++) {
    char ch = str1[i];
    str1[i] = str1[k];
    str1[k] = ch;
    print_permutations (str1, k+1);
  }
}
}
```

IOIOIOIOIOIOIOIOIOIOIOIOIOIOIOIOIOIOIOIOIOIOIOIOIOIOIOIOIOIOI

E. Structures, Unions, Enumerated Types

True/False Questions

E1   Members of a 'struct' can be of different datatypes. _____

E2   Members of a 'struct' share storage. _____

E3   Storage for the members of a 'struct' may not be allocated contiguously. _____

E4   A 'struct' cannot have another 'struct' as a member. _____

E5   A 'struct' can have itself as a member. _____

E6   A 'struct' can have a pointer to itself as a member. _____

E7   A 'struct' cannot have a 'union' as a member. _____

E8   A 'struct' can have an 'enum' as a member. _____

E9   A 'struct' cannot have an array as a member. _____

E10   Structs can have function definitons. _____

E11   The names of members (fields) of a struct must be distinct. _____

E12   Members of a 'struct' cannot be qualified with **const**. _____

E13   Defining a 'struct' and declaring a variable of its type cannot be done at the same time. _____

E14   Two different 'struct' definitions, even with identical member names and types are considered different. _____

E15   Members of a 'struct' cannot be initialized with values at the time of struct definition. _____

E16   Members of a 'struct' variable cannot be initialized with values at the time of declaration. _____

E17   Two 'structs' cannot be compared for equality by a single operator.
_____

E18   Two variables of the same struct type can be directly assigned to one another. _____

E19   It is not possible to have pointers to individual members (fields) of a 'struct'. _____

E20   The declaration of a 'struct' within a block is not visible outside of the block. _____

E21   The definition of a 'struct' will not allocate any memory. _____

E22   The **sizeof** operator cannot be used with structures. _____

E23   The **sizeof** operator can be used with 'struct' members. _____

E24   The members of a 'union' share storage. _____

E25   The members of a 'union' can be of different datatypes. _____

E26   A 'union' cannot contain itself as a member. _____

E27   A union may contain a pointer to an instance of itself. _____

E28   A union may not contain a 'struct' as a member. _____

E29   A union holds atmost one component (member) at a time. ____

E30   Two components (members) of a union may have the same name.
_____

E31   The **sizeof** operator cannot be used with unions. _____

E32   The datatype of enumeration constants could be any one of the integer types. _____

E33   The members of a 'enum' type cannot be explicitly assigned values.
_____

E34   The members of a 'enum' type must have unique values. _____

E35 The values assigned to members of a 'enum' type are integers. _____

E36 The value assigned to a member of a 'enum' type cannot be a negative integer. _____

E37 The members (enumeration constants) of a 'enum' type, can be explicitly assigned only increasing values. _____

E38 The values of the members (enumeration constants) of a 'enum' type must be distinct. _____

E39 An enumeration constant cannot be used in place of an integer expression. _____

IOIOIOIOIOIOIOIOIOIOIOIOIOIOIOIOIOIOIOIOIOIOIOIOIOIOIOIOI

Fill-in the-blanks Questions

E1 The name used between the keyword **struct** and the opening brace (**{**) is known as the _____

E2 The storage allocated for a variable of a 'struct' containing members requiring 20 bytes, 4 bytes, 2 bytes, 8 bytes is _____

E3 Given that **DATE** is a 'struct' with member 'year' of type 'int', and **d1** is a variable of type **DATE**, then the statement to set the 'year' of **d1** to 1976 is _____

E4 Given that **DATE** is a 'struct' with member 'month' of type 'int', then for **d1->month = 9;** to be syntactically correct, the declarartion of **d1** should be _____

E5 Given that **DATE** is a 'struct' with member 'month' of type 'int', and the declaration **DATE d2,*dp**, then, to set the 'month' value of **d2** to 4 using **dp->month = 4**, **dp** should be initialized using the statement _____

E6 Given that **DATE** is a 'struct' with member 'date' of type 'int', and **dp** is a pointer to a variable **d3** of type **DATE**, then the statement to set the 'date' of **d3** to 27 is _____

E7 Given that **DATE** is a 'struct' with member 'date' of type 'int', and **dp** is a pointer to a variable **d4** of type **DATE**, then the statement to set the 'date' of **d4** to 19 without using the -> operator is

_____

E8 The storage allocated for a variable of a 'union' containing members requiring 20 bytes, 4 bytes, 2 bytes, 8 bytes is _____

E9 Given **enum device {phone, smart_phone, tablet, laptop, pc};** the value of **phone** is ____

E10 Given **enum device {phone, smart_phone, tablet, laptop, pc};** the value of **laptop** is ____

E11 Given **enum device {phone, smart_phone=5, tablet, laptop, pc=10};** the value of **laptop** is ___

E12 Given **enum device {phone=1, smart_phone, tablet, laptop=2, pc};** the value of **pc** is ____

IOIOIOIOIOIOIOIOIOIOIOIOIOIOIOIOIOIOIOIOIOIOIOIOIOIOIOIOIOIOIOI

Essay-type Questions

E1 Given the following 'struct' and the variable **book_list**
```
typedef struct book_str {
    char title[80];
    char authors[80];
    char publisher[30];
    int year, ISBN;
    float price;
} Book;

Book book_list[12];
```

how much storage is allocated to **book_list** assuming 1 byte for character, 4 bytes each for integer and floating point number?

E2 What is the statement to assign 11.95 to the 'price' of the 6th book in **book_list** ? (Note that the arrays are 0-indexed)

E3   What is the statement to assign **"Horizon"** to the 'publisher' field of the 3rd book in **book_list** ?

E4   What is the statement to print the book title and the price in the same line for the 10th book in **book_list** ?

E5   Given **BOOK b1, b2, *pb1**; what are two possible statements to assign to the 'price' member of 'b2', the value of 'price' of 'b1' using 'pb1'?

E6   What is the output of the following code segment?

```
typedef struct time{
      int hr, min;
   } TIME;
TIME t1, t2 = {10, 20};
printf ("%2d:%2d\n", t1.hr, t1.min);
printf ("%2d:%2d\n", t2.hr, t2.min);
```

E7   Given the following declarations,
```
typedef struct date_str {
   int hour, min, sec;
} DATE;
DATE d1, *dp1;
d1.hour = 5; d1.min = 36; d1.sec = 24;
dp1 = &d1;
```

What is the error in the following statement? What is the fix?
```
DATE d2;
d2.hour = *dp1.hour;
```

E8   What is the output of the following program?
```
typedef struct test_str {
      char c;
      int a;
      float x;
} Test;

void print_test_str(Test t){
      printf ("%c %d %.2f\n", t.c, t.a, t.x);
}
int main()
{
   Test t1, t2, t3;
   char *cp; int* ip; float* fp;
   t1.c = 'x'; t1.a = 5; fp = &(t1.x);
```

```
*fp = 12.34;
t2.c = 'Q'; t2.x = 6.29; ip = &(t2.a);
*ip = 24;
t3.a = 17; t3.x = 3.14; cp = &(t3.c);
*cp = 'M';
print_test_str(t1);
print_test_str(t2);
print_test_str(t3);
return 0;
}
```

Use the following 'struct' definition for E9 – E11.

```
typedef struct date_str {
    int day, month, year;
} DATE;
```

E9   Write a function **get_date1** which takes no argument, and returns a variable of struct DATE, with fields initialized using values input via the keyboard by the user.

E10   Write a function **get_date2** which takes as argument a pointer to a struct of type DATE, and initializes the fields using values input via the keyboard by the user.

E11   Write a function **print_date** which takes as argument a struct of type DATE, and prints in the format: <month name> day, year. For example, if a variable of type DATE with values 8/22/1989 were given as argument, it should print out "August 22, 1989".

E12   What is the output of the following code segment?
```
typedef union mult_type
{
    char c1;
    int i1;
    float f1;
    double d1;
} MULTTYPE;

MULTTYPE mt1;

printf("c1: %lu, i1: %lu, f1: %lu, d1: %lu\n",
sizeof(char), sizeof(int), sizeof(float), sizeof
(double));

printf("Space for mt1 is: %lu\n", sizeof(mt1));
```

The following definitions are used for problems E13 – E17.

```
typedef struct {
  float monthly_sal;
} SAL_TYPE1;

typedef struct {
  float commission, weekly_sal;
} SAL_TYPE2;

typedef struct {
  float hr_rate, num_hrs;
} SAL_TYPE3;

typedef struct date {
  int month, day, year;
} DATE;

typedef struct {
  char name[30], dept[20];
  int id;
  DATE join_date;
  short sal_type;
  union {
    SAL_TYPE1 salary1;
    SAL_TYPE2 salary2;
    SAL_TYPE3 salary3;
  } salary;
} EMP_REC;


main ()
{
  EMP_REC emprec;
  DATE date = {11, 3, 93};
}
```

E13 Give the declaration for an array **emp_list** of **NUM_EMPS** records of type **EMP_REC**.

E14 Give the statement to initialize the 'dept' field of element at index 5 of emp_list to "Marketing".

E15 Give the statements to initialize the 'commission' to 15 and 'weekly_sal' to 1,150 of element at index 7 of emp_list.

E16 Give the statements to initialize the 'join_date' field of the element at index 4 of emp_list to 4/23/1992.

E17 Give the declaration and initializer to declare a variable **er1** of type **EMP_REC** which is initialized at declaration to the field values: 'name': "Adam Adams"; 'dept': "Sales"; 'id': 341; 'join_date': 5/22/1978; 'sal_type': 2; (salary2): 'commision': 12.5; 'weekly_sal': 995.0.

Consider the following declaration for E18 – E24.

```
typedef union {
  char a[15];
  int n;
  float x;
} U;
```

E18 What is the output of the following code segment?

```
U u1;
strcpy(u1.a,"Programming");
u1.n = 25;
u1.x = 22.50;
printf("Union u1: %s %d %f\n",u1.a,u1.n,u1.x);
```

E19 What is the output of the following code segment?

```
U u1;
strcpy(u1.a,"Programming");
u1.x = 22.50;
u1.n = 25;
printf("Union u1: %s %d %f\n",u1.a,u1.n,u1.x);
```

E20 What is the output of the following code segment?

```
U u1 = {101};
printf("Union u1: %s %d %f\n",u1.a,u1.n,u1.x);
```

E21 What is the output of the following code segment?

```
U u1 = {"Test string"};
printf("Union u1: %s %d %f\n",u1.a,u1.n,u1.x);
```

E22 What is the output of the following code segment?

```
U u1 = {"Test string", 101, 12.3};
printf("Union u1: %s %d %f\n",u1.a,u1.n,u1.x);
```

E23 What is the output of the following code segment?

```
U u1 = {.a = "Test string", .n=101, .x=12.3};
printf("Union u1: %s %d %f\n",u1.a,u1.n,u1.x);
```

E24 What is the output of the following code segment?

```
U u1 = { .n=101, .x=12.3, .a = "Test string"};
printf("Union u1: %s %d %f\n",u1.a,u1.n,u1.x);
```

IOIOIOIOIOIOIOIOIOIOIOIOIOIOIOIOIOIOIOIOIOIOIOIOIOIOIOI

F. Functions

True/False Questions

F1   A C program can have more than one **main()** function. _____

F2   **main()** is never invoked by any other function. _____

F3   **main()** can call itself. _____

F4   There can be more than one function with the same name in a program. _____

F5   A local variable and a formal parameter in a function cannot have the same name. _____

F6   A local variable in a function cannot have the same name as a global variable. _____

F7   In a function declaration, the formal parameters need not have names. _____

F8   The number of arguments passed to a function call must exactly match the number of parameters in the function definition. _____

F9   Any mismatch of the type of argument and the corresponding type of formal parameter will always result in error. _____

F10   A function definition must have at least one parameter. _____

F11   In a function call, if a default value is used for an argument, the subsequent arguments must have default values. _____

F12   A struct can be passed as argument to a function. _____

F13   A struct cannot be returned from a function. _____

F14   When the formal parameter is passed by value, the actual parameter (argument) must be a constant value. _____

F15   When the formal parameter is passed by reference, the actual parameter (argument) can be an expression. _____

F16   Pointer to a 'union' cannot be returned from a function. _____

F17   Pointer to a 'struct' can be returned from a function. _____

F18   C supports both pass-by-value and pass-by-reference for primitive types. _____

F19   C supports only pass-by-reference for structs. _____

F20   The first statement to be executed always is the first executable statement in **main()**. _____

F21   Call-by-value is more efficient than Call-by-reference. _____

F22   An inline function is expanded at runtime. _____

F23   An inline function can have loops. _____

F24   An inline function cannot have static variables. _____

F25   A recursive function cannot be an inline function. _____

F26   Default parameters can be listed anywhere in the parameter list of a function declaration/definition. _____

F27   A constant parameter with the 'const' keyword cannot be a parameter of a function. _____

F28   In C the parameter passing for arrays is call-by-value. _____

F29   In pass-by-value, it is possible for the called subprogram to change the values of the actual parameters of the calling subprogram. _____

F30   Individual 'structs' are passed by reference if they contain arrays. _____

F31   A function may contain more than one **return** statement. _____

F32   A function can return multiple results back to the calling subprogram. _____

F33   In C, a function definition can have further nested function definitions. _____

F34 In C, the local variables of functions are always stack dynamic variables. _____

F35 In C, the local variables of functions are always stack dynamic variables, *by default.* _____

F36 In C, the lifetimes of local variables declared with **static** keyword extend beyond the time the function is active. _____

F37 In a recursive call of a subprogram, there are multiple instances of its activation record. _____

F38 C supports both functions and procedures. _____

F39 In C, a function defined in a file cannot be called in another function in a different file. _____

F40 A function must be defined before it can be called. _____

F41 In C, function names can be passed as arguments. _____

F42 In C, pointers to functions can be passed as arguments. _____

F43 The argument in a function call must have the same name as the corresponding formal parameter in the function definition. _____

F44 A function's declaration and definition must be in the same file. _____

F45 The order of evaluation of a function's arguments is from left to right. _____

F46 An expression cannot be used as an argument to a function. _____

F47 A function call cannot be used as an argument to a function. _____

F48 All the arguments of a function are evaluated before control transfers to the called function. _____

F49 For a one dimensional array used as an argument in a function call, specifying the dimension is optional. _____

F50 For a multi-dimensional array used as an argument in a function call, specifying all dimensions is optional. _____

IOI

Fill-in the-blanks Questions

F1   The number of parameters and their data types of a function are together known as the _____

F2   The function that is invoked first when a program starts is _____

F3   The function that is the last to finish in a program (under normal circumstance) is _____

F4   The function that is not callable by any other function is _____

F5   The default return type of a function is _____

F6   The default parameter passing mechanism for primitive types is _____

F7   The default parameter passing mechanism for arrays is _____

F8   A 'struct' passed as argument to a function uses pass by _____

F9   C does not allow _____ and _____ as return types in functions.

F10   A function whose statements are executed, but without causing a 'jump/return' (save/restore of activation record) is known as _____ function.

F11   A function, say A, calling itself, is known as _____

F12   A function A, calling function B, which in turn calls A, is known as _____

F13   All C programs must have a function named _____ where the execution starts.

F14   The 'special' function that cannot be called from any other function is the _____

F15 The deault parameter passing for 'structs' is _____

IOIOIOIOIOIOIOIOIOIOIOIOIOIOIOIOIOIOIOIOIOIOIOIOIOIOIOIOI

Essay-type Questions

F1 What does the following function compute for $n \geq 0$?

```
int fun1 (int m, int n)
{
  if (n == 0)
    return m;
  else
    return (1 + fun1 (m, n-1));
}
```

F2 What does the following function compute for $n \geq 0$?

```
int fun1 (int n, int m)
{
    if (m == 0 || n == 0)
        return 0;
    if (n == 1)
        return m;
    else
        return (m + fun1 (n-1, m));
}
```

F3 What does the following function compute for $n > 0$?

```
int fun1 (int n)
{
  if (n == 1)
    return 1;
  return n + fun1(n-1);
}
```

F4 What does the following function compute for $n \geq 0$?

```
int fun1 (int n)
{
  if (n < 10)
    return 1;
  return (1 + fun1 (n/10));
}
```

```
    }
```

F5 What does the following function compute for $n \geq 0$?

```
int fun1 (int num)
{
  if (num < 10)
    return (num);
  return (num % 10 + fun1 (num / 10));
}
```

F6 What does the following function compute (given that MAX returns the larger of its two arguments)?

```
int fun1 (int num)
{
  if (num < 10)
    return (num);
  return MAX(num % 10, fun1 (num / 10));
}
```

F7 What does the following function compute?

```
int fun1(int num){
    static int sum=0,rem;
    if(num > 0){
        rem = num%10;
        sum = sum*10+rem;
        reverse_dgts(num/10);
    }
    return sum;
}
```

F8 What does the following function compute?

```
int fun1 (int n)
{
  if ((n == 0) || (n == 1))
    return 1;
  return (1 + fun1 (n / 2));
}
```

F9 What does the following function compute?

```
int fun1 (int n)
{
```

```
    if (n == 0)
        return 0;
    else if (n % 2 == 0) // n is Even
        return fun1(n/2);
    else
        return 1 + fun1(n/2); // integer division
}
```

F10 What does the following function compute, for $n \geq 0$?

```
int fun1 (int n)
{
    if (n == 0 || n == 1)
        return 1;
    return (n * fun1 (n-1));
}
```

F11 What does the following function compute?

```
int fun1 (int n)
{
    if (n == 1) || (n == 2)
        return 1;
    return (fun1(n-1) + fun2(n-2));
}
```

F12 What does the following function compute?

```
int fun1 (int n){
    if (n == 0)
        return 1;
    else
        return fun1(n-1) + fun1(n-1);
}
```

F13 What does the following function compute?

```
int fun1 (int n)
{
    if (n == 0)
        return 1;
    else
        return 2 * fun1(n-1);
}
```

F14   What does the following function compute?

```c
int fun1 (int n, int m)
{
    if (n == 0)
        return 0;
    if (m == 0)
        return 1;
    if (n == 1)
        return 1;
    else
        return (n * fun1 (n, m-1));
}
```

F15   What does the following function compute?

```c
int fun1 (int n, int m) {
    if (m == 0 || m == n)
        return 1;
    return fun1(n-1, m-1) + fun1(n-1, m);
}
```

F16   What does the following function compute (given that MAX returns the larger of its two arguments)?

```c
int fun1 (int A[], int L, int R)
{
    if (L == R)
        return (A[L]);

    return MAX(A[L], fun1(A, L+1, R));
}
```

F17   What does the following function compute?

```c
int fun1 (int A[], int L, int R)
{
    if (L == R)
        return (A[L]);

    int M = (L + R) / 2;
    return MAX(fun1(A,L,M), fun1(A,M+1,R));
}
```

F18   What does the following function compute?

```
int fun1 (int A[], int L, int R)
{
  if (L == R)
    return A[L];

  return A[R] + fun1(A,L,R-1);
}
```

F19 What does the following function compute?

```
int fun1 (int A[], int L, int R)
{
  if (L == R)
    return A[L];

  int M = (L + R) / 2;
  return fun1(A,L,M) + fun1(A,M+1,R);
}
```

F20 What is the output of the following function?

```
void fun1 (int N)
{
  if (N/2 == 0) {
    if (N == 0)
      putchar ('0');
    else

      putchar ('1');
    return;
  }
  fun1 (N / 2);
  printf("%d", (N % 2));
}
```

F21 What is the output of the following function?

```
void fun1 (int N) {
  if (N == 1) {
    printf("1 ");
    return;
  }
  fun1 (N-1);
  printf("%d ", N);
}
```

F22   What is the output of the following program?

```
void fun1 (int A[], int L, int R){
  if (L == R){
    printf("%d ", A[L]);
    return;
  }
  fun1(A, L+1, R);
  printf("%d ", A[L]);
}
int main()
{
  int arr[]= {3, 4, 7, 2, 9, 1, 8, 5, 6};
  fun1 (arr, 0, 8);
}
```

F23   What does the following function compute?

```
#define FALSE 0
#define TRUE 1

unsigned fun1 (char str[], int L, int R])
{
  if (L >= R)
    return TRUE;
  if (str[L] != str[R])
    return (FALSE);
  return (fun1(str, L+1, R-1));
}
```

F24   What is the output of the following program?
```
void fun(int *p, int *q) {
  p = q;
  *p = 7;
}

int main() {
  int i = 3, j = 5;
  fun(&i, &j);
  printf("i=%d j=%d\n", i, j);
  return 0;
}
```

F25   What is the output of the following program?
```
void fn1 (int a, int* b)
{
  int *x, y;

  x = &a;
```

```
    *x += *b;
    *b += *x;
    x = b;
    b = &y;
    *b = 5;
    *x += y;
}
main ()
{
    int n, m;

    n = 10; m = 20;
    fn1 (n, &m);
    printf ("n=%d m=%d\n", n, m);
    fn1 (n, &m);
    printf ("n=%d m=%d\n", n, m);
}
```

F26 What is the output of the following program segment?

```
int i, num, fac=1, inc=1;
for (i=1; i<=6; i++) {
    num = 4*fac;
    inc++;
    fac += inc;
    printf("%d\n", num);
}
```

F27 What is the output of the following program segment?

```
int a = 156, b = 273;
printf ("a=%d, b=%d\n", a, b);
a = a ^ b;
b = a ^ b;
a = a ^ b;
printf ("a=%d, b=%d\n", a, b);
```

F28 What is the output of the following program segment?

```
char s1[] = """";
char s2[] = "\"\"";
char s3[] = "\\\"\\\"";

printf ("%s\n", s1);
printf ("%s\n", s2);
printf ("%s\n", s3);
```

F29 What is the output of the following program segment?

```
char c1, c2;
float n1, n2;
c1 = 'a'; c2 = c1+16;
printf ("%c  %c\n", c1, c2);
c1 = 127; c2 = c1+5;
printf ("%d  %d\n", c1, c2);

n1 = 26.13283476;
n2 = 728.8382108348;
printf ("%f %f\n", n1, n2);
printf ("%6.2f %6.2f\n", n1, n2);
```

F30 What is the output of the following program?

```
fn2 (int x, int* y, int z, int *w)
{
  x += *y + *w;
  *y += x + z;
  z = x + *y;
  *w = *y + z;
  printf ("%d %d %d %d\n", x, *y, z, *w);
}

main ()
{
  int a=3, b=5, c=4, d=6;
  printf ("%d %d %d %d\n", a, b, c, d);
  fn2 (a, &b, c, &d);
  printf ("%d %d %d %d\n", a, b, c, d);
}
```

F31 What is the output of the following program?

```
int fn1 (int a, int *b)
{
  int *x, y;

  x = &y;
  *b += 5;
  a += 3;
  *x = a;
  return (y);
}

void fn2 (int *x, int y)
{
  int a, *b;
```

```
  a = 5;
  b = &a;
  *b += 3;
  *x = fn1(y, b);
  printf ("%d\n", *x);
  y = fn1(a, x);
  printf ("%d\n", y);
}

main ()
{
  int n, m;

  n = 10; m = 20;
  fn2 (&n, m);
  printf ("n=%d m=%d\n", n, m);
}
```

F32   What is the output of the following program?

```
int fn1 (int a, int b)
{
  int x;

  a += b;
  b += a;
  x = a + b;
  return (x);
}

void fn2 (int a, int *b)
{
  int *x, y;

  x = b;  y = a;
  *x += y;  y += *x;
  printf ("fn2: (*x)=%d y=%d\n", *x, y);
}

void fn3 (int *a, int b)
{
  int x, *y;

  x = *a;  y = &b;
  *a += *y; b += x;
  printf ("fn3: x=%d (*y)=%d\n", x, *y);
}
```

```
int main()
{
  int n = 5, m = 12, p;

  p = fn1 (n, m);
  printf ("n=%d m=%d p=%d\n", n, m, p);
  fn2 (n, &m);
  printf ("n=%d m=%d\n", n, m);
  fn3 (&n, m);
  printf ("n=%d m=%d\n", n, m);
}
```

F33   What is the output of the following program?

```
void fun(int x, int y){
   x += x;
   y += y;
   printf("Values in fun: %d %d\n", x, y);
}
int main(){
   int list[2] = {1, 3};
   fun(list[0], list[1]);
   printf("Values in main: %d %d\n", list[0],
list[1]);
}
```

F34   What is the output of the following code?

```
int fun1 (int x){
  int a;
  x = x * 2;
  a = x + 3;
  x = a - 5;
  printf("fun1: x = %d a = %d\n", x, a);
  return a;
}

int main (){
  int a = 5, b;
  b = fun1 (a);
  a = fun1 (b);
  printf("main: a = %d b = %d\n", a, b);
  return 0;
}
```

F35   What is the output of the following code?

```
int fun1 (int x, int y){
```

```
  int a;
  x = y * 2;
  y = x * 3;
  a = y - x;
  printf("fun1: x = %d y = %d a = %d\n", x,y,a);
  return a;
}
int main (){
  int a = 5, b = 4, c, d;
  c = fun1 (a, b);
  d = fun1 (b, a);
  printf("main: a = %d b = %d c = %d d = %d\n", a, b,
c, d);
  return 0;
}
```

F36 What is the output of the following program?

```
void fn1 ()
{
  int i=0;
  i++;
  printf ("fn1: i=%d, ", i);
}

void fn2 ()
{
  static int i=0;
  i++;
  printf ("fn2: i=%d\n", i);
}

int main ()
{
  int i;

  for (i=1; i<=3; i++){
    printf ("[Call %d] ", i);
    fn1 ();
    fn2 ();
  }
}
```

F37 What is the output of the following code?

```
int fun1 (int* x, int c)
{
   c--;
```

```
        if (c == 0) return 1;
        (*x)++;
        return fun1(x, c) * (*x);
}
int main()
{
    int a = 4;
    printf ("%d\n", fun1(&a, a));
    return 0;
}
```

F38 What is the output of the following code?

```
int* fun1()
{
    static int x = 10;
    x += 5;
    return &x;
}
int main()
{
    printf("%d\n", *fun1());
    printf("%d\n", *fun1());
    return 0;
}
```

F39 What is the output of the following code?

```
int fun1 (int a)
{
    return 2*a+3;
}
void fun2 (int a, int b)
{
    a += 2*b;
    printf ("fun2: a = %d\n", a);
}
int main()
{
    int x = 7, y = 5;
    fun2 (x, fun1(y));
    return 0;
}
```

F40 What is the output of the following code?

```
void fun (){
    static int i = 2;
    while (i-- > 0){
        printf ("%d ", i);
        fun ();
    }
```

```
}
int main(){
  fun();
  return 0;
}
```

F41 What is the output of the code of the previous problem if the **static** keyword of 'i' is removed?

F42 What is the output of the following code?
```
int main()
{
  void fun();
  fun();
  (*fun) ();
}
void fun() {
  printf("In fun()\n");
}
```

F43 What is the output of the following code?
```
void fun1(){
  printf ("fun1 called.\n");
  return;
}
void fun2(){
  printf ("fun2 called.\n");
  return;
}
void fun3(void (*fun) ()){
  fun();
  return;
}
int main(){
  fun3(fun1);
  fun3(fun2);
  return(0);
}
```

F44 What is the output of the following code?

```
int fun1(int a){
    return 3*a;
}
int fun2(int (*fun) (), int a){
  return fun(a);
}
```

```
int main(){
  int i;
  i = fun2(fun1, 5);
  printf ("i = %d\n", i);
  return(0);
}
```

F45 What is the output of the following code?
```
int fun1(int a){
    return 3*a;
}
float fun2(int (*fun)(), int a){
  return 2.35 + fun(a);
}
int main(){
  int i=5; float z;
  z = fun2(fun1, i);
  printf ("z = %.2f\n", z);
  return(0);
}
```

IOIOIOIOIOIOIOIOIOIOIOIOIOIOIOIOIOIOIOIOIOIOIOIOIOIOIOIOIOIOIOIOIOIOI

G. Dynamic Storage Management

True/False Questions

G1   The **malloc** function will always be able to allocate storage. _____

G2   The **malloc** function returns an address. _____

G3   The **malloc** function returns a pointer to a specific type. _____

G4   Consecutive calls to **malloc** are guaranteed to allocate storage contiguously. _____

G5   Dereferencing a pointer whose memory has been deallocated causes runtime error. _____

G6   The size of storage to be allocated by **malloc** must be specified at compile time. _____

G7   The pointer returned by **realloc()** will always be the same as the original pointer. _____

G8   Memory allocated using the **malloc** operator must be explicitly released when it is no longer needed. _____

G9   The memory allocation using the **malloc** operator is done in the stack area of memory. _____

G10   The memory allocation using the **calloc** operator is done in the data area of memory. _____

G11   The statement **free(ptr)**, when the **ptr** is NULL, causes an error. _____

G12   Given **p1** is a pointer to memory allocated using 'malloc' operator, **free(p1)** would release memory allocated by 'malloc' and also that for **p1**. _____

G13   The **free(ptr)** function does not delete the pointer variable **ptr**. _____

G14 The **free()** function can be used to release storage allocated to any variable. _____

G15 **malloc** does not clear the memory that it allocates. _____

G16 **calloc** clears (zeros out) the memory before returning. ____

G17 The **realloc()** function reallocates memory previously allocated using **malloc** or **calloc**. _____

G18 The **realloc()** function can only increase the memory allocation, but not decrease it. _____

G19 The **realloc()** function leaves the existing data unchanged up to the smaller of the old and new size. _____

G20 The **realloc()** function always makes a new allocation. _____

G21 The **realloc()** function cannot be called with a **NULL** pointer. _____

G22 The **realloc()** function cannot be called with a zero size. _____

G23 After dynamic memory is freed up using **free(ptr)**, the pointer **ptr** is set to NULL. _____

IOIOIOIOIOIOIOIOIOIOIOIOIOIOIOIOIOIOIOIOIOIOIOIOI

Fill-in the-blanks Questions

G1 The function used to allocate a block of storage is _____

G2 If the **malloc** function fails to allocate memory, it returns _____

G3 The type returned by **malloc** function is _____

G4 The **malloc** function call required to allocate storage for 10 unsigned integers is _____

G5 The **malloc** function call required to allocate storage for 25 chaacters is _____

G6   The type returned by **calloc** function is _____

G7   The function used to release (deallocate) a block of storage is _____

G8   The function used to increase or decrease the size of dynamically allocated storage is _____

G9   Objects created dynamically using the 'malloc' function are allocated in the _____ area of memory.

G10   The functions used for dynamic allocation of memory in the heap area are _____ and _____

G11   The function used to release the memory allocated by the 'malloc' and 'calloc' operators is _____

G12   The functions **malloc, calloc** and **free** manage storage in the _____ area of memory.

IOIOIOIOIOIOIOIOIOIOIOIOIOIOIOIOIOIOIOIOIOIOIOIOIOIOI

Essay-type Questions

G1   What is the argument expected by a malloc function?

G2   What is the return value of a malloc function?

G3   What are the arguments and return value/type of the calloc function?

G4   What is a dangling pointer?

G5   What is memory leak?

G6   What is the effect of the following statement?
      ```
      int* ip = malloc(10*sizeof(int));
      ```

G7   What is the effect of the following statement?
      ```
      char* cp = (char *)malloc(25*sizeof(char));
      ```

G8 What is the effect of the following statement?
```
int* ptr = calloc(len, sizeof(int));
```

G9 Give the equivalence of **ptr** = **calloc(m, n);** to the combination of **malloc** and **memset**.

G10 What is the output of the following program? Describe the salient steps of the program.

```
#include <stdio.h>
#include <stdlib.h>
int main(void) {
    int* iptr1 = NULL;
    int* iptr2 = NULL;
    iptr1 = (int*) malloc (sizeof(int));
    iptr2 = (int*) malloc (sizeof(int));
    printf ("Type two integers: ");
    scanf("%d", iptr1);
    scanf("%d", iptr2);
    printf("iptr1 deref. = %d, iptr2 deref. = %d\n",
*iptr1, *iptr2);
    printf("iptr1 content = %p, iptr2 content = %p\n",
iptr1, iptr2);
    free(iptr1);
    free(iptr2);
    return 0;
}
```

G11 What is the output of the following code segment? Describe the behavior.
```
int *p;
p = (int*) calloc(10, sizeof(int));
printf ("%p\n", p);
free(p);
printf ("%p\n", p);
```

IOIOIOIOIOIOIOIOIOIOIOIOIOIOIOIOIOIOIOIOIOIOIOIOIOIOIOIOI

H. Input / Output and Library Functions

True/False Questions

H1   **stdin**, **stdout**, and **stderr** are binary streams. _____

H2   The number of expressions following the format string must be exactly same as the number of format specifiers in the string of **printf**. _____

H3   The expressions following the format specifiers in **scanf** need to be memory addresses of where the scanned data is to be stored. _____

H4   **printf** cannot handle a 'struct' argument. _____

H5   Structs and unions can be directly read by **scanf**. _____

H6   Given **str** is a character string, **printf("%s", &str)** results in error. _____

H7   Given **str** is a character string, **printf("%s", str)** outputs a newline character after printing **str**. _____

H8   Given **str** is a character string, **printf("%s", &str[0])** prints **str**. _____

H9   Given **str** is a character string, **puts(str)** outputs a newline character after printing **str**. _____

H10 **printf** cannot handle structured types (arrays, structs, unions). _____

H11 **fprintf** outputs formatted data in variables into an output stream. _____

H12 **fprintf** cannot output formatted data in variables on standard output (monitor). _____

H13 **sprintf** outputs formatted data in variables into memory (buffer). _____

H14 **sprintf** can also output formatted data in variables on standard output (monitor). _____

H15 **scanf** can only be used for reading primitive types and character strings. _____

H16 The **scanf** statement to read into an integer variable **num**, is **scanf("%d", num);** _____

H17 **getchar()** reads characters from the keyboard after the 'Enter' key has been pressed. _____

H18 **scanf** reads in a string of characters up to the first newline character. _____

H19 **scanf** appends the encountered a newline character to the end of the character string stored. _____

H20 **scanf** appends a null character to the end of the character string stored. _____

H21 **scanf** has only side-effect, and no return value. _____

H22 **fscanf** can read from keyboard (stdin) also. _____

H23 **sscanf** can read from keyboard (stdin) also. _____

H24 The **gets** function continues to read strings of characters even after encounting space ot tab characters. _____

H25 A limit on the number of characters read by **gets** can be specified. _____

H26 **fputs** writes a string to a file, but not on the terminal. _____

H27 A NULL return value of **fgets** always indicates error. _____

H28 A limit on the maximum number of characters read using **fgets** can be specified. _____

H29 **fgets** can be used to read from a file but not from the keyboard. _____

H30 After encounting a newline character, **fgets** stops reading and stores the newline character. _____

H31 **fprintf** is always returns a posiive number. _____

H32 When **fopen** is used in **"r"** mode, the file must be existing. _____

H33 When **fopen** is used in **"r"** mode, the file cannot be written into. _____

H34 When **fopen** is used in **"w"** mode, the file must be existing. _____

H35 When **fopen** is used in **"w"** mode, the existing contents of a preexisting file with the given name is erased. _____

H36 When **fopen** is used in **"a"** mode, the file must be existing. _____

H37 When **fopen** is used in **"a"** mode, the existing contents of a preexisting file with the given name is erased. _____

H38 When **fopen** is used in **"a"** mode, writing into the file can be done anywhere. _____

H39 When **fopen** is used in **"r+"** mode, it expects a preexisting file. _____

H40 When **fopen** is used in **"r+"** mode, the file can be written into. _____

H41 When **fopen** is used in **"w+"** mode, it expects a preexisting file. _____

H42 When **fopen** is used in **"w+"** mode, reading from the file is not allowed. _____

H43 When **fopen** is used in **"a+"** mode, it expects a preexisting file. _____

H44 When **fopen** is used in **"a+"** mode, both reading and writing are allowed. _____

H45 When **fopen** is used in **"a+"** mode, reading and writing are allowed anywhere in the file. _____

H46 When **fopen** is used in **"a+"** mode, reading/writing can be done anywhere in the file. _____

H47 There are library functions for converting strings of lower/upper case characters fron one to the other. _____

H48 The value of **tolower(toupper(ch))** is the same as **tolower(ch)** for any character. _____

H49 The value of **tolower(tolower(ch))** is the same as **tolower(ch)** for any character. _____

H50 The functions **tolower** and **toupper** have no effect on character 'ch' for which **isalpha(ch)** is true. _____

IOIOIOIOIOIOIOIOIOIOIOIOIOIOIOIOIOIOIOIOIOIOIOIOIOIOIOIOIOIOIOI

Fill-in the-blanks Questions

H1 The three text streams which are predefined when a C program begins execution are _____, _____, and _____.

For H2 – H8: Given **char str[] = "SAMPLE STRING";**

H2 The output of **printf("%s", str)** is _____

H3 The output of **printf("%s", &str[0])** is _____

H4 The output of **printf("%s", &str[1])** is _____

H5 The **printf** statement to print **RING** (part of **str**) is

_____

H6 The **printf** statement to print **M** (3rd letter of **str**) is

_____

H7 The output of **puts(str)** is _____

H8 The **puts** statement to print **STRING** (part of **str**) is

_____

H9 The **gets** function reads a string of characters from
_____

H10 When fscanf encounters the end of the file before the desired number of items are be scanned in, it returns _____

H11 The file I/O function which flushes buffers from RAM out to disk is _____

H12 The function which returns a character at a time, read from the **stdin** stream is _____

H13 Functions to read a character at a time from a given input stream are _____ and _____

H14 The function which outputs a character at a time onto the **stdout** stream is _____

H15 Functions which output a character at a time to a given output stream are _____ and _____

H16 The function which puts back a character read from an input stream is _____

H17 The function which reads characters into a character array from standard input is _____

H18 The function which prints from a character array to standard output (screen) is _____

H19 The library function to output a character at a time onto standard output (screen) is _____

H20 The library function to output a character string (buffer of characters) at a time to an output stream is _____

H21 The function to output/transfer formatted data from variables to standard output (monitor) only is _____

H22 The function to read/transfer formatted data from only standard input (keyboard) into variables is _____

H23 The function to output/transfer formatted data from variables to an output stream is _____

H24 The function to read/transfer formatted data from an input stream into variables is _____

H25 The function to output/transfer formatted data from variables to memory (buffer) is _____

H26 The function to read/transfer formatted data from memory (buffer) into variables is _____

H27 When **fopen** is unable to open a requested file it returns _____

H28 The fopen modes where the stream pointer is placed at the beginning of the file are _____

H29 The fopen modes where the stream pointer is placed at the end of the file are _____

H30 The function to check end-of-file in an input stream is _____

H31 The function to check for the error bit in a stream is _____

H32 The function to clear error bit in a stream is _____

H33 The function to get the file descriptor associated with a given file is _____

H34 The function to reset a file to the beginning is _____

H35 The function to directly jump to a certain position in a file is _____

H36 The function which gives the position (for reading/writing) in a file is _____

H37 The argument of **feek** to specify the offset relative to the file beginning is _____

H38 The argument of **feek** to specify the offset relative to current position is _____

H39 The argument of **feek** to specify the offset relative to current position is _____

H40 The function to read from a binary file is _____

H41 The function to write to a binary file is _____

Library Functions

H42 Function to check whether a character is alphabetic is _____

H43 Function to check whether a character is alphanumeric is _____

H44 Function to check whether a character is a digit is _____

H45 Function to check whether a character is a space or tab is _____

H46 Function to check whether a character is tab or a control code is _____

H47 Function to check whether a character is tab or space or whitespace control code is _____

H48 Function to check whether a character is printable is _____

H49 Function to check whether a character is punctuation mark is _____

H50 Function to check whether a character is hexadecimal is _____

H51 The value of **islower(toupper(c))** for any alphabetic character is _____

H52 The value of **iscntrl(c) && isalnum(c)** for any character 'c' is _____

H53 When **isalnum(c) && isalpha(c) && isupper(c)** is 'true', the value of 'c' is between _____ and _____

H54 When **isalnum(c) && isdigit(c)** is 'true', the value of 'c' is between _____ and _____

H55 The value of **abs(3 - 5 - abs (2 - 9))** is _____

H56 The value of **fabs(2.3 - 4.5 + fabs(3.2-7.1))** is _____

H57 The value of **round(1.49)** is _____

H58 The value of **round(1.5)** is ____

H59 The value of **rint(1.49)** is ____

H60 The value of **rint(1.5)** is ____

H61 The value of **ceil(1.01)** is ____

H62 The value of **ceil(1.99)** is ____

H63 The value of **floor(1.99)** is ____

H64 The value of **floor(1.01)** is ____

H65 The statement to compute $e^{2.3}$ (where e is the base of the natural logarithm) is _____

H66 The statement to compute $\log_e 5.7$ is _____

H67 The statement to compute $\log_{10} 7.3$ is _____

H68 The statement to compute $\sqrt{4.5}$ is _____

H69 The statement to compute $3.2^{4.5}$ is _____

H70 The value of **pow(9, 1/2)** is ____

H71 The value of **pow(9, 1.0/2)** is ____

H72 The function to initialize the pseudo-random-number generator is _____

H73 **rand()** returns a random number (integer) between ____ and _____

H74 The statement to generate a random number between 1 and 100 (inclusive) is _____

H75 The statement to generate a random number between −273 and 200 (inclusive) is _____

H76 The statement to generate a random number between 0 and 1 is _____

H77 The statement to generate random integers 0 or 1 is _____

H78 The statement to generate random integers in the range 18 to 65 is _____

H79 To obtain a random integer between values **a** and **b**, a possible statement would be _____

H80 The function used to parse a string of numeric characters into a number of type int is _____

H81 The function used to parse a string of numeric characters into a number of type double is _____

H82 The function used to parse a string of numeric characters into a number of type long int is _____

H83 Given **str** is a character array of size 20, and **str** contains the string "**Test String**", the value of **strlen(str)** is _____

H84 Given **str1** contains the string "**Test** ", **str2** contains the string "**String**", the value of **strcat(str1, str2)** is _____

H85 Given **str1** contains the string "**Test** ", **str2** contains the string "**String**", the value of **strncat(str1, str2, 3)** is _____

H86 Given **str1** contains the string "**Test** ", **str2** contains the string "**String**", the value of **strlen(strcpy(str2, str1)** is _____

H87 The value of **strcmp("Sang", "Sing")** is _____

H88 The value of **strcmp("sing", "Sing")** is _____

H89 For any valid character string str, The value of **strcmp(str,str)** is _____

H90 The value of **strncmp("Singular", "Single", 4)** is ____

H91   Given **str** = **"BICYCLING"**, **char* s1=strchr(str, 'C')**; the output of **printf("%s\n", s1)** is _____

H92   Given **str** = **"BICYCLING"**, **char* s1=strrchr(str, 'C')**; the output of **printf("%s\n", s1)** is _____

H93   Given **str** = **"INSIDER"**, **char* s1=strstr(str, "SIDE")**; the output of **printf("%s\n", s1)** is _____

IOIOIOIOIOIOIOIOIOIOIOIOIOIOIOIOIOIOIOIOIOIOIOIOIOIOIOIOIOI

Essay-type Questions

H1   What is the behavior of the following program?

```
int main ()
{
  FILE *infile;
  char c, fname[80];

  printf ("Type the file name: ");
  scanf ("%s", fname);

  if ((infile = fopen (fname, "r")) == NULL){
    printf ("Can't open file\n");
    exit (1);
  }

  while ((c=getc (infile)) != EOF)
    putchar (c);
}
```

H2   What is the behavior of the following program?

```
int main (int argc, char* argv)
{
  FILE *infile, *outfile;
  char c;

  if (argc != 3) {
    fprintf (stderr, "Number of args should be
two.\n");
    exit (1);
  }
  if ((infile = fopen (argv[1], "r")) == NULL {
```

```
        fprintf (stderr, "Can't read file %s\n",
argv[1]);
        exit (2);
    }
    if ((outfile = fopen (argv[2], "w")) == NULL) {
        fprintf (stderr, "can't write to file %s\n",
argv[2]);
        exit (3);
    }

    while ((c=getc (infile)) != EOF)
        putc (c, outfile);
}
```

H3   What is the behavior of the following program?

```
#define BUFSIZE 80

main ()
{
    FILE *infile;
    char fname[80], buf[BUFSIZE];

    printf ("Type the file name: ");
    scanf ("%s", fname);

    if ((infile = fopen (fname, "r")) == NULL) {
        printf ("Can't open file\n");
        exit (1);
    }

    while (fgets (buf, BUFSIZE, infile) != NULL)
        fputs(buf, stdout);
}
```

H4   Write statement to open an existing file named "sales_07.dat" for reading only.

H5   Write statement to open an existing file named "sales_09.dat" for reading and writing.

H6   Write statement to create a new file named "sales_07.dat" for wriring into it. An already existing file may be overwriten

H7   Write statement to create file named "sales_09.dat" for writing and reading. An already existing file may be overwriiten.

H8   Write statement to open a file named "sales_07.dat" for appending (only writing after the end of existing file). If the file does not exist, it should create it.

H9   Write statement to open a file named "sales_09.dat" for reading and writing after the end of existing file. If the file does not exist, it should create it,

H10   Write statements to create a file named "emp_records_01.dat" with a file pointer named "empf", and write to the file "num_recs" records, each record of type "EMPREC", the data given in an array pointed to by "emp_recs".

H11   Write statements to open an existing file named "emp_records_03.dat" with a file pointer named "empf", and read from the file "num_recs" records, each of type "EMPREC", into an array pointed to by "emp_recs".

H12   Write statement to position the file pointer named "fp" to the byte number "byte_num" from the start of file.

H13   Write statement to position the file pointer named "fp" to the byte number "byte_num" from the current position in the file.

H14   Write statement to position the file pointer named "fp" to the byte number "byte_num" backwards from the current position.

H15   Write statement to position the file pointer named "fp" to the end of file.

H16   Write statement to position the file pointer named "fp" to the byte number "byte_num" before the end of file.

IOIOIOIOIOIOIOIOIOIOIOIOIOIOIOIOIOIOIOIOIOIOIOIOIOIOIOIOI

I. Programming Problems

I1   Write the code segment to determine if a given 'year' is leap year or not, and return a Boolean value accordingly. Note that a year is leap year if it is divisible by 4 or if it is a century boundaries, it must be divisible by 400. For example, 1976 is a leap year, 1982 is not a leap year, 1900 is not a leap year, and 2000 is a leap year.

I2   Write a 'for-loop' for printing the 'N' numbers of the sequence given below for a given N.
     1 2 5 10 17 26 .. ..

I3   Write the code segment for printing the numbers of the sequence given below as long as the numbers are less than or equal to a given positive integer 'N'.
     1 2 5 10 17 26 .. ..

I4   Write a function which takes an array of integers and its size as arguments, and determines and returns the number of times the maximum element occurs in the array, using only one pass through the array.

I5   Write the statements to assign to variable 'max3' the maximum of three numbers in variables a, b, and c.

I6   An interval (*b*, *e*) is a pair of real numbers (*b*: begin, *e*: end). Intervals (2.7, 5.3) and (4.8, 12.2) overlap, (3.4, 6.6) and (6.6, 7.3) do not overlap, and (2.7, 5.3) and (7.1, 9.5) do not overlap. Declare a struct **Interval** with fields **begin** and **end**. Write a function **overlap** which takes two intervals as arguments, and returns the extent of overlap (0 if no overlap).

I7   An interval (*b*, *e*) is a pair of real numbers (*b*: begin, *e*: end). Write a function **interval_pos** which takes two intervals as arguments, and returns the relative positions of the two intervals: 1. The intervals do not overlap; 2. The intervals just touch (end of one interval equals the beginning of the other); 3. The intervals overlap; 4. One interval completely contains the other.

1. No Overlap (Disjoint)   2. No Overlap (End of 1 = Begin of 2)   3. Overlap   4. Containment

I8   Write a function which takes two arguments: (1) a 'struct' representing a circle containing fields (a) 'center' which is a 'struct' of type 'point' consisting of two real numbers, and (b) 'radius' which is a real number, and (2) a 'point', and returns an integer: 1. If the point is on the circle (circumference); 2. If the point is inside the circle; 3. If the point is outside the circle.

I9   Write a function which takes as arguments three real numbers representing the sides of a triangle, and determines and returns true or false, based on whether it is a valid triangle or not. **Note:** In a valid triangle, the sum of the lengths of any two sides is greater than the length of the third side. For example, if the given side lengths are 10.7, 5.6, and 2.9, it should return false.

I10   Write a program, without using the 'pow' library function, to print all the odd powers of 3 less than or equal to a given N, obtained as user input. (ex. It should print 3 27 243 ... as long as the odd power of 3 is $\leq N$)

I11   Write a program which prints the following sequence up to a given length. The length of the sequence is read from the keyboard.
Sequence: 1 2 4 7 11 16 22 29 ……..
The program should prompt: "Type the sequence length: ". If 5 is typed in, then the output should be: "1 2 4 7 11".

I12   Write a program that calculates and prints the sequence, as shown below.

```
        9
       89
      789
     6789
      : :
      : :
123456789
```

I13   Write a program to determine the least number of coins using quarters, dimes, nickels, pennies to be given as change.

I14   Write a program which reads the number of seconds elapsed since the clock has 'struck 12' and prints the number of hours, minutes and seconds.
For example, if the number is **371**, it should print **0:6:11**; for **36522**, it should print **10:8:42**

I15   Write a function which takes an integer argument and returns the number of digits in the number. Use main() as a driver to test it.

I16   Write a function which takes an integer argument and returns the sum of digits in the number. Use main() as a driver to test it.

I17   Write a function which takes an integer as argument and returns 'true' if it has any of the digits repeated, 'false', otherwise. Assume the input to be within the valid range of integers.
Example: for 3538291, it should return 'true'; for 7384961, it should return 'false'.

I17   Write a function which takes a number 'n' and a digit 'd' as arguments and determines and returns the number of occurrences of the digit in the number.
Ex. Input: (536714, 3), Output: 1;   Input: (2354392, 3), Output: 2; Input: (2352, 6), Output: 0

I18   Write a function which takes two integers 'num' and 'pos' as arguments, and returns the digit at position 'pos' of the number 'num'. Note that pos = 1 denotes the unit's position. For example, Input: (6753, 3), Output: 7; Input: (372519, 4), Output: 2. Use main() as a driver to test it.

I19   Write a function which takes an integer as argument and returns an integer with the digits reversed. For example, if the input is 536327, the output is 723635.

I20   Given an integer, adding the digits of the number yields another integer. Repeating this process results in a single digit number. Write a function which takes an integer argument, and returns the number of 'stages' required to obtain the single digit number. For example, if the number is 798, after one stage, the number obtained is 7+9+8 = 24. After the second stage, the number is 2+4 = 6. Thus, two stages are required. A typical output is given below.

```
Type in a number: 7383926
Stage: 1 Stage sum: 38
Stage: 2 Stage sum: 11
Stage: 3 Stage sum: 2
The number of stages: 3
```

I21   The overview of Russian Peasant multiplication to find the product P of two integers N and M, is as follows:

```
1) Initialize product: P to 0.
2) While N is greater than 0 do
   a) If N is odd, add M to P
   b) Double M and halve N
3) Return P
```

Write a function which takes two integers as arguments, and computes and returns their product using the Russian Peasant multiplication scheme. Use main() as a driver to test it.

I22   Write a function which reads an integer limit and determines and prints out all 'Armstrong numbers' within the limit. An Armstrong number is one which equals the sum of the cubes of its digits. A sample output is shown below.

I23   Write a function to calculate and print all the well-ordered numbers of a given number of digits. It should take as input the number of digits, and return the number of well-ordered numbers of that many digits. A well-ordered number is one whose digits strictly increase from left to right. A sample output is given below.

```
Type the number of digits [1-9]: 2
12 13 14 15 16 17 18 19 23 24
25 26 27 28 29 34 35 36 37 38
39 45 46 47 48 49 56 57 58 59
67 68 69 78 79 89
Number of well ordered numbers of 2 digits = 36
```

I24   Write a recursive function for fast power computation of a^N using the facts that:
  • when $N = 0$, then the result is 1.
  • when N is even, the result is $(a^{N/2})^2$.
  • when N is odd, the result is $(a^{(N-1)/2})^2 * a$.
Assume the availablity of a function $SQR(x)$ which computes x^2. 'a' and 'N' are obtained as user input. Use the 'main()' as the driver function.

I25   Write a recursive function which checks for the presence of digit 'd' in a given number 'N', and returns a Boolean value accordingly. 'd' and 'N' are obtained as user input. Use the 'main()' as the driver function.

I26   Write a recursive function which computes, and prints out the number of different partitions of a given integer. Partition of an integer is the number of distinct ways of representing it as a sum of natural numbers.

I27 Write a program that computes and prints the square root 'r' of a number 'x' using Newton's method, and the number of iterations required. Compare it with the value given by the library function. An example output is given below.

```
Type the number: 57
Square root of 57.000000 using Newton's method is
7.549835
The number of iterations required was 6
Square root computed by library function = 7.549834
```

Newton's method: Start with r = 1. If 'r' is an approximation to the square root of 'x', then a better approximation to the square root is given by: (x/r + r)/2 . This is iterated till the error converges (*i.e.* keep itearating until error becomes less than a small number ε, say 0.001.

I28 Write a function which takes as argument a number N (integer), and returns the sum of the sequence: $1/2 + 2/3 + 3/4 + \ldots + N/(N+1)$. Note that the sequence sum is a real number. For example, if $N = 100$, it should output 95.8027.

I29 Write a program to determine the value of N (sequence length) when the sum of the sequence: $1/2 + 2/3 + 3/4 + \ldots + N/(N+1)$ exceeds a given value which is read from the keyboard. Assume that the entered sequence sum is > 0.

I30 Write a program to read a number N (integer) from the terminal, and compute π using the first N terms of the approximation given below.

$$\pi = 4\left(1 - \frac{1}{3} + \frac{1}{5} - \frac{1}{7} + \frac{1}{9} - \frac{1}{11} + \cdots + \frac{(-1)^{N+1}}{2N-1}\right)$$

I31 Write a program to read a number N (integer) from the terminal, and compute e, the base of the natural logarithm, using the first N terms of the approximation given below.

$$e = 1 + \frac{1}{1!} + \frac{1}{2!} + \frac{1}{3!} + \cdots + + \frac{1}{N!}$$

I32   Write a program prints the first "N" numbers of the *Padovan* series. "N" is read from the keyboard. The *Padovan* series is `1,1,1,2,2,3,4,5,7,9,12,16,21,28,37,...` Each number is obtained by skipping the previous one and adding the two before that. Have the program also print the ratio of two successive *Padovan* numbers.

I33   Write a program to compute the amounts after compounding of interest quarterly, monthly, and daily, over a range of years.

A sample output is given below.

```
Type in the principal: 10000
Type in the Interest rate (%): 6.5
Type in the term range (ex. 5 10): 6 12
Yield on 10000.0 at 6.5%
                 Quarterly      Monthly        Daily
 6  Years       14,723.58      14,754.27      14,769.30
 7  Years       15,704.19      15,742.39      15,761.10
 8  Years       16,750.12      16,796.69      16,819.50
 9  Years       17,865.70      17,921.60      17,948.97
10 Years        19,055.59      19,121.84      19,154.30
11 Years        20,324.72      20,402.46      20,440.57
12 Years        21,678.38      21,768.85      21,813.21
```

I34   The formula for the future value of an Annuity is given below:

$$ A = \frac{R\left[\left(1+\frac{r}{n}\right)^{nt} - 1\right]}{\frac{r}{n}} $$

Where A is the future value of the annuity, R is the regular periodic payment, r is the annual interest rate, n is the number of payments made per year, t is the term of the annuity in years.

Write a program which reads the values of A, r, and printout a table which gives the monthly payment required to reach the target with the given interest rate over 5, 10, 15, 20, 25, and 30 years. A sample output is given below.

```
Type in the target amount: 35000
Type in the interest rate (%): 7.5

Years   Monthly Payment
----------------------
  5        482.58
 10        196.71
```

```
15      105.70
20       63.21
25       39.90
30       25.98
```

I35   Write a function which takes as input an Integer N, and prints out N down to 1 in the first row, (N – 1) down to 1 in the second row, etc., and 1 in the last row. For example, if the input value of N is 5, the output should be:

```
5 4 3 2 1
4 3 2 1
3 2 1
2 1
1
```

I36   Write a program which determines the 'day number', given the date. For example, given Dec 18, 1973, it should determine that it is the 352nd day

I37   Write a program to determine the 'date', given the 'year' and 'day number'. For example, given year as 1973 and day number as 352, the program should print the corresponding date as Dec 18.

I38   Write a program to print the Gray code of a given number of bits. The number of bits is specified via user input.

I39   Give a code segment to initialize an integer variable **x** to a given power N of 2 (*i.e.* x = 2^N).

I40   Give a code segment to store in a signed integer variable **x**, the largest positive number which is a power of 2.

I41   Suppose an integer variable **x** contains the lowest integer value (**INT_MIN**). Write one statement which will store the maximum integer value (**INT_MAX**) without direct assignment of **INT_MAX**, but using bit operations.

I42   Write a function which takes an integer as argument, and returns the the number of 1's in it.

I43   Write a function which takes an integer as argument, and returns the the number of 0's in it.

I44 Write a function which takes a positive integer as argument, and returns the exponent if it is a power of 2, and returns −1, otherwise.

I45 Give a code segment to check if bit number 6 of an unsigned integer variable **x** is a 1 or 0, and sets a string variable **status** to "Error" or "Okay", accordingly. (Note that the rightmost bit is bit 0)

I46 Write a program which generates a random integer between 1 and 1,000 and have the user guess the number. Based on the input, it should notify the user whether the guess was lower/higher than the generated number. There should be a maximum of 10 guesses allowed.

I47 Write a function which takes as argument two numbers (rows and columns), and prints a rectangle of '*'s.

I48 Write a function which takes an integer argument which specifies the height of a triangle and prints it using '*'s and spaces.
Examples:

```
height 1:        *


                 *
height 2:       ***


                 *
height 3:       ***
               *****
```

I49 Write a program to read a number (integer) N from the terminal, and print an arrow of '*'s of a given height.
Examples:

```
height 1:    *


             *
height 2:   **
             *


             *
height 3:   **
           ***
            **
             *
```

I50 Write a function which takes two integer arguments (rows and columns), and prints a "hollow" rectangle of '*'s. (The boundary consists of single '*'s)

I51   Write a function which takes an integer argument N indicating the number of nested boxes, and prints N nested boxes. The output for values 1, 2 and 3 are given below.

```
                                     +----+
                        +--+         |+--+|
           ++           |++|         ||++||
           ++           |++|         ||++||
                        +--+         |+--+|
                                     +----+
```

I52   Write a function to print an "X" shape of '*'s of a given height.

```
h=1              *


                *  *
h=2              *
                *  *


             *     *
              *  *
h=3            *
              *  *
             *     *
```

I53   Write a function to print an "Z" shape of '*'s of a given height.

```
                 **
h=2              **


              *  *
h=3              *
              *  *


              ****
                *
h=4             *
              ****
```

I54   Write a function to print an "N" shape of '*'s of a given height.

```
h=2              **
                 **


              *  *
h=3           ***
```

```
                    * *

                  *   *
h=4               ** *
                  * **
                  *   *
```

I55   Write a function to print an "M" shape of '*'s of a given height.

```
h=2                 *  *
                    ***


                  *      *
h=3               **  **
                  *  *  *


                *         *
h=4             **       **
                *  *   *  *
                *   *   *
```

I56   Write a function to print an "V" shape of '*'s of a given height.

```
h=1                   *

h=2                 *   *
                      *


                  *       *
h=3                 *   *
                      *


                *         *
h=4               *       *
                    *   *
                      *
```

I57   Write a function to print an "K" shape of '*'s of a given height.

```
h=1                 **


                  *  *
h=2               **
                  *  *
```

I58   Write functions to (i) print time in HH:MM format, (ii) add two 'times', (iii) subtract two 'times', where 'times' are struct variables. The 'time' struct has two integer members representing hours and minutes. Test them in the main program.

I59   Write a function which takes as arguments (i) an array of integers, (ii) the number of elements of the array, (iii) a given number (say, target), and returns the index of the array element which is 'closest' to the target.

I60   Write a function which takes (i) an array of integers, (ii) the array size, and (iii) an integer item, and determines and returns the 'rank' of the given item in the array. In an array of N elements, the smallest element has a rank of 1, the next smallest has a rank of 2, ... and the largest element has a rank of N. If the item is not found, it returns a rank of 0.

I61   Write a program which determines the first common element, if any, in three sorted lists and prints that element and the indices of the three arrays where it occurs. Otherwise, it prints a "Not Found" message. (For simplicity you may assume that elements in each array are distinct. You may use arrays initialized at declaration)

I62   Write a program to check if a given point is (a) inside, (b) on a border, or (c) outside of a given rectangle.

I63   Write a program to compute the solutions of the quadratic equation $ax^2 + bx + c$, given a, b, and c.

I64   Write a function which maintains a sorted list of K largest integer values in an array. The function takes as input (a) a sorted array of K integers, (b) the array length, and (c) a key Q, and places Q in the appropriate position. For example, suppose the array is {3, 5, 11, 15, 23}. If the input Q is 2, nothing changes in the array. If Q is 11, nothing changes in the array, If Q is 25, the array becomes {5, 11, 15, 23, 25}. If Q is 19, the array becomes {5, 11, 15, 19, 23}.

I65 Write a program to simulate the tossing of a fair coin for different number of tosses, which is read from the keyboard. A sample output is shown below:

I66 Write a program to simulate the tossing of a fair coin for different number of tosses, N: 100, 1,000, 10,000, 100,000. Display the number of outcomes of exactly 3 and exactly 5 consecutive heads coming up.

I67 Write a program to simulate the tossing of a fair coin and determine the minimum number of trials required for exactly 3 consecutive heads coming up. Also determine the number of tails and heads. Have the program to run a certain number of runs as specified by an input. A sample output for 2 runs is shown below.

```
Enter the no. of runs: 2
Run number: 1
T T T H H T T H H H H T H T H T T H H H H T H H H T
Number of Trials: 26
Number of Tails: 11
Number of Heads: 15
Run number: 2
H T H H H T
Number of Trials: 6
Number of Tails: 2
Number of Heads: 4
```

I68 Write a program to simulate the roll of a fair die, and to count the number of times each of the faces comes up in a given number of trials. The number of trials is given as user input. A sample output is shown below.

```
Enter the no. of trials: 10000
Number of trials = 10000
Face   No. of times
1         1635
2         1714
3         1680
4         1653
5         1675
6         1643
```

I69 Simulate and determine the number of throws of a single die until all faces have come up. A sample output is shown below. Note that the theoretical expected number of throws is $6/6 + 6/5 + 6/4 + 6/3 + 6/2 + 6/1 \approx 14.7$

Sample output:
```
2 5 2 1 3 4 2 3 4 4 2 4 3 5 6
Number of trials required for all faces to come up
was 15
```

I70   Write a function which takes an array of integers and its length as arguments and checks if it has duplicates. It and returns true or false based on whether the array has duplicates or not.

I71   Write a function which takes an array of integers and its length as arguments, and prints out the elements such that repeating (duplicate) elements are printed just once. For example, if the input is:

5 2 7 2 4 7 8 12 3 2 3 2 9 2 4 the output should be: **5 2 7 4 8 12 3 9**

I72   Write a function which takes an array of integers and its length as arguments, and prints out only the unique (non-repeating) and returns a count of the unique elements. For example, if the input is: **5 2 7 2 4 7 8 12 3 2 3 2 9 2 4** the output should be: **5 8 12 9** and the return value should be 4.

I73   Write a function which takes a sorted array and its length as arguments, and prints the starting index of the most occurring number, the number, and the number of occurrences. If all the elements are distinct, then it does not print anything.

I74   Write a program to determine and print out the elements of an array of integers that are repeated, along with the indices of the first occurrence and the repetitions. For example, if the input array is:

```
17, 7, 18, 2, 3, 18, 18, 16, 3, 18, 17, 4, 10, 19, 3,
11, 10, 8, 16, 8
```

the output should be:

```
17 at [0] repeated at indices:  10
18 at [2] repeated at indices:  5 6 9
3 at [4] repeated at indices:  8 14
16 at [7] repeated at indices:  18
10 at [12] repeated at indices:  16
8 at [17] repeated at indices:  19
```

I75   Write a function which takes an array and its length as arguments, and prints a 'histogram' based on values in the array. It. A sample output for array of {5, 3, 2, 7, 4} is shown below.

```
    *
    *
*   *
*  **
** **
*****
*****
```

I76   Write a function to partition an array into ODD and EVEN integers. After partition, the array will have all odd elements followed by all even elements. It takes an array as an argument and partitions it in-place.

I77   Write a function to print common elements in two sorted arrays, each having distinct values.

I78   Write a function which takes (i) an array 'a' of integers, (ii) the size of the array, and (iii) an array 'permu_arr' which specifies a permutation of the indices, and permutes the data in array 'a' in-place, based on the specified permutation.

I79   Write a program to simulate the fall of marbles in a Galton board. Show the outcome graphically. Shown below is a 3-level Galton board.

I80   Mathematically, a square matrix A is said to be symmetric if $A(i, j) = A(j, i)$ for all valid i, j. Write a function which takes a 2D array and its size as arguments, and checks if the matrix is symmetric or not, and returns 'true' or 'false' accordingly.

I81   Write a function which takes a square matrix and its size as arguments, and transposes the matrix. The transpose A^T of a matrix A is such that $A^T(i, j) = A(j, i)$.

I82   Write a function to initialize a square matrix to an Identity matrix, where all diagonal elements are 1's and all the remaining elements are 0's.

I83   Write a function which takes a square array and its size as arguments, and rotates it clock-wise by 90 degrees. The rotation is done in-place, without using any temporary array. Test this by using functions for creating a dynamic array of a given size (given as user input), initializing with random numbers, and printing the array.

I84   Write a function which takes a string as argument, and checks if the string is a palindrome or not, and returns 'true' or 'false'accordingly.

I85   Write a function which takes an integer 'N' (≥ 1) as argument, and generates the 'Pascal triangle' of height 'N', and returns it. 'Pascal triangle' is a triangular array of binomial coefficients. An example with N = 5 is shown below.

```
1
1 1
1 2 1
1 3 3 1
1 4 6 4 1
```

I86   Write a function which takes a 2D array as argument, and determines the minimum and maximum elements, and returns them in an array of two elements.

I87   An N x N unit matrix is a matrix of N rows and N columns where all the diagonal elements are '1's and all the remaining elements are '0's. Write a function which takes a 2D array of integers and its size as arguments, and returns 'true' or 'false' if the matrix corresponding to the 2D array is a unit matrix or not.

I88   Write a function which takes as arguments a 2D square array of integers and its size (number of rows), and returns 'true' if all the elements are distinct, and 'false', otherwise.

I89   A Magic Square is N x N matrix of integers such that the sum of every row, column, and diagonal is the same. Write a function which takes a 2D array as an argument and returns true/false depending on whether the array is a magic square or not.

190 The pair-wise distances between 'N' cities are given in a triangular array, as shown below. Write a function which takes the 'distance' array and its size as inputs, and prints out the farthest pair of cities and their distance. An example of pair-wise distance of 10 cities, and the expected output is given below. (Note: The C's marked in red are not part of the array).

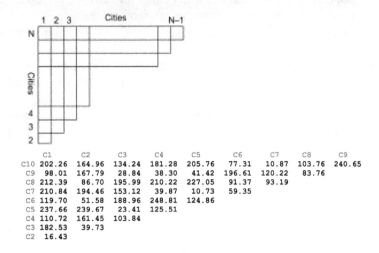

	C1	C2	C3	C4	C5	C6	C7	C8	C9
C10	202.26	164.96	134.24	181.28	205.76	77.31	10.87	103.76	240.65
C9	98.01	167.79	28.84	38.30	41.42	196.61	120.22	83.76	
C8	212.39	86.70	195.99	210.22	227.05	91.37	93.19		
C7	210.84	194.46	153.12	39.87	10.73	59.35			
C6	119.70	51.58	188.96	248.81	124.86				
C5	237.66	239.67	23.41	125.51					
C4	110.72	161.45	103.84						
C3	182.53	39.73							
C2	16.43								

Max distance is 248.81 between cities 6 and 4

IOIOIOIOIOIOIOIOIOIOIOIOIOIOIOIOIOIOIOIOIOIOIOIOIOIOIOIOIOIOI

Answers

A. Data Types, Operators, Expressions

True/False Questions

A1   Software maintenance is the most expansive component of the entire software cycle. **_True_**

A2   Inline functions do not do type checking of parameters. **_False_**

A3   Inline functions have the same performance as normal functions. **_False_**
[Inline functions do not have the overheads (saving/restoring activation records) of normal function calls, and therefore have better performance]

A4   The sizes of the generated binary files (generated by the compiler) increase with the use of Inline functions. **_True_**

A5   The compilation time of a source file decreases with the use of Inline functions. **_False_**
[Inline functions add the code of the function in all the places they are called, thus increasing the code size, and correspondingly increasing the compilation time. Note that the keyword 'inline' is a recommendation to the compiler to generate inline code]

A6   Inline functions cannot return values. **_False_**

A7   Macros can return values. **_False_**
[Macros cannot have return statement]

A8   **`typedef`** can only be used with user-defined types, but not built-in types. **_False_**
[**`typedef`** can be used provide synonyms for both built-in and user-defined types]

A9   A variable declared in the main() function is visible (accessible) anywhere in the program. **_False_**
[A variable declared in the main() function is visible only within the scope of main(), i.e., between the {} enclosing the statements of main()]

A10   A global variable and a local variable cannot have the same name. **_False_**

[A global variable and a local variable cannot have the same name. The local variable is not visible outside of the scope that it is declared in. The global variable will not be visible (will be 'shadowed') in the scope of the local variable with the same name]

A11   A variable with block scope declared with the keyword **static** is allocated in the same area of memory as a global variable. *True*

A12   A 'static' variable is never visible in more than one file. *True*

A13   The rules for the linkage of identifiers are not applicable to function names. *False*
[Function names are identifiers, so the linkage rules are applicable]

A14   A variable declared with the 'static' keyword is unique within its source file, and is invisible in other source files. *True*

A15   No storage is allocated to an identifier declared with the keyword **extern**. *True*

A16   All variables are not automatically initialized to a default values when declared. *True*.

A17   C provides garbage collection (implicit/ automatic reclamation of unreferenced storage). *False*

A18   C is dynamically typed. *False*
[C is statically typed. The datatypes of variables must be known at compile time]

A19   All the letters in a C keyword is in lowercase. *True*

A20   C keywords may be used as variable names. *False*

A21 $amount is a valid identifier. *True*

A22 $576 is a valid identifier. *True*

A23   **_amt** is a valid identifier. *True*

A24   _273 is a valid identifier. *True*

A25   **current_sum** is a valid identifier. *True*

A26 $6,379 is a valid identifier. *False*

[The ',' (comma) symbol is not permitted]

A27 **74Points** is a valid identifier. *False*
[Cannot start with a numeral]

A28 **total-count** is a valid identifier. *False*
[The '−' symbol is not permitted]

A29 Floating point arithmetic does not cause overflow. *False*

A30 Integer computations do not cause rounding errors. *True*

A31 Arithmetic overflow causes a run-time error. *False*
[Upon arithmetic overflow, the execution continues. However, the condition can be caught and handled suitably by an exception handler]

A32 Local variables must be initialized before their values are used in an expression. *True*

A33 C requires all variables to have a type declared before they can be used in a program. *True*

A34 In C, string is a primitive type. *False*
['string' is not a type defined in the language]

A35 A 'double' to 'float' promotion of primitive type is allowed to occur. *False*

A36 The operands of an operator are always evaluated from left to right. *False*

A37 C supports overloading of operators. *False*

A38 Recursion is often more efficient than iteration. *False*

A39 C has different variations of integer datatype. *True*
[Some of the variants of the integer datatype are short, unsigned, int, long]

A40 An array may contain only primitive types. *False*
[An array may contain both primitive and structure types]

A41 The sub-expressions are evaluated from left to right. *False*

A42   Array index range checks are not done in C. *True*

A43   C does not have a preprocessor. *False*
[#include, #ifndef, #define, etc. are preprocessor directives]

A44   The **#include** files cannot be nested. *False*

A45   Macros are processed by the compiler. *False*
[Macros are processed by the Preprocessor]

A46   A macro can take variable number of arguments. *True*
[The variable number of arguments is specified by "..." at the end of argument list]

A47   The Preprocessor has knowledge of C's syntax. *False*

A48   The **#define** directive must appear at the beginning of a program. *False*
[The **#define** directive may appear anywhere in the program]

A49   The **#define** directive cannot have arithmetic expressions. *False*
[**#define TWO_PI 2*3.14159** is valid]

A50   No storage is allocated for **MAX_SIZE** using **#define MAX_SIZE 25**. *True*

A51   Variables defined using **#define** do not have the scope rules. *True*

A52   Local variables are initialized with default values when they are declared. *False*

A53   Use of an uninitialized variable in statement gives compilation error. *False*

A54   C does not require declaration of variables before use. *False*

A55   Variables declarations can be anywhere a statement can be. *True*

A56   A variable in a nested block cannot have the same name as a variable in the enclosing block. *False*
[A variable in a nested block having the same name as a variable in the enclosing block is allowed, and is known as shadowing]

A57   C does not support multiple-selection statement. ***False***
[The switch-case supports multiple selection]

A58   Arrays are not initialized at the time of allocation. ***False***

A59   C does not have the **goto** control structure. ***False***
[C supports 'goto' control structure]

A60   In C, the control expression must be Boolean. ***False***
[**while (i+j) { }** is valid, where i and j are integer variables]

A61   C has built-in support for exception handling. ***False***

A62   An expression cannot be an argument to a function. ***False***

A63   The **++** and **--** operators can be applied to a 'char' variable. ***True***

A64   The ++ and -- operators are binary operators. ***False***
[They are unary operators. They have only one operand]

A65   The '%' operator is not valid on floating point numbers. ***True***

A66   Relational operators are (generally) used for primitive types. ***True***

A67   There is no value of x for which the expression **(x < 10) && (x > 10)** would be true. ***True***

A68   There is no value of x for which the expression **(x < 10) || (x > 10)** would be false. ***False***
[The compound expression would be false for x = 10, since both x < 10 and x > 10 would be false]

A69   The value of the expression **(x <= y ^ x >= y)** would always be true. ***False***
[When x equals y, both **x <= y** and **x >= y** are true, and therefore, the expression would be false]

A70   The value of the expression **(x < y ^ x > y)** would always be true. ***False***
[When x equals y, both **x < y** and **x > y** are false, and therefore, the expression would be false]

A71 The value of the expression **((x%y == 0) ^ (y%x == 0))** would always be true. ***False***
[For x = 4 and y = 7, x % y is 4 and y % x is 3, and thus the expression is false]

A72 For integers x and y, the value of the expression **(x/y == 0 ^ y/x == 0)** would always be true. ***False***
[When x = y, each of the conditions is false, and the expression is false]

A73 For integers x and y, the value of the expression **(x/y == 1 ^ y/x == 1)** could never be false. ***False***
[When x = y, each of the conditions is true, and the expression is false]

A74 For integers x and y, the value of the expression **(x/y == 0 ^ x/y != 0)** is always true. ***True***

A75 The value of **(x < y || x > y)** is always true. ***False***
[The value of the expression is false when x equals y]

A76 The value of **(x <= y && x >= y)** is always true. ***False***
[The value of the expression is false when x equals y]

A77 The value of **(x < y && x > y)** is always false. ***True***

A78 The value of **(x == y || x != y)** is always true. ***True***

A79 The value of **(x == y && x != y)** is always false. ***True***

A80 The value of **(x == y ^ x != y)** is always true. ***True***

A81 The value of **(x % y == y % x)** is always false. ***False***
[When x = y, the LHS and RHS are both equal to 0]

A82 For integer values of x and y, the expression **(x/y == y/x)** would never be true. ***False***
[When x and y are equal, then x/y = y/x = 1]

A83 In C, arithmetic overflow does not result in run-time error. ***True***

A84 When x ≠ y, it is never the case that **x % y** is 0. ***False***
[When x is evenly divisible by y, then x % y is 0]

123

A85   When x < y, it is always the case that **x / y** is 0. *__True__*

A86   When x < y and x ≠ 0, it is never the case that **x % y** is 0. *__True__*

A87   For integer values of x and y, when x ≥ y, it is always the case that **x / y** is not 0. *__True__*

A88   When x ≠ y, it is never the case that **x % y** and **x / y** are equal. *__False__*
[For x = 12 and y = 5, x % y is 2 and x/y is 2]

A89   **(x != y)** is equivalent to **!(x == y)**. *__True__*

A90   **!(x < y)** is equivalent to **(x >= y)**. *__True__*

A91   **(x > y || x < y)** is equivalent to **(x == y)**. *__False__*
[This is equivalent to x ≠ y]

A92   The value of the expression **(x < y ^ x > y)** would always be true. *__False__*
[When x = y, each part of the expression is false, and the value of the expression is false]

A93   Integer arithmetic is always gives the correct result. *__False__*

A94   All integer values in the range supported are accurately represented. *__True__*

A95   Floating point arithmetic is always accurate. *__False__*

A96   The output of dividing a nonzero floating-point number by zero causes an error. *__False__*
[It does not cause an error. It returns either **inf** or **-inf**]

A97   Variables declared with **const** keyword must be initialized during declaration. *__True__*

A98   Variables declared with **const** keyword can be assigned a value after declaration. *__False__*
[Variables declared with 'const' keyword must be initialized at declaration]

A99   A variable declared with **const** keyword has no associated storage cell. *False*
[A variable declared with 'const' keyword is allocated storage]

A100 No storage is allocated for the declaration **extern int i**. *True*
[The keyword extern indicates that the identifier refers to a variable declared and defined in another file]

A101 The values of global variables are implicitly initialized when declared. *True*

A102 The values of local variables are implicitly initialized when declared. *False*

A103 All local variables are not initialized when declared. *False*
[Local variables declared with the keyword static are initialized]

A104 Literals are treated as constants. *True*

A105 A variable of type bool takes 1-bit of storage. *False*
[Even though a variable of type 'bool' has only two possible values, it is stored in a byte]

A106 The '−' (subtraction) operator is right associative. *False*
[It is right associative. a − b − c is evaluated as (a − b) − c]

A107 The '=' (assignment) operator is right associative. *True*
[a = b = c is evaluated as a = (b = c)]

A108 In C, files containing one or more subprograms can be independently compiled. *True*

A109 The '*' operator in C has operation(s) other than multiplication. *True*

A110 C allows variable declarations to be anywhere a statement can be. *True*

A111 C supports **union** type. *True*

A112 C does not support enumeration types. *False*

A113 C does not support default parameters. *False*

A114 Local variables in the functions, by default, are stack-dynamic. **_True_**
[The default can be overridden using the reserved word 'static']

A115 A local variable (auto or static) inside a block cannot have the same name as an 'extern' variable. **_False_**
[A local variable can have the same name as an 'extern' variable. The local variable is said to shadow the extern variable with the same name, since the latter will not be visible within that block]

A116 Two variables with the same name cannot be declared within the same block. **_True_**

A117 C language does not support concurrency. **_True_**

A118 C supports implicit type conversions (coercions). **_True_**

A119 C does not support explicit type conversions (casts). **_False_**

A120 C uses short circuit evaluation of Boolean expressions. **_True_**

A121 In C, control expressions can be arithmetic. **_True_**

A122 C does not allow mixed-mode expressions. **_False_**

A123 C performs type checks at compile time. **_True_**

A124 C supports nested subprogram definitions. **_False_**

A125 C has exponentiation operator. **_False_**
[The exponentiation operation is supported via library function]

A126 Initialization of global variables is done at compile time. **_True_**

A127 Initialization of variables declared with 'static' keyword is done at runtime. **_False_**
[Initialization of static variables is done at compile time]

A128 Initialization of global and static variables are done before the **main()** starts execution. **_True_**

A129 A heap–dynamic variable must be explicitly deallocated. **_True_**

A130   Multiple variables of the same name but with different scopes can be used in the same program. *True*

A131   A variable can be defined anywhere in the program where a statement can appear. *True*

A132   No arithmetic operation at all can be done on a pointer type. *False*
[C supports pointer arithmetic operations]

A133   A character string variable can be assigned a string literal at any time using the '=' assignment operator. *False*
[A string literal can be assigned to a character string variable using the '=' assignment operator only at declaration. At other times, library function (strcpy/strncpy) need to be used]

A134   The **sizeof** operator can only be used on types, but not on actual variables. *False*
[If 'x' is a variable of type 'double', then **sizeof(double)** and **sizeof(x)** are both valid]]

A135   The bit shift operators (**<<, >>**) cannot be used on floating point variables. *True*

A136   The bitwise operators (**|**, **&**, **^**) can be used on integer variables. *True*

A137   The is no logical XOR operator. *True*

A138   A variable declared with **static** keyword is visible across files. *False*

A139   An **extern** variable with the same name may be declared in multiple files. *True*

A140   An **extern** variable must be defined in only one file. *True*

IOIOIOIOIOIOIOIOIOIOIOIOIOIOIOIOIOIOIOIOIOIOIOIOIOIOIOIOIOIOI

Fill-in the-blanks Questions

A1   The high-level language code / program written by the programmer is known as *source* code.

A2   The code / program executed by the computer is known as *machine* code.

A3   The software which translates high-level language program into machine language program is known as *compiler*.

A4   The software which manages various resources and activities in a computer is known as the *operating system*.

A5   A(n) *Integrated Development Environment (IDE)* provides facilities such as editing, compiling, running, and debugging during program development.

A6   Program that processes the source code before compilation is known as *preprocessor*.

A7   Macros are processed by *preprocessor*.

A8   Inline functions are processed by *compiler*.

A9   The Black Box test is also known as *Functional test*.

A10   In *black box* testing, program unit is treated as a 'black box' whose Inner workings are not visible.

A11   The White Box test is also known as *Structural test*.

A12   In *white box* testing, the internal structure of program unit is transparent, and specific parts can be tested.

A13   A program which does not compile is said to have *syntax* error(s).

A14   A program which compiles without error(s) but terminates abnormally when run is said to have *runtime* error.

A15   A program which compiles without error(s) but produces incorrect result(s) is said to have *logic* (*logical*) error.

A16   A variable declared outside of any function (including main()) is known as *global* variable.

A17   A variable visible (accessible) anywhere in the program is known as *global* variable.

A18   The section of a program where a (variable) name is visible of known as its *static scope*.

A19   All C programs must have a function named **main** where the execution starts.

A20   Although **void** is a valid type, no variable can be declared of that type.

A21   An expression containing operands of different data types is known as a *mixed mode* expression.

A22   Implicit type conversion which is automatically done by the compiler is known as *coercion*.

A23   Explicit type conversions done by the programmer is known as *cast*.

A24   The two ways of representing a string (sequence of characters) are as *array of characters* and as *string type*.

A25   A block is enclosed between *braces*.

A26   The two broad categories of data types of C are *simple* (or *primitive*) and *structured*.

A27   Data types such as int, char, long, double etc. are known as *simple* or *primitive* types.

A28   Data types such as arrays, structures, and unions are known as *structured* types.

A29   An identifier declared with the keyword **extern** refers to an entity declared in another file.

A30   A variable declared with the **const** keyword cannot be modified.

A31   A variable with block scope declared with no keyword is allocated in the ***stack*** area of memory.

A32   A variable with block scope declared with the keyword **static** is allocated in the ***data*** area of memory.

A33   A global variable (declared outside of any function) is allocated in the ***data*** area of memory.

A34   Variables which are allocated once, and stay in the same memory location for the duration of a program's execution are known as ***static*** variables.

A35   A(n) **extern** variable can have multiple declarations, but only one definition.

A36   A sequence of characters contained between quotes (") is known as a ***string literal***.

A37   The datatype of the result of adding an int, a byte, a long, and a double, is ***double***.

A38   The contents of the location pointed to by a pointer is accessed using the ***dereferencing (*)*** operator.

A39   The ternary (or conditional operator) is **?** **:**

A40   The datatype size operator is **sizeof**.

A41   The keyword required to declare a constant of a primitive type (ex. int, double, etc.) is **const**.

A42   Given **#define SQR(x) x*x**, **a = 3**, and **b = 5**, the value of **SQR(a+b)** is $\underline{23}$.
[**SQR(a+b)** expands to $3 + 5 * 3 + 5 = 23$]

A43   Given **#define SQR(x) (x)*(x)**, **a = 3**, and **b = 5**, the value of **SQR(a+b)** is $\underline{64}$.
[**SQR(a+b)** expands to $(3 + 5) * (3 + 5) = 64$]

A44   Given **#define MOD(x, y) (x % y)**, **a = 19**, and **b = 5**, the value of **MOD(a+b, b)** is $\underline{19}$.
[**MOD(a+b, b)** expands to $19 + 5 \% 5 = 19 + 0 = 19$]

A45   Given **#define MOD(x, y)   ((x) % (y))**, **a = 19**, and
      b = 5, the value of **MOD(a+b, b)** is <u>4</u>.
      [**MOD(a+b, b)** expands to **(19 + 5) % (5) = 24 % 5 = 4**]

Given the declarations **int i, long int l, float f, double**
d, (and assuming suitable initializations) what are the types of the
following expressions?

A46   **i + 2** is <u>int</u>

A47   **2.56 - i** is <u>float</u>

A48   **i / l** is <u>long</u>

A49   **l + f** is <u>float</u>

A50   **i/l + f** is <u>float</u>

A51   **f/2** is <u>float</u>

A52   **f - d** is <u>double</u>

A53   **i/(l + d)** is <u>double</u>

A54   **l + f** is <u>float</u>

A55   **l * d** is <u>double</u>

A56   **l/(i*3.7)** is <u>float</u>

A57   **f/l - d** is <u>double</u>

A58   What are the values of the following expressions?

      int a = 2, b = 3, c = 5;

      a > b || c > b   <u>1</u>

      b < a + 2 && c <= a + b   <u>1</u>

      (b > c - a) || (a < c / b + 1)   <u>0</u>

$$b == b \% c \mid\mid a + b > c \quad \underline{\textbf{1}}$$

$$(b <= c)\ \&\&\ (b + c \% a == 0)\ \underline{\textbf{0}}$$

A59 The value of 3 / 4 is **0**

A60 The value of (double) (3 / 4) is **0**

A61 The value of (double) 3 / 4 is **0.75**

A62 The value of 3 / (double) 4 is **0.75**

A63 The value of 3.0 / 4 is **0.75**

A64 The value of 3 / 4.0 is **0.75**

A65 The value of 19 / 5 is **3** [integer division]

A66 The value of 19 / 5.0 is **3.8** [floating point division]

A67 The value of (double)19 / 5 is **3.8** [floating point division]

A68 The value of 5 % 1 is **0**.

A69 The value of 17 % 3 is **2**.

A70 The value of 3 % 17 is **3**.

A71 For **x % n** to be 0 for all values of **x**, the value of **n**, should be **1**. [Note that **x % n** gives the remainder of dividing **x** by **n**. Any number divided by I has a remainder of 0. Therefore **n** is I]

A72 The value of (int)(12.345 * 100) / 100.0 is **12.34**.

A73 The value of (int)(12.345 * 100 / 100) is **12**.

A74 The output of dividing a nonzero floating-point number by zero is **inf** or **-inf**.

A75 The output of dividing zero by zero is **NaN** (Not a Number).

A76 The value of x for which the expression **(x <= 10) && (x >= 10)** would be true, is **10**.

A77   The value of x for which the expression **(x < 10) || (x > 10)** would be false, is **10**.

A78   Given x = 5, the value of **(x << 5)** would be **160**.
[The '<<' operator does a left shift of the bits of the left operand by the specified times. One left shift is equivalent to multiplication by 2. Left shift by 5 is equivalent to multiplication by $2^5 = 32$ times, which, in the example would be 5 x 32 = 160]

A79   Given x = 84, the value of **(x >> 3)** would be **10**.
[The '>>' operator does a right shift of the bits of the left operand by the specified times. One right shift is equivalent to division by 2. In this example, it is equivalent to $84 / 2^3 = 84 / 8 = 10$. Note that it is integet divison]

A80   The value of **(x == y && x != y)** is always **false**.

A81   The value of **(x == y || x != y)** is always **true**.
[The Boolean values of 'true' and 'false' are represented by '0' and '1', respectively]

A82   When x ≠ y, the value of the expression **(x <= y && x >= y)** would always be **false**.

A83   The value of **(x <= y || x >= y)** is always **true**.

A84   The value of **(x == y || x != y)** is always **true**.

A85   The value of **(x == y ^ x != y)** is always **true**.

A86   When x ≠ y, the value of the expression **(x < y ^ x > y)** would always be **true**.

A87   The value of **(x == y && x != y)** is always **false**.

A88   The value of **(x <= y && x >= y)** is true only under the condition **x == y**.

A89   The value of **(x < y ^ x > y)** is false only under the condition **x == y**.

A90   The value of **(x >= 0) || (x < 0)** is always **true**.

A91   The value of **(x < y && x > y)** is always **false**.

A92   The value of **(x == y ^ x != y)** is always **true**.

A93   For integers x and y, the expression **(x/y == y/x)** would be true only under the condition **x _equals_ y**.

A94   The value of **(x > 0) || (x < 0)** is always false except when x is **0**.

A95   The value of **(x > 0) && (x < 0)** is always **false**.

A96   The value of **!(x > 0) && (x > 0)** is always **false**.

A97   The value of **(x != 0) || (x == 0)** is always **true**.

A98   The expression to check if the value of **age** is at least 18 is **(age >= 18)**

A99   The expression to check if the value of **age** is between 18 and 65 (inclusive) is **(age >= 18 && age <= 65)**

A100   The expression to check if the value of **x** is at least 3 and at most 10 is **(x >= 3 && x <= 10)**

A101   The expression to ckeck if **x** is evenly divisible by 3 and 7 is **(x % 3 == 0 && x % 7 == 0)**

A102   The expression to check if the value of **count** is not in the range 25 to 35 (inclusive) is **(count < 25 || count > 35)**

A103   Given **x = 3**, the value of ~x is **-4**.

A104   Given **x = 0**, the value of ~x is **-1**.
[The 2's complement representation of 0 is all 0 bits. The ~ operator complements all the bits, and all 1's is -1 in 2's complement]

A105   The value of **x | x** for any integer **x** is **x**.

A106   The value of **x & x** for any integer **x** is **x**.

A107   The value of **x ^ x** for any integer **x** is **0**.

A108   The value of **x | ~x** for any integer **x** is **-1**.

[The bits of **x** | **~x** would be all 1's, which is −1 in 2's complement]

A109 The value of **x & ~x** for any integer **x** is <u>0</u>.

A110 The value of **x ^ ~x** for any integer **x** is <u>−1</u>.

A111 The value of **x | −1** for any integer **x** is <u>−1</u>.
[Note that the bits of −1 is all 1's]

A112 The value of **x & −1** for any integer **x** is <u>x</u>.

A113 The value of **x ^ −1** for any integer **x** is <u>−(x+1)</u>.

A114 The value of **x | 0** for any integer **x** is <u>x</u>.

A115 The value of **x & 0** for any integer **x** is <u>0</u>.

A116 The value of **x ^ 0** for any integer **x** is <u>x</u>.

A117 Given x = 3 and y = 5, the value of **(x = y)** is <u>5</u>.

A118 Given x = 3 and y = 5, the value of **(x = y == y)** is <u>1</u> [The assignment x = y returns y which is compared with y for equality, returning 'true', which is represented by '1']

A119 Given x = 3 and y = 5, the value of (x = y == x) is <u>0</u> (false).

A120 Given x = 7 and y = 5, the value of **x-- - --y** is <u>3</u>.
[The value of x is used before decrementing (7), and the value of y is decremented and used (4), thus, 7 − 4 = 3]

A121 Given x = 7 and y = 5, the value of **--x - --y** is <u>2</u>.

A122 Given x = 7 and y = 5, the value of **++x + ++y** is <u>14</u>.

A123 Given x = 7 and y = 5, the value of **x++ + y++** is <u>12</u>.

A124 Given x = 3 and y = 7, the value of y after evaluating the expression **(x >= 3) && (y-- > 5)**, is <u>6</u>.

A125 Given x = 3 and y = 7, the value of y after evaluating the expression **(x > 3) && (y-- > 5)**, is <u>7</u>.

[Note that (**x > 3**) evaluates to **false**, and since the value of the entire expression would be false irrespective of the second term, the evaluation of the second term is 'short-circuited' (is not evaluated)]

A126   Given x = 5 and y = 9, the value of y after evaluating the expression (**x > 5**) || (**y++ >= 12**), is <u>10</u>.

A127   Given x = 5 and y = 9, the value of y after evaluating the expression (**x >= 5**) || (**y++ >= 12**), is <u>9</u>.
[Note that (**x >= 5**) evaluates to **true**, and since the value of the entire expression would be true irrespective of the second term, its evaluation of the second term is 'short-circuited' (is not evaluated)]

A128   Given x = 5 and y = 9, the value of y after evaluating the expression (**x >= 5**) | (**y++ >= 12**), is <u>10</u>.
[The '|' operator is non-short-circuit operator. Therefore, even when its left term is true, the right term is evaluated, which increments y]

A129   Given x = 3 and y = 7, the value of the expression (**x >= 3**) **&&** (**y-- <= 6**), is <u>**false**</u>.

A130   Given x = 3 and y = 7, the value of the expression (**x >= 3**) **&&** (**y-- == 6**), is <u>**false**</u>.

A131   Given x = 3 and y = 7, the value of the expression (**x >= 3**) **&&** (**y-- >= 7**), is <u>**true**</u>.

A132   Given x = 3 and y = 7, the value of the expression (**x >= 3**) **&&** (**y-- == 7**), is <u>**true**</u>.

A133   Given x = 3 and y = 7, the value of the expression (**x >= 3**) **&&** (**--y <= 6**), is <u>**true**</u>.

A134   Given x = 3 and y = 7, the value of the expression (**x++ == 3**) **&&** (**y-- == 7**), is <u>**true**</u>.

A135   Given x = 3 and y = 7, the value of the expression (**++x >= 4**) **&&** (**--y == 6**), is <u>**true**</u>.

A136   Given x = 3 and y = 7, the value of the expression (**x++ > 3**) **&&** (**y-- == 7**), is <u>**false**</u>.

A137   Given x = 5 and y = 9, the value of the expression **(x > 5) ||
(y++ > 9)**, is **false**.

A138   Given x = 5 and y = 9, the value of the expression **(x > 5) ||
(++y > 9)**, is **true**.

A139   Given x = 3 and y = 7, the value of the expression **(x > 3) &&
(--y <= 6)**, is **true**.

A140   Given **j** is 0, the value of **j++ + j * 5** is **5**.
[Operands are evaluated from left to right in C++. The left-hand operand of a binary
operator is evaluated before any part of the right-hand operand is evaluated. Therefore,
j++ is evaluated first. j is now 1. However, since j++ is postincrement, the old value
of j is returned for j++. So j++ + j * 5 equals 0 + 1 * 5, and the value is 5]

A141   Given **j** is 0, the value of **++j + j * 5** is **6**.
[Since j++ is preincrement, j is first incremented and the value of j (=1) is returned.
So ++j + j * 5 equals 1 + 1 * 5, and the value is 6]

A142   Given **x** is 1, the value of **x++ + x** is **3**.

A143   Given **x** is 1, the value of **++x + x** is **4**.

A144   For any values of **a** and **b**, after executing the statements **a = b
+ a; b = a - b; a = a - b;**, the value of **a** would be **b**
and the value of **b** would be **a**.

A145   The size in bytes of the data type long is **8**, short is **2**, byte is **1**,
and int is **4**.

A146   The declaration of a constant named PI with value
3.14159265358979, is **const double PI =
3.14159265358979;**

A147   Unary arithmetic operators are **+, -, ++, --**

A148   Unary logical operator is **!**

A149   Unary bitwise operator is **~**

A150   The operators which are both unary and binary (although with
different semantics) are **+, -, *, &**.

A151 To assign to x the larger of the values of x and y, in one statement, is **x = (x > y) ? x : y;**

A152 The possible range of values returned by **rand() % 10** is between **0** and **9**.

A153 The short-circuit operators are **&&** and **||**.

A154 The difference between the computed value in a program and the exact mathematical value is known as ***round-off* (or *rounding*)** error.

A155 The number of bytes required to store '**x**' is **1**.
[A character literal takes one byte of storage]

A156 The number of bytes required to store "**x**" is **2**.
["**x**" is a string literal takes two bytes of storage — one for the character 'x' and another for the terminating NULL character]

A157 The output of **putchar(55)** is **7**
[The ASCII value of character '0' is 48. Thus, character corresponding to the ASCII value of 55 is 7]

A158 The output of **putchar('5')** is **5**

A159 The output of **putchar('5'+ 12)** is **A**

A160 The output of **printf("%d",'A')** is **65**

A161 The output of **printf("%d",'Z'-'A'+1)** is **26**

A162 The output of **putchar('A'+7)** is **A**

A163 The output of **putchar('1' + 16)** is **A**

A164 Given **string s = "NOT"**, **t = "ABLE"**, the value of **s+t** is **"NOTABLE"**

A165 Given **string s = "able"**, the value of **'t'+s+'s'** is **"tables"**

A166   Given a sring **s1** to be **"Program"**, the value of **s1.length()** is **7**.

A167   Given a sring s1 to be **"Inhabit"**, the value of **s1.substr(0)** is **"Inhabit"**.

A168   Given a sring s1 to be **"Inhabit"**, the value of **s1.substr(2)** is **"habit"**

A169   Given a sring s1 to be "Transportation", the statement using **substr** which returns "sport" is **s1.substr(4,5)**.

A170   The output of **printf("%.2f", 1234.567)** is **1234.57**.
[The **%.2f** specifies up to 2 decimal places]

A171   The output of **printf("%.4e", 1234.56)** is **1.2346e+03**
[The **%.4e** specifies up to 4 decimal places and scientific notation]

A172   The output of **printf("%3d", 123456)** is **123456**
[The **%3d** specifies an integer with display width 3. The width is automatically expanded if the number of digits is more than the specified width]

A173   The allocation of memory to variables at runtime is known as *dynamic* allocation.

A174   The unary '*' operator in C is used for the *dereferencing* operation.

A175   The relational operator **!=** is equivalent to logical XOR operation (in the absence of logical XOR operator).

A176   Multiple names bound to the same entity at the same time is known as *aliasing*.

A177   The value of **sizeof("A")** is **2**.

A178   The value of **sizeof('Z')** is **4**.

A179   The value of **sizeof('\0')** is **4**.

A180   The value of **sizeof(char)** is **1**.

A181 The value of **sizeof("")** is <u>1</u>.
[It is a **NULL** string, and 1 byte is required for the null terminator]

A182 The value of **sizeof("\0\0\0\0")** is <u>5</u>.
[The memory required is 4 bytes for the 4 null characters, and 1 byte for the null terminator]

IOIOIOIOIOIOIOIOIOIOIOIOIOIOIOIOIOIOIOIOIOIOIOIOIOIOIOIOIOI

Essay-type Questions

A1 Give examples of common syntax errors in C.
1) Not having a closing quotation mark on a string.
2) Not having a semicolon at the end of a statement
3) Use of misspelt reserved words (ex. 'brake' in place of 'break')
4) Using reserved words with capitalization (ex. "While" in place of "while")
5) Not having a corresponding closing brace (}) for an opening brace ({)
6) Putting spaces between some relational operators ("!=", "<=", ">=", "==")
7) Using the modulus operator, %, with non-integer operands.
8) Not having a return statement in a function that is defined to return a value.

A2 Give examples of common run-time errors in C.
1) Division by 0.
2) Termination due to excessive memory use (Memory leak).
3) Caught in an infinite loop

A3 Give examples of logical errors in C.
1) Use of '=' where an equality check ('==') is intended.
2) Having an 'else' for an unintended 'if'.
3) Using "<=" in place of ">=" (and vice versa)
4) Mixing variables of different types (ex. integer and double types) in expressions without explicit cast.
5) Omitting the **break** clause from **switch** statements.

A4 What are the four areas of memory of a typical C program and data, and what do they contain?
1) Code area: This contains the instructions of the program.

2) Static data area: This contains the global variables, and the variables declared with the **static** keyword.
3) Stack area: This contains the local (non-static) variables of functions, the arguments passed to functions, variables declared with in blocks (delimited by '{' and '}').
4) Heap area: This contains the dynamic memory allocated, such as by the use of 'malloc' and 'calloc' operators.

A5   Give examples of two operators that are not associative.

Subtraction (–) and division (/) are not associative.
$9 - 3 - 1$: when left associative would be $(9 - 3) - 1 = 5$;
when right associative would be $9 - (3 - 1) = 7$
$8 / 4 / 2$: when left associative would be $(8 / 4) / 2 = 1$
when right associative would be $8 / (4 / 2) = 4$

A6   What is the difference between coercion and cast?

Coercion is implicit type conversion which is automatically done by the compiler. Cast is explicit type conversion done by the programmer.

A7   What is short-circuit evaluation?

In the case of compound expressions made up of sub-expressions, the value of the entire expression may be determined without evaluation all of the component sub-expressions, based on rules of Logic. For example, if any one of the subexpressions of a 'conjunction' (logical 'and') is false, then the entire expression is false.This is known as short-circuit evaluation.

A8   Write a macro **DIV_10(x)** which tests if an integer argument is evenly divisible by 10. It should be usable in an 'if' statement, as in **if (DIV_10(a))**.

```
#define DIV_10(x)  ((x) % 10 == 0)
```

Give declarations for variable of the following types.

A9   **i**   integer
      int i;

A10 **pf**   pointer to float

141

```
float* pf;
```

A11 **darr**   array of 10 double precision numbers
```
double darr[10];
```

A12 **names**   array of 5 pointers to char
```
char* names[5];
```

A13 **ip**   pointer to an array of 5 pointers to int
```
int * (*ip)[5];
```

A14 **pfn1**   pointer to a function returning double
```
double (*pfn1)();
```

A15 **pfn2**   pointer to a function returning pointer to int
```
int* (*pfn2)();
```

A16 **apfn3**   array of pointers to functions returning float
```
float (*apfn3())[];
```

A17 **pfn1** Function taking a pointer to char as argument, and returning a pointer to an array of floats
```
float(*(pfn1(char*)))[];
```

A18 **pfn2** Pointer to a function taking a pointer to char as argument, and returning a pointer to an array of ints
```
int (*(*pfn2(char*)))[];
```

A19 **apfn4**   pointer to an array of 2 functions returning float
```
float (*apfn4[2])();
```

A20 **ap**   array of 5 integer pointers
```
int* ap[5];
```

A21 **pai**   pointer to an array of 5 integers
```
int (*pai)[5];
```

A22 **pap**   pointer to array of 5 integer pointers
```
int* (*pap)[5];
```

A23 **fp**   pointer to a function returning a pointer to array of 3 floats
```
float* (*fp())[3];
```

A24 **fpp**   pointer to a function which takes an argument of type 'int', and returns a pointer to a function which takes an argument of type 'double', returning an int

```
int (*(*fpp)(int))(double);
```

Determine the data types for the following variables.

A25 `int i`
    i is an integer

A26 `int *j`
    j is a pointer to an integer

A27 `char * t[10]`
    t is an array of 10 pointers to char

A28 `double s[4][7]`
    s is a 2D array of 4 rows and 7 columns of double values

A29 `int (*h)()`
    h is a pointer to a function with no parameters, returning int

Determine the data types for the following variables.

A30 `int a[5];`
    a is an array of 5 integers

A31 `int *b[5];`
    b is an array of 5 integer pointers

A32 `int (*c)[5];`
    c is a pointer to an array of 5 integers

A33 `int* (*d)[5];`
    d is a pointer to an array of 5 integer pointers

A34 `int * (*(*e)[5]);`
    e is a pointer to an array of 5 pointers to integer pointers

A35 `int * (*(f[5]));`
    f is an array of 5 pointers to integer pointers

Determine the data types for the following variables.

A36 `int (*fp)(char*)`
fp is a pointer to a function taking a char* as an argument and returning int.

A37 `int(*fparr[5])();`
fparr is array of 5 pointers to function which returns an int.

A38 `double (*fp)(double*)`
fp is a pointer to a function which takes a pointer to double as argument and returns a double value.

A39 `double* (*fp)(double*)`
fp is a pointer to a function which takes a pointer to double as argument and returns a pointer to type double.

A40 `float* * fp2(int, float)`
fp2 is a pointer to a function which takes an int and double as arguments and returns a pointer to a float.

A41 `double * f(double)`
f is a function which takes an argument of type double, and returns a pointer to type double.

A42 `int **fun(float*, char**)`
fun is a function with parameters (i) pointer to a float, (ii) pointer to a pointer to a char, and returns a pointer to a pointer to a integer.

A43 `int (*fun[3])(char*, int)`
fun is an array of pointers to functions with parameters (i) pointer to a char, (ii) int, which return an integer.

A44 `float* (*fun(int, float))[]`
fun is a pointer to function with parameters (i) int, (ii) float, and returns a pointer to an array of floats.

A45 `char* pri_colors[] = {"Red", "Green", "Blue"};`
pri_colors is an array of pointers to strings (arrays of characters).

A46 Write a statement using **printf** to print the following:
`String literal is delimited by " character`

```
printf ("String literal is delimited by \"
character");
```

A47 Write a statement using **printf** to print the following:
'\n' is the newline character

```
printf ("'\\n' is the newline character");
```

A48 Write a statement using **printf** to print the following:
The "\" character serves as an escape character

```
printf ("The \"\\\" character serves as an escape
character\n");
```

A49 What is happening in the following assignment statement (assuming compatible datatypes)?

```
int a = fn(x);
```

The function **fn** is called with argument **x**, and value returned is assigned to **a**.

A50 What is happening in the following assignment statement (assuming compatible datatypes)?

```
int a = (*pfn) (x, y);
```

The function pointed to by **pfn** is called with arguments **x** and **y**, and the value returned is assigned to **a**.

A51 What is happening in the following assignment statement (assuming compatible datatypes)?

```
int a = (*apfn[i]) (x, y);
```

apfn is an array of pointers to functions. The function pointed to by **apfn[i]** is called with arguments **x** and **y**, and the value returned is assigned to **a**.

A52 What is the output of the following code segment?

```
const int i=10;
i=12;
printf("%d\n", i);
```

145

It gives a compilation error, since a variable declared with 'const' keyword is a read-only variable (immutable).

A53 What are the values of **a** and **n** after the execution of the following statements?

```
a = 2; n = a++; a = n++; n = a++;
```

n = a++; → **n** is assigned 2, and **a** is then incremented to 3, since it is post-increment.
a = n++; → **a** is assigned 2, and **n** is then incremented to 3, since it is post-increment.
n = a++; → **n** is assigned 2, and **a** is then incremented to 3, since it is post-increment.
Therefore, the values are: **a = 3** and **n = 2**

A54 What are the values of **a** and **n** after the execution of the following statements?

```
a = 2; n = a++; a = ++n; n = a++;
```

n = a++; → **n** is assigned 2, and **a** is then incremented to 3, since it is post-increment.
a = ++n; → **n** is incremented to 3, since it is pre-increment, and then **a** is assigned 3.
n = a++; → **n** is assigned 3, and **a** is then incremented to 4, since it is post-increment.
Therefore, the values are: **a = 4** and **n = 3**

A55 What are the values of **a** and **n** after the execution of the following statements?

```
a = 2; n = ++a; a = n++; n = ++a;
```

n = ++a; → **a** is incremented to 3, since it is pre-increment, and then **n** is assigned 3.
a = n++; → **a** is assigned 3, and **n** is then incremented to 4, since it is post-increment.
n = ++a; → **a** is incremented to 4, since it is pre-increment, and then **n** is assigned 4.
Therefore, the values are: **a = 4** and **n = 4**

A56 What are the values of **a** and **n** after the execution of the following statements?

```
a = 2; n = ++a; a = ++n; n = ++a;
```

n = ++a; → **a** is incremented to 3, since it is pre-increment, and then **n** is assigned 3.
a = ++n; → **n** is incremented to 4, since it is pre-increment, and then **a** is assigned 4.
n = ++a; → **a** is incremented to 5, since it is pre-increment, and then **n** is assigned 5.
Therefore, the values are: **a** = 5 and **n** = 5

A57 What is the output of the following code segment?

```
int n = 08;
printf("n = %d", n);
```

It gives a compilation error. Any number with the prefix 0 is treated as an octal number, and a valid octal digit is 0 – 7.

A58 What is the output of the following code segment?

```
int n = 027;
printf("n = %d", n);
```

n = 23
[It prints the decimal equivalent of the octal number 27, which is 23]

A59 What is the output of the following code segment?
```
int n = 1000 * 1000 * 2000;
printf("n = %d", n);
```

n = 2000000000

A60 What is the output of the following code segment?
```
int n = 1000 * 1000 * 3000;
printf("n = %d", n);
```

Gives a warning about integer overflow, and prints out:
n = -1294967296

The result of 1000 * 1000 * 3000 is too large to be stored in the int variable n. This causes an overflow and gives erroneous results. However, the program continues to run because C reports only a warning on overflow errors.

A61 What is the output of the following program?

```c
int main( void )
{
   int a = 1;
   int b = 2;
   {
     int b = 3;
     printf ("a = %d b = %d\n", a, b);
   }
   printf ("a = %d b = %d\n", a, b);
}
```

```
a = 1 b = 3
a = 1 b = 2
```

Variable 'b' with value 3 in the inner block shadows the variable 'b' with value 2 in the enclosing block. Variable 'a' in the inner block refers to the one in the enclosing block.

A62 What is the output of the following program?

```c
int main()
{
   int i = 3;
   printf ("block0: i = %d\n", i);
   {
     int i = 5;
     printf ("block0: i = %d\n", i);
     {
       int i = 7;
       printf ("block0: i = %d\n", i);
     }
   }
}
```

```
block0: i = 3
block1: i = 5
block2: i = 7
```

A63 Write the statements to assign to variables **min2** and **max2** the minimum and maximum of two numbers in variables **n1** and **n2**, using the ternary operator.

```
min2 = n1 < n2 ? n1 : n2;
max2 = n1 > n2 ? n1 : n2;
```

A64 Write the statements to assign to variables **min3** and **max3** the minimum and maximum of three numbers in variables **n1**, **n2**, and **n3**, using the ternary operator.

```
max3 = n1 > n2 ? (n1 > n3 ? n1 : n3)
               : (n2 > n3 ? n2 : n3);

min3 = n1 < n2 ? (n1 < n3 ? n1 : n3)
               : (n2 < n3 ? n2 : n3);
```

A65 What is the output of the following code segment?
```
int i=5, j;
j = i++;
printf ("j=%d\n", j);
j = ++i;
printf ("j=%d\n", j);
j = i--;
printf ("j=%d\n", j);
j = --i;
printf ("j=%d\n", j);
```

```
j=5
j=7
j=7
j=5
```

A66 What is the output of the following code?
```
int main() {
  int i;
  for (i = 1; i <= 3; i++) {
    int a = 1;
    static int b = 1;
    printf("a = %d, b = %d\n", a, b);
    a++;
    b++;
  }
  return (0);
}
```

```
a = 1, b = 1
a = 1, b = 2
a = 1, b = 3
```

Note that 'a' is an 'auto' / temporary variable. It is initialized at the beginning of each iteration of the loop, and 'b' is a 'static' variable which is initialized only once.

A67 Given **x** is an 'int' variable, and assuming that 'int' takes 4 bytes, what is the value of N such that **x >> N;** results in 0, for any value of **x**?

The value of N is 31. Given 'int' takes 4 bytes = 32 bits, the MSB (Most Significant Bit) is used for the sign. Thus, the right shift operator '>>' is applied to the remaining 31 bits. Every right shift fills the leftmost bits with 0's. Thus, after 31 shifts, for any integer, the result would be 0.

IOIOIOIOIOIOIOIOIOIOIOIOIOIOIOIOIOIOIOIOIOIOIOIOIOIOIOIOIOIOIOI

B. Control Structures

True/False Questions

B1   The **for** loop is more powerful (in terms of controlling the flow of statement executions) than a **while** loop. *False*

B2   Any **for** loop can be rewritten as a **while** loop. *True*

B3   The **for**, **while**, and **do-while** loops do not have equivalent expressive power. *False*

B4   Any of the **for**, **while**, and **do-while** loops can be transformed to the other having the same effect. *True*

B5   The **do-while** loop always executes at least once. *True*

B6   The **while** loop always executes at least once. *False*

B7   The **for** loop always executes at least once. *False*

B8   The index variable of a **for** loop cannot be of type double. *False*

B9   **for (; ;);** is equivalent to **for (; true;);** *True*

B10 The **for** statement in C can be rewritten as an equivalent **while** loop. *True*

B11 The **for**, **while**, and **do-while** loops do not have equivalent expressive power. *False*

B12 Any of the **for**, **while**, and **do-while** loops can be transformed to the other having the same effect. *True*

B13 The **do-while** loop always executes at least once. *True*

B14 The **while** loop always executes at least once. *False*

B15 The **for** loop always executes at least once. *False*

B16 The **switch** statement cannot be rewritten by using multiple **if-else** statements. *False*

B17 The **break** statement inside an inner loop of a nested loop will pass control out of the all the nested loops to the statement outside of the outermost loop. *False*
[The **break** statement passes control to the first statement outside of the (innermost) loop where it is executed]

B18 The **break** statement inside a loop of a nested loop will pass control out of the entire loop. *False*
[The **break** statement will pass control out of the loop at that level and to the enclosing loop, if any]

B19 Assignment statements always produce side effects. *True*

B20 All the three expressions of the **for** statement must be present. *False*
[Each of the three expressions of the **for** statement is optional]

B21 The **exp1** in **for (exp1; exp2; exp3)** can be executed more than once. *False*
[The 'exp1' is executed exactly once, and is the first to be executed at the start of 'for' loop]

B22 The **exp1** in **for (exp1; exp2; exp3)** cannot consist of multiple statements. *False*
[Multiple statements separated by commas is valid]

B23 The **exp3** in **for (exp1; exp2; exp3)** can consist of multiple statements. *True*
[Multiple statements separated by commas is valid]

B24 Given the loop: **for (exp1; exp2; exp3) {BODY}** **exp2** and **exp3** are executed exactly the same number of times. *False*
[**exp2** is executed one more time than **exp3**]

B25 Given the loop: `for (exp1; exp2; exp3) {BODY}` exp3 is executed before the 'body' of the loop is executed. *False* [`exp3` is executed after the 'body' of the loop is executed]

B26 The `continue` control statement transfers control to the the outermost loop. *False*

B27 The `continue` control statement transfers control to the start of the loop, ignoring further statements after the `continue`. *True*

B28 Nesting of `switch` statements ('switch' statement(s) inside another 'switch") are not allowed. *False*

B29 The `default` must be at the end of the `switch` statement, after all the `case` statements. *False*

B30 The expression associate with the case in switch–case statement cannot be a variable expression. *True*

B31 The '`case`'s cannot be combined and share the same code block. *False*

IOIOIOIOIOIOIOIOIOIOIOIOIOIOIOIOIOIOIOIOIOIOIOIOIOIOIOIOI

Fill-in the-blanks Questions

B1 Statement that is used to modify the order of execution is known as *control* statement.

B2 A control statement together with its associated block of statements is known as *control structure*.

B3 A loop whose number of iterations is determined by the numeric value of a variable is known as *counter-controlled* loop.

B4 A loop whose number of iterations is determined by the Boolean condition of an expression is known as *condition-controlled* loop.

B5   In a ***post-test*** (***do-while***) loop control structure, the loop body is executed at least once.

B6   It is more natural to use the **`for`** loop when the number of iterations is known *a priori* (before hand).

B7   The statement block in a ***post–test*** (or ***do–while***) control structure is executed at least once.

B8   The ***multiple–selection* (`switch-case`)** construct allows the selection of one of a number of statements or statement groups.

B9   ***Pre–test loop* (ex. *while loop*)** causes a (compound) statement to be executed zero or more times.

B10   The **`break`** control statement transfers control out of the smallest enclosing loop.

B11   The **`continue`** control statement transfers control to the top of the loop.

B12   An optional **`else`** clause in an **`if–then`** [**`–else`**] statement resulting in nested conditionals being ambiguous is known as ***dangling-else*** problem.

B13   The first statement to be executed in **`while`** **`(cond_exp)`** **`{stmt1; ... stmt17;}`** is **`cond_exp`**.

B14   The last statement to be executed in **`while`** **`(cond_exp)`** **`{stmt1; ... stmt17;}`** is **`cond_exp`**.

B15   The first statement to be executed in **`do`** **`{stmt1; ... stmt17;}`** **`while (cond_exp);`** is <u>**`stmt1`**</u>.

B16   The last statement to be executed in **`do`** **`{stmt1; ... stmt17;}`** **`while (cond_exp);`** is **`cond_exp`**.

B17   The effect of the statement: **`for ( ; ; );`** is ***an infinite loop***.

B18   The numbet of times the **STATEMENT BLOCK** is executed in the following loop is <u>**25**</u>.

```
for (int i=23; i <= 47; i++)
{
    STATEMENT BLOCK
}
```

B19 The numbet of times the **STATEMENT BLOCK** is executed in the following loop is **15**.

```
for (int i=51; i > 36; i--)
{
    STATEMENT BLOCK
}
```

B20 The numbet of times the **STATEMENT BLOCK** is executed in the following loop is **1**. (Note that there is ';' at the end of 'for')

```
for (int i=1; i <= 25; i++);
{
    STATEMENT BLOCK
}
```

B21 Given the loop: **for (exp1; exp2; exp3) {BODY}** is itrerated 20 times, the number of times **exp1** is evaluated is **1**.

B22 Given the loop: **for (exp1; exp2; exp3) {BODY}** is itrerated 20 times, the expression to be evaluated last is **exp2**.

B23 Given the loop: **for (exp1; exp2; exp3) {BODY}** is itrerated multiple times, the order of execution of the different components of the loop, after the first iteration is **exp2**, **BODY**, and **exp3**.

B24 Given the loop: **for (exp1; exp2; exp3) {BODY}** is itrerated multiple times, the components of the loop which are executed exactly the same number of times are **BODY** and **exp3**.

IOIOIOIOIOIOIOIOIOIOIOIOIOIOIOIOIOIOIOIOIOIOIOIOIOIOIOIOI

Essay-type Questions

B1   The following loop was intended to compute $1/2 + 2/3 + 3/4 + ... + 99/100$. What is the error and what is a fix?

```
double sum = 0;
for (int i = 1; i <= 99; i++) {
  sum += i / (i + 1);
}
```

In each iteration, the division in `i / (i + 1)` is performed on integers, and each of them results in a 0. Thus, sum remains 0. Each of the following code segments shows a fix.

```
double sum = 0;
for (int i = 1; i <= 99; i++) {
  sum += (double)i / (i + 1);
}
```

```
double sum = 0;
for (int i = 1; i <= 99; i++) {
  sum += i / ((double)i + 1);
}
```

```
double sum = 0;
for (int i = 1; i <= 99; i++) {
  sum += i / (i + 1.0);
}
```

```
double sum = 0;
for (int i = 1; i <= 99; i++) {
  sum += 1.0 * i / (i + 1);
}
```

B2   Do the following loops result in the same value of sum?

```
for (int i = 1; i <= 10; ++i) {
  sum += i;
}
```

```
for (int i = 1; i <= 10; i++) {
  sum += i;
}
```

Here, ++i and i++ are used standalone with no side-effect. So, they are equivalent.

B3   What is the flaw with the 'while' condition in the following code segment? How could it be fixed?

```
double sum = 0;
double n = 0;
while (n != 10.0) {
   n += 0.1;
   sum += n;
}
```

There is no guarantee that the value of n will be exactly 10.0 because real numbers are represented using approximation in computers. Thus, the code could get caught in an infinite loop.

The important point to note is to not compare floating point numbes for "equality/non-equality" whose values are based on a sequence of computations. One way is to see if they are arbitrarily "close to each other" by using ABS $(x - y) < \varepsilon$ (for some ε, say 0.001).

```
double sum = 0;
double n = 0;
while (abs(n - 10.0) > 0.001) {
   n += 0.1;
   sum += n;
}
```

B4   The following code which was intended to print 1, 2, ... 10 has a flaw. What does it print? What is the correction required?

```
int i;
for (i = 1; i <= 10; i++);
   printf("%d ", i);
```

The program prints 11. Note that there is a ";" after the **for** statement. Thus, there is no body of statements in the **for** loop. After the loop exits, the value of i is 11, which is printed. The corrected code is shown below.

```
int i;
```

```
for (i = 1; i <= 10; i++)
    printf("%d ", i);
```

B5 How many times does the **while** loop execute in the following code segment?

```
int x = 0;
while (x < 5)
   x++;
```

5 times.

B6 How many times does the **while** loop execute in the following code segment?

```
int x = 10;
while (x < 5)
   x++;
```

0 times.

B7 How many times does the **while** loop execute, and what will be the value of **sum** after the loop has finished?

```
double n = 0, sum = 0;
while (n <= 1.0) {
   n += 0.1;
   sum += n;
}
```

The loop executes 11 times. The value of **sum** after the loop has finished is 6.6.

B8 Does the following code segment result in an infinite loop?

```
int x = 0;
while (x >= 0)
   x++;
```

No. x keeps on incrementing, and after it reaches the maximum representable integers, further increment results in an overflow, which results in x becoming negative, at which time the condition becomes false, and the loop exits. Note that the largest representable positive integer (in 32 bits) is $2^{31} - 1 = 2147483647$, and the largest representable negative integer (in 32 bits) is $-2^{31} = -2147483648$. When the value of x reaches the largest representable value, and it is incremented, there will be an overflow.

B9   What is the output of the following code segment?

```
int i=0, x = 0;
while (x >= 0){
  x++;
  i++;
}
printf("i=%d x=%d\n", (i-1), x);
```

Output: i = 2147483647 x = -2147483648

[The number 2147483647 which is hexadecimal 7FFFFFFF is the maximum positive value for a 32-bit signed binary integer. After it is incremented by 1, there will be an overflow, and the number representation will be a negative number]

B10   What is the output of the following code segment? Rewrite the following code segment using a **for** loop with the same effect.

```
int x = 0;
while (x < 5) {
  x++;
  printf("%d ", x);
}
```

Output: 1 2 3 4 5

There are several ways of using a **for** loop. A couple of ways are given below.

```
int x = 0;
for (int i=0; i < 5; i++) {
  x++;
  printf("%d ", x);
```

```
    }

    int x = 0;
    for (x++; x <= 5; x++)
        printf("%d ", x);
```

B11 Convert the following 'for' loop to 'while' loop.

```
    for (int i=low; i <= high; i++){
        /* STATEMENT BLOCK */
    }

    int i=low;
    while (i <= high){
        /* STATEMENT BLOCK */
        i++;
    }
```

B12 Convert the following 'while' loop to 'do-while' loop, assuming low ≤ high.

```
    int i=low;
    while (i <= high){
        /* STATEMENT BLOCK */
        i++;
    }

    int i=low;
    do {
        /* STATEMENT BLOCK */
        i++;
    } while(i <= high);
```

For arbitrary values of 'low' and 'high',

```
    int i=low;
    if (low <= high){
        do {
            /* STATEMENT BLOCK */
            i++;
        } while(i <= high);
    }
```

B13 What is the output of the following code segment?

```
double sum = 0;
while (sum != 10)
  sum += 0.1;
printf("%d\n", sum);
```

It is likely that it gets caught in an infinite loop. Unlike integer arithmetic, due to the nature of floating point arithmetic, the result of adding 0.1 to the variable sum, may not result in an exact value of 10. Thus the value of sum may never equal to 10

B14   What is the output of the following code segment?

```
double sum = 0;
while (sum < 10)
  sum += 0.1;
printf("%d\n", sum);
```

Output: **10.1**

B15   What is the output of the following code segment?

```
int i, j;
for (i=1, j=5; i<=5; ++i, --j)
  printf ("i= %d j= %d\n", i, j);
```

Output:
```
i= 1 j= 5
i= 2 j= 4
i= 3 j= 3
i= 4 j= 2
i= 5 j= 1
```

B16   What is the output of the following code segment?

```
int i, j;
for (i=1, j=5; i<=j; ++i, --j)
  printf ("i= %d j= %d\n", i, j);
```

Output:
```
i= 1 j= 5
i= 2 j= 4
i= 3 j= 3
```

B17 What is the output of the following code segment?

```
double sum = 0, incr = 0.01;
for (int i=1; i<=100; i++)
    sum += incr;
printf ("%.18f", sum);
```

Output: **1.000000000000000666**

B18 What is the output of the following code segment?

```
double sum = 0, incr = 0;
for (int i=1; i<=100; i++){
    incr += 0.01;
    sum += incr;
}
printf ("%.18f", sum);
```

Output: **50.500000000000028422**

The basic objective of this (and similar problems) is for the reader to run these and see the results. The point to be noted is that the values resulting from floating point opcratons may not be exact, as with integer operations.

B19 What is the output of the following code segment?

```
double sum = 0, decr = 1;
for (int i=1; i<=100; i++){
    sum += decr;
    decr -= 0.01;
}
printf ("%.18f\n", sum);
```

Output: **50.499999999999950262**

B20 What is the output of the following code segment?

```
double sum = 0, incr = 0, decr = 1.0;
for (int i=1; i<=50; i++){
    incr += 0.01;
    sum = sum + incr + decr;
    decr -= 0.01;
```

```
}
printf ("%.18f\n%.18f\n ", incr, sum);
```

Output:
```
0. 500000000000000222
50.499999999999992895
```

B21 What error does the following code segment have?

```
int x;
double d = 1.5;

switch (d) {
  case 1.0: x = 1;
  case 1.5: x = 2;
  case 2.0: x = 3;
}
```

It results in a compilation error. The switch control variable cannot be 'double'.

B22 What error does the following code segment have?

```
int x;
double d = 1.5;

switch ((int)d) {
  case (int)1.0: x = 1;
  case (int)1.5: x = 2;
  case (int)2.0: x = 3;
}
```

It results in a compilation error due to duplicate 'case' values.

B23 What error does the following code segment have, if any?

```
int x;
double d = 1.5;

switch ((int)d) {
  case (int)1.5: x = 1;
  case (int)2.5: x = 2;
  case (int)3.5: x = 3;
```

```
    }
```

There is no error.

B24 What is the output of the following program?

```
int main() {
  int i, j;
  for (i=1; i<=3; i++) {
    for (j=1; j<=3; j++) {
      if ((i+j) % 4 == 0) {
         printf("Iteration (%d, %d) is not done\n", i, j);
         break;
      }
      else
         printf("Iteration (%d, %d) is done\n", i, j);
    }
  }
}
```

Output:
```
Iteration (1, 1) is done
Iteration (1, 2) is done
Iteration (1, 3) is not done
Iteration (2, 1) is done
Iteration (2, 2) is not done
Iteration (3, 1) is not done
```

B25 What is the output of the following program?

```
int main() {
  int i, j;
  for (i=1; i<=3; i++) {
    for (j=1; j<=3; j++) {
      if ((i+j) % 4 == 0) {
         printf("\nIteration (%d, %d) is not done\n", i, j);
         continue;
      }
      else
         printf("(%d, %d) is done ", i, j);
    }
    printf("\n");
  }
}
```

Output:
```
(1, 1) is done (1, 2) is done
Iteration (1,3) is not done

(2, 1) is done
```

```
Iteration (2,2) is not done
(2, 3) is done

Iteration (3,1) is not done
(3, 2) is done (3, 3) is done
```

B26 What is the output of the following program?

```
int main() {
  for (int i = 0; i < 10; i++){
    for (int j = 0; j < 10; j++){
      if ((i+j) % 3 == 0)
        break;
      printf("(%d, %d) ", i, j);
    }
    printf("\n");
  }
}
```

Output:
```
(1,0) (1,1)
(2,0)

(4,0) (4,1)
(5,0)

(7,0) (7,1)
(8,0)
```

B27 Rewrite the following code segment using multiple-selection (switch-case).

```
if (k == 1 || k == 2) j = 2*k - 1;
if (k == 3 || k == 5) j = 3*k + 1;
if (k == 4) j = 4*k - 1;
if (k == 6 || k == 7 || k == 8) j = k - 2;
```

Answer:
```
switch (k) {
   case 1:
   case 2: j = 2*k - 1; break;
   case 3:
   case 5: j = 3*k + 1; break;
   case 4: j = 4*k - 1; break;
   case 6:
   case 7:
   case 8: j = k - 2; break;
}
```

B28 What is the output of the following code segment?

```
int i=0;
do {
  if (i < 10) {
    i += 2;
    printf ("%d ", i);
    continue;
  }
  else
    printf ("%d\n", ++i);
} while (i < 15);
```

Output:
```
2 4 6 8 10 11
12
13
14
15
```

B29 What is the output of the following code segment?

```
for (i=0; i<3; i++) {
  for (j=0; j<3; j++) {
    for (k=0; k<3; k++) {
      printf ("i=%d j=%d k=%d\n", i, j, k);

      if ((i+j+k) % 2 == 0)
```

```
        goto label1;
    }
  }
  label1: continue;
}
```

Output:
```
i=0 j=0 k=0
i=1 j=0 k=0
i=1 j=0 k=1
i=2 j=0 k=0
```

B30 What is the output of the following code segment?

```
for (i=0; i<3; i++) {
  for (j=0; j<3; j++) {
    for (k=0; k<3; k++) {
      if ((i+j+k) % 2 == 0)
        break;
      printf ("i=%d j=%d k=%d\n", i, j, k);
    }
  }
}
```

Output:
```
i=0 j=1 k=0
i=1 j=0 k=0
i=1 j=2 k=0
i=2 j=1 k=0
```

B31 Rewrite the following code segment using a 'for' loop.

```
k = (j + 10) / 15;
loop:
    if k > 5 then goto out
    k = k + 1
    i = 3 * k - 1
    goto loop
out: ...
}
```

Answer:

```
for (k = (j+10)/15; k <= 5; k++)
    i = 3*(k+1) - 1;
```

B32 Rewrite the following code segment without using **switch-case**.

```
j = -3;
for (i = 0; i < 3; i++){
        switch (j + 2){
          case 0: j += 2; break;
          case 2:
          case 3: j--; break;
          default: j = 0;
        }
        if (j > 0)
          break;
        else j = 3 - i;
}
```

Answer:
```
j = -3;
k = j + 2;
for (i = 0; i < 3; i++){
        if (k == 0)
          j += 2;
        else if ((k == 2) || (k == 3))
          j--;
        else j = 0;
        if (j > 0)
          break;
        else j = 3 - i;
}
```

B33 What is the output of the following code segment?

```
int a, b, c, m;
a= 352; b = 56; c = 173;
if (a < b){
  if (a < c)
    m = a;
  else
    m = c;
}
else if (b < c)
  m = b;
else
  m = c;
}
printf("%d\n", m);
```

Output:
56

B34   What is the output of the following code segment?

```
int n, p;
n = 1; p = 1;
while (n < 1000){
  printf("%d ", n);
  p ++;
  n = n * p;
}
```

Output:
1 2 6 24 120 720

B35   What is the output of the following code segment?

```
int x = 1, y = 1;
do {
  printf("%d ", x);
  x = x + y;
  y ++;
} while (y < 10);
```

Output:
1 2 4 7 11 16 22 29 37

B36   What is the output of the following code segment?

```
int i, num, term, inc;
term = 1; inc = 1;
for (i = 1; i <= 10; i++){
  num = 2 * term;
  inc ++;
  term += inc;
  printf("%d ", num);
}
```

Output:
2 6 12 20 30 42 56 72 90 110

B37   Write a 'while' loop which prints out the following sequence of numbers. It starts at 10 and the difference between successive numbers increases by 1 (ex. 1 2 3 4)

```
        10   9   7   4   0
```

```
int n = 10, i = 1;
```

```
while (n >= 0) {
  printf("%d ", n);
  n = n - i;
  i++ ;
}
```

B38 How many times does the following loop execute?

```
int x, y;
x = 10; y;
do {
  x = x - 1;
  y = x / 2;
} while (y <= 3);
```

Answer: **Loop is done once**

B39 In the following C program segment, how many times is **<Statement block1>** executed?

```
for (i = 1;  i <= 5; i++) {
  for (j = 1;  j <= 4; j++) {
    if (i%2 != 0 && j%2 == 0)
      continue;
      <Statement block1>
  }
}
```

The total number of iterations is 20. The **continue** statement is executed when i is even and j is odd. This happens 6 times. When **continue** statement is not executed, the **<Statement block1>** is executed. Thus, **<Statement block1>** is executed 14 times.

IOIOIOIOIOIOIOIOIOIOIOIOIOIOIOIOIOIOIOIOIOIOIOIOIOIOIOIOIOIOI

C. Pointers

True/False Questions

C1 The name of an integer array can be assigned to a variable of type int* (pointer to integer). *True*
[Array name represents the base address of array. So it can be treated as pointer to the first element of the array, and therefore can be assigned to a int*]

C2 Subscripts cannot be used with a pointer variable. *False*
[Given char str[25], *pstr; pstr[i], $(0 \leq i \leq 24)$, is valid]

C3 A pointer to an object of a certain datatype cannot be cast to point to another object of a different type. *False*

C4 The pointers to simple types and pointers to structured types have different sizes. *False*

C5 The size of a pointer is guaranteed to be the size of 'int' or 'long. *False*

C6 A pointer can be defined for only for non-primitive types. *False*
[A pointer can be defined to point to a variable of any datatype]

C7 Pointers cannot be used with multidimensional arrays. *False*

C8 Function pointers and data pointers may have different representations. *True*

C9 A 'void' pointer can hold the address of any data type. *True*

C10 A 'void' pointer cannot be cast to point to any data type. *False*

C11 A 'void' pointer cannot be dereferenced. *True*

C12 Pointer arithmetic can be done on 'void' pointers. *False*

C13 A void pointer can be dereferenced after casting it to a data type pointer. *True*

C14   Pointer arithmetic can be done on a pointer to a variable of type double. ***True***

C15   Pointer arithmetic can be done on a function pointer. ***False***

C16   Pointer arithmetic uses only integer values. ***True***

C17   Relational operators can be used with pointer variables. ***True***

C18   A pointer may not be declared with the type qualifier `const`. ***False***

C19   A pointer must be initialized when declared. ***False***

C20   A pointer variable always points to a valid memory address. ***False***

C21   A pointer variable can have a value of NULL. ***True***

C22   A pointer variable cannot be reassigned. ***False***

C23   An array of references is not valid. ***True***

C24   A variable can have more than one pointer. ***True***

C25   A pointer and variable it is pointing to, share the same address. ***False***

C26   Pointers can be declared to point to both primitive types as well as to structures and arrays. ***True***

C27   There is no generic pointer to functions. ***True***

Given the declaration `char ch1='G', ch2='T', *cp1, *cp2;`

C28   `ch1 = ch2;` is valid. ***True***

C29   `cp1 = ch1;` is valid. ***False***

C30   `cp2 = cp1;` is valid. ***True***

C31   `cp1 = &ch2;` is valid. ***True***

C32   `ch2 = cp2;` is valid. ***False***

C33   `ch1 = *cp2;` is valid. ***True***

C34 &cp1 = ch2; is valid. *False*

C35 *cp2 = *cp1; is valid. *True*

C36 *ch1 = &cp1; is valid. *False*

C37 &cp2 = &cp1; is valid. *False*

C38 Given the declaration int* ap, *ap cannot be on the left-hand side of an assignment. *False*
[The sequence int a; ap = &a; *ap = 5; is valid]

C39 Given the declaration int a, &a cannot be on the left-hand side of an assignment. *True*

C40 The declaration int*** ap3; is a valid declaration. *True*

C41 The declaration int& a; is a valid declaration. *False*

C42 The set of declarations: int **ap2; int a = 5; *ap2 = &a; is valid. *True*

C43 Given the definition int fn (float x){ } and the declaration int (*pf)(float); the assignment pf = &fn; is valid. *True*

C44 Given the definition int fn (float x){ } and the declaration int (*pf)(float); the assignment pf = fn; is not valid. *False*
[Both assignments pf = &fn; and pf = fn; are valid. In the latter, there is implicit conversion to pointer]

IOIOIOIOIOIOIOIOIOIOIOIOIOIOIOIOIOIOIOIOIOIOIOIOIOIOIOIOIOIOIOI

Fill-in the-blanks Questions

C1 Pointer arithmetic is not valid on *'void'* and *function* pointers.

C2 Given a datatype DT, the declaration DT a, *pa; and the statement pa = &a; pa++ increments pa by sizeof (DT) bytes.

C3   Given **int a = 5**, the declaration of a pointer variable 'ap' to point to 'a' is **int* ap = &a;**

C4   Given 'bp' to be a pointer with the address of a valid integer variable 'b', the statement to assign the contents of 'b' using 'bp' to an integer variable 'c' is **c = *bp;**

C5   Given **double x = 5.3712**, the declaration of a variable 'xp' which is initialized to the address of 'x' is **double* xp = &x;**

C6   Given **char c = '@'; char* cp = &c;** the statement using **putchar** to print the contents of 'c' using 'cp' is **putchar(*cp);**

C7   Given **double x = 7.26; double* xp = &x;** the declaration of a variable 'xpp' to contain the address of 'xp' is **double** xpp = &xp;**

C8   Given **int a = 5; int* ap = &a; int** app = ≈** the statement to assign the value of 'a' to an integer variable 'c' using 'app' is **c = **app;**

C9   Given the declaration **int **ap2;** the datatype of **ap2** is *pointer to pointer to integer*.

C10   Given the set of declarations: **int **ap2; int a = 5; *ap2 = &a;** the content of **ap2** is *address of a location containing the address of a*.

C11   Given **char* p**, assuming that the size of 'char is 1 byte and pointer to 'char' is 8 bytes, the value of **sizeof(p)** is **8 bytes**.

C12   Assuming that a character takes 1 byte and a pointer takes 8 bytes, given the declaration **char *b[5];** the number of bytes allocated to **b** is **40**.
[**b** is an array of 5 character pointers. Therefore 5 x 8 = 40 bytes]

C13   Assuming that a character takes 1 byte and a pointer takes 8 bytes, given the declaration **char (*c)[5];** the number of bytes allocated to **c** is **8**.
[**c** is a pointer to an array of 5 characters, and a pointer takes 8 bytes]

C14 Assuming that a character takes 1 byte and a pointer takes 8 bytes, given the declaration **char* (*d)[5];** the number of bytes allocated to **d** is <u>8</u>.
[**d** is a pointer to an array of 5 character pointers , and a pointer takes 8 bytes]

C15 Assuming that a character takes 1 byte and a pointer takes 8 bytes, given the declaration **char* (*(*e)[5]);** the number of bytes allocated to **e** is <u>8</u>.
[**e** is a pointer to an array of 5 pointers to character pointers, and a pointer takes 8 bytes]

C16 Assuming that a character takes 1 byte and a pointer takes 8 bytes, given the declaration **char* (*(f[5]));** the number of bytes allocated to **f** is <u>8</u>.
[**f** is an array of 5 pointers to character pointers. Therefore 5 x 8 = 40 bytes]

C17 Given **char* str = " INCORPORATION ";** the **puts** statement to output **CORPORATION** using index of **str** is **puts (&str[2]);**

C18 Given **char* str = " INCORPORATION ";** the **puts** statement to output **RATION** using pointer arithmetic on **str** is **puts (str+7);**

C19 Given **char* str = " INCORPORATION ";** the statement to assign the character 'P' in **str** to a character variable **ch**, using index of **str** is **ch = str[5];**

C20 Given **char* str = " INCORPORATION ";** the statement to assign the character 'T' in **str** to a character variable **ch**, using pointer arithmetic on **str** is **ch = *str+9;**

C21 Given **char* str = " INCORPORATION ";** the output of **putchar (*str)** is <u>I</u>.

C22 The value of **"HABIT" + 2** is **BIT**.
[The pointer to the start of a string is used in address arithmetic and subscripts. In the above expression the pointer is offset by 2 positions, and it will be pointing at 'B']

C23 The value of *** ("HABIT"+2)** is **B**.
[The above expression refers to the contents of the pointer offset by 2 positions, which is 'B']

C24 The value of **"HABIT"[2]** is **B**.

IOIOIOIOIOIOIOIOIOIOIOIOIOIOIOIOIOIOIOIOIOIOIOIOIOIOIOI

Essay-type Questions

C1 Given the declaration **char* str = "Test String";** and the size of a character is 1 byte, the size of an address is 4 bytes, how many bytes are allocated to **str**?

Note that **"Test String"** is allocated in some area of memory, and it's start address is assigned to **str**. Thus, **str** is allocated 4 bytes.

C2 What is the output of the following code segment?
```
int a, *b=&a, **c=&b;
a = 5;
**c = 7;
printf ("a = %d\n", a);
```

Output: **a = 7**

C3 What is the error in the following code segment?
```
float **fp2, *fp1;
fp1 = &fp2;
```

'fp1' is a pointer to 'float'. The correct contents of 'fp1' is address of a float variable. However, it is being set to the address of a pointer to pointer to float.

C4 What is the error in the following code segment?
```
char ch, **fc2, *fc1;
ch = '$';
fc1 = &ch;
**fc2 = *fc1;
```

fc2 is being dereferenced without properly being initialized.

C5 What is the error in the following code segment?
```
float x = 3.75, **fp2, *fp1;
```

```
fp2 = &x;
```

fp2 is of type pointer to pointer to a float. However, **fp2** is assigned the address of 'x', which essentially is assignining to **fp2** a pointer to float, leading to type incompatible assignment.

C6   What is the error in the following code segment? What is the fix?

```
int fn (float x){ }
int *p;
p = &fn;
```

Note that **p** is a pointer to integer, and it is being set to the address of a function **fn**, which is not valid. The valid declaration for 'p' is **int (*p)(float);**

C7   What is the error in the following code segment?

```
int fn (float x){ }
int fn1();
fn1 = &fn;
```

Note that **fn1** is a function which returns an integer, and it is being set to the address of a function **fn**, which is not valid.

C8   What is the error in the following code segment?

```
int fn (float x){ }
int *fn2();
fn2 = &fn;
```

Note that **fn2** is a function which returns an integer pointer (**int ***), and it is being set to the address of a function **fn**, which is not valid.

C9   What is the error in the following code segment? What is the correction required in the declaration of **pfn**?

```
int fn (float x){ }
int (*pfn)();
pfn = &fn;
```

Note that **pfn** is a pointer to a function whose parameter type is unspecified, and by default will be assumed to be **int**, and it is being set to the address of a function **fn**, whose parameter is of type float. Thus, although **pfn** and **&fn** are pointers, the pointer types are incompatible. The declaration **int (*pfn) (float) ;** would be correct.

C10 What is the error in the following code segment? What is the correction required in the assignment?

```
int fn (float x){ }
void (*pfn)(float);
pfn = &fn;
```

Note that **pfn** is a pointer to a function whose return type is **void**, and **&fn** is the address of (pointer to) function **fn** whose return type is **int**. Thus, although **pfn** and **&fn** are pointers, the pointer types are incompatible. The assignment **pfn = (void *)&fn;** would be correct.

C11 What is the output of the following code segment?
```
float x = 3.75, *fp1, **fp2;
fp1 = &x;
fp2 = &fp1;
printf ("%.2f\n", **fp2);
```

It outputs **3.75**. Note that **fp1** is set to the address of **x**, and **fp2** is set to the address of **fp1**. The double dereferencing of **fp2** gives the contents of **x** which is printed.

C12 Given 'dp1' is a pointer to double, 'dp2' is a pointer to a pointer to double, and 'x' is a double, what are the declarations and assignments required to have ****dp2** to have a value 5.12?

```
double **dp2, *dp1;
double x = 5.12;
dp1 = &x;
dp2 = &dp1;
```

C13 What is the output of the following code segment?
```
char *ptr;
char str[] = "pancake";
ptr = str + 3;
printf("%s\n", ptr);
```

Output: **cake**

C14 What is the output of the following code segment?
```
int a = 5;
int *p = &a;
*p = 7;
printf("a: %d\n", a);
```

Output: **a: 7**
[‘p’ is a pointer which contains the address of ‘a’. When ‘p’ is dereferenced and set to 7, it effectively changes the contents of ‘a’]

C15 What is the output of the following code segment?
```
int x = 10;
int* p = &x;
*p = 20;
printf("x: %d\n", x);
x = 30;
printf("(*p): %d\n", *p);
```

Output:
x: 20
(*p): 30

C16 What is the output of the following code segment? What is the difference between the two declarations?

```
char* p = "Test";
char s[] = "Best";
puts(p);
puts(s);
```

Output:
Test
Best

‘p’ is a variable of type pointer to ‘char’, which contains the pointer to the start address of the location where the string “Test” is stored, ‘s’ refers to the starting location of the memory which stores the array of characters.

C17 What is the output of the following code segment?

```
double x = 3.678;
double *dp = &x;
```

```
printf("(*dp): %lf, dp: %p\n", *dp, dp);
dp++;
printf("(*dp): %lf, dp: %p\n", *dp, dp);
```

Output:
*dp): 3.678, dp: 0x7fff53e9a2c0
(*dp): 0.000, dp: 0x7fff53e9a2c8
[When 'dp' is incremented, the address that 'dp' is pointing to increases by 8 bytes (64 bits)]

C18 What is the output of the following code segment?

```
char* p = "Test";
putchar(p[0]); putchar(p[1]);
putchar(p[2]); putchar(p[3]);
```

Output: **Test**.
'p' is a pointer which contains the start address of the location where the string "Test" is stored. 'p' can also be treated as an array of characters, and the elements can be accessed using subscripts.

C19 What is the output of the following code segment?

```
char* p = "Test";
char* q = p;
q[0] = 'B';
printf("p: %s q: %s\n", p, q);
```

Output: **p: Test q: Best**

'p' and 'q' are two different string variables. Assigning a value to q[0] does not change 'p'.

C20 What is the output of the following code segment?

```
char s[] = "Test";
char* q = s;
q[0] = 'B';
printf("s: %s q: %s\n", s, q);
```

Output: **s: Best q: Best**

'q' is a character pointer which is initialized to the same value as in 's'. Now, both 's' and 'q' point to the same area of memory where the string "Test" is stored. `q[0] = 'B'` changes the string.

C21 What is the output of the following code segment?

```
char* s = "C is fun and useful";
char* p = s;
puts(p);
```

Output: `C is fun and useful`

C22 What is the output of the following code segment?

```
char* s = "C is fun and useful";
char* p = &s[0];
puts(p);
```

Output: `C is fun and useful`

In this case, `&s1[0]` represents the address of the first element of s, which is synonymous with a pointer.

C23 What is the output of the following code segment?

```
int a = 10;
void *ptr = &a;
printf("%d", *ptr);
```

Error. 'void' pointer has to be cast to int * in oder for proper dereferencing.

C24 What is the output of the following code segment?

```
int a = 10;
void *ptr = &a;
printf("%d", *(int *)ptr);
```

Output: `10`
'void' pointer has been cast to (int *) for proper derefencing.

C25 What is the output of the following code segment?

```
int a = 3, * p1;
p1 = &a;
*p1 = 5;
printf("a: %d, (*p1): %d\n", a, *p1);
```

Output: a: 5, (*p1): 5
Note that p1 = &a sets the contents of 'p1' to the address of 'a', which is valid location. Subsequently, when *p1 = 5 is executed, 5 is assigned to the location pointed to by 'p1'.

C26   What is the output of the following code segment?

```
int* p1;
*p1 = 5;
printf("p1: %p, (*p1): %d\n", p1, *p1);
```

This results in segmentation fault. int* p1 declares 'p1' as a pointer to an integer. The contents of 'p1' would be an address, but it is as yet uninitialized – it is not pointing to a valid location. When *p1 = 5 is attempted, the assignment of 5 is attempted to an invalid location, and hence the error.

C27   What is the output of the following code segment?

```
int a = 3, *p1;
p1 = &a;
free (p1);
```

It gives a runtime error, since 'p1' is pointing to 'a' – a valid memory location, there is an attempt to delete a valid memory location.

C28   What is the output of the following code segment?

```
char * p1;
p1 = calloc(10, sizeof(char));
p1[0]= 'a'; p1[1]='b';p1[2]='c';p1[3]='\0';
printf("%p\n", p1);
printf("%s\n", p1);
```

Output:
0x20b3010 (address in memory where the 10 'char's are allocated
a b c

C29   What is the output of the following code segment?

```
int * p1;
p1 = calloc (10, sizeof(int));
p1[0]= 1; p1[1]=2;p1[2]=3;p1[3]=4;
printf("%p\n", p1);
printf("%d %d %d\n", *p1, *(p1+1), *(p1+2));
```

Output:
`0x1f6ec20` (address in memory where the 10 'int's are allocated
`1 2 3`

C30 What is the output of the following code segment?

```
char * p1 = "Test";
puts(p1);
putchar(*p1); putchar(*p1+1);
putchar(*p1+2); putchar(*p1+3);
putchar('\n');
putchar(*p1); putchar(*(p1+1));
putchar(*(p1+2)); putchar(*(p1+3));
```

Output:
```
Test
TUVW
Test
```

C31 What is the output of the following code segment?

```
int a[]={2, 3, 5, 7, 11};
int* pi = a+3;

printf("%lu\n", pi - a);
printf("%lu\n", ((int *)pi - (int *)a) *
(sizeof(int)));
```

Output:
3
12
['pi' and 'a' contain addresses. 'pi' is offset by 3 positions from 'a', where a position corresponds to the index (subscript) of the array. In the second 'printf', the difference in the address values is multiplied by the size of an 'int'. Since each integer takes up 4 bytes, three integers correspond to 12 bytes]

C32 What is the output of the following code segment?

```
int* pi = calloc(2, sizeof(int));
double* pd = calloc(2, sizeof(double));
unsigned long a1 = (unsigned long) (pi+1) -
(unsigned long) pi;
unsigned long a2 = (unsigned long) (pd+1) -
(unsigned long) pd;

printf("a1: %lu, a2: %lu\n", a1, a2);
```

Output:
```
a1: 4, a2: 8
```

'a1' is the difference between the byte addresses of two consecutive integers in memory. Since an integer takes 4 bytes, this difference is 4. Similarly, since a double takes 8 bytes of memory, 'a2' is 8.

C33   What is the output of the following code segment?

```
int a[]={10, 20, 30};
int* pi = a;

printf("pi: %p, a: %p\n", pi, a);
printf("*pi: %d, a: %p\n", *pi, a);
printf("pi: %p, *a: %d\n", pi, *a);
```

Output:
```
pi:0x7ffdffc92f14, a:0x7ffdffc92f14
*pi:10, a:0x7ffdffc92f14
Pi:0x7ffdffc92f14, *a:10
```

'pi' is a pointer to an integer, 'a' is an array of integers, and 'a' is also treated as an address to the first element of the array. Thus, assignment of 'pi' to 'a' is valid. 'p' and 'a' refer to addresses, *p, *a, a[0] refer to the first element of array 'a'.

C34   What is the output of the following code segment?

```
int a[]={2, 3, 5, 7, 11, 13, 17};
int* pi = a+3;

printf("*pi: %d, a[3]: %d, *(a+3): %d\n", *pi,
a[3], *(a+3));
```

Output:
```
*pi:7, a[3]:7, *(a+3):7
```

184

'pi' is a pointer to an integer, 'a' is an array of integers, and 'a' is also treated as an address to the first element of the array. Thus, assignment of 'pi' to 'a+3' is valid, and 'pi' will be pointing to the fourth element of 'a' (note the 0-indexing of array). Thus, in order to access the fourth element, *pi, a[3] and *(a+3) are equivalent.

IOIOIOIOIOIOIOIOIOIOIOIOIOIOIOIOIOIOIOIOIOIOIOIOIOIOIOIOI

D. Arrays

True/False Questions

D1   When an array of primitive type is declared, the elements have undefined values. *True*

D2   An array cannot be passed as argument to a function. *False*

D3   An array cannot be returned from a function. *True*
[Pointer to a dynamic or static arrays can be returned from a function]

D4   The number of elements of an array must be specified at array declaration. *True*

D5   The elements of an array are allocated consecutively in memory. *True*

D6   When an array is passed as argument to a function, the function receives a copy of the array. *False*
[Arrays can be passed as argument to a function. The pass-by-reference is used for array arguments]

D7   Pointers cannot be used with multidimensional arrays. *False*

D8   The parameter passing mechanisms of arrays and array elements are the same. *False*
[The parameter passing mechanism used for arrays is pass-by-reference, and that for array elements is pass-by-value]

D9   When a 2-dimensional array is passed as argument to a function, the row and column sizes must be specified. *False*
[Ex. if 'A' is the array with 'N' rows and 'M' columns, the argument should be A[][M] – the number of columns of the array must be specified along with the array name. The number of rows need not be specified]

D10   Arrays cannot be returned from functions. *True*

[An array cannot be returned from a function. A pointer to an array can be returned from a function]

D11 Array elements can be strings. **_True_**

D12 Array sizes are fixed at compile time. **_True_**

D13 The name of an array variable is equivalent to a pointer to the first element of the array. **_True_**
[Given int a[10], 'a' is synonymous with &a[0] which is the address of a[0]. The assignment *a = 5 is equivalent to a[0] = 5]

D14 Pointer arithmetic cannot be done on array names. **_False_**
[Since array name holds the address of the first element of the array, it is equivalent to a pointer to the first element of the array. Therefore, address arithmetic can be done on array names]

D15 An array subscript can be a valid expression (evaluating to an integer value). **_True_**

D16 The length of a static array known at compile time is also known to the C runtime system. **_False_**

D17 Strings stored as character arrays must be terminated by a '0'. **_False_**
[The termination character is the 'null' character, with ASCII value 0, is denoted by '\0']

D18 The elements of an array of primitive type can be heterogeneous. **_False_**
[All elements of an array of primitive type must be of the same type]

D19 When an array is created using the 'calloc' statement, the element values are automatically initialized to 0. **_True_**

D20 The size of an array can be changed after it is created. **_False_**

D21 The datatype of an array must be specified at the time of declaration. **_True_**

D22 An array of a generic type can be declared. **_False_**
[At the time of declaration of an array, the datatype must be specified]

D23 The datatype of an array could be changed during run time. **_False_**

D24   There are no operators to perform array operations. **_True_**
[Array operations (ex. addition, multiplication, etc. are performed using user-defined functions]

D25   The declaration **int arr [3] = {12, 3, 5, 2}** results in error. **_True_**
[The initializing list has more elements than the array size]

D26   The declaration **int arr[] = {2, 3, 9, 1, 7}** is valid. **_True_**

D27   Given **int a[5] = {12, 3, 5, 2, 7}**, the values of **&a[2]** and **a+2** are the same. **_True_**
[**&a[2]** gives the address of **a[2]**. **a** represents the address of the start of array **a. a** is equivalent to **[&a[0]**. Thus **a** and **a+2** are the same]

D28   Given **int b, a[] = {12, 3, 5, 2, 7}**, **b = a** is a valid assignment. **_False_**

D29   Given **int b[5], a[] = {12, 3, 5, 2, 7}**, **b = a** is a valid assignment. **_False_**

D30   Given **int *b, a[] = {12, 3, 5, 2, 7}**, **b = a** is a valid assignment. **_True_**

IOIOIOIOIOIOIOIOIOIOIOIOIOIOIOIOIOIOIOIOIOIOIOIOIOIOIOIOIOI

Fill-in the-blanks Questions

D1   An array whose size is determined at compile time is known as **_static array_**.

D2   When an array needs to be returned from a function, **_the pointer to the array_** is returned.

D3   When an array is passed to a function, the function receives **_the pointer to the array_**.

D4   When an array is passed as argument to a function, what is actually passed is the *__starting address of the array__*.

D5   The parameter passing mechanism used, when arrays are passed as arguments to functions, is *__pass-by-reference__*.

D6   The parameter passing mechanism used, when array elements are passed as arguments to functions, is *__pass-by-value__*.

D7   The parameter passing mechanism used, when primitive types are passed as arguments to functions, is *__pass-by- value__*.

D8   The parameter passing mechanism used, when structs are passed as arguments to functions, is *__pass-by- value__*.

D9   The parameter passing mechanism used, when unions are passed as arguments to functions, is *__pass-by- value__*.

D10 The parameter passing mechanism used, when arrays are passed as arguments to functions, is *__pass-by- reference__*.

D11 A locally declared array within a function is allocated in the *__stack__* area of memory.

D12 An array created using the 'calloc' operator is allocated in the *__heap__* area of memory.

D13 Given `int a[] = {2, 9, 5, 4, 7}`, a[2] is _5_.

D14 Given `int a[] = {12, 9, 5, 14, 25}`, element with value 14 is accessed using __a[3]__.

D15 Given `int a[5] = {12, 3, 5, 2, 7}`, the value of `*&a[2]` is _5_.
     [`&a[2]` gives the address of `a[2]`, and the '*' dereferences it giving the value contained at that address, which is a[2] = 5]

D16 Given `int *ap, a[5] = {12, 3, 5, 2, 7}`, and `ap = a;` the value of `*ap` is _12_.

D17 Given `int *ap, a[5] = {12, 3, 5, 2, 7}`, and `ap = a;` the value of `*ap++` is _12_.

D18 Given **int *ap, a[5] = {12, 3, 5, 2, 7}**, and **ap = a;** the value of *++ap is **3**.

D19 Given **int *ap, a[5] = {12, 3, 5, 2, 7}**, in order to replace 2 by 8 in the array **a** using **ap[3] = 8**, the statement to initialize **ap** is **ap = a;**.

D20 Given **int *ap, a[5] = {12, 3, 5, 2, 7}**, in order to access 2 using *(**ap+2**), the statement to initialize **ap** is **ap = &a[1];** or **ap = a+1;**

D21 The expression to increment the element at index **i** of array **numlist** is **numlist[i]++**

D22 The number of bytes allocated for **str** in the declaration **char str[] = "Test"** is **5**.
[One byte for each character of "Test", and one for the terminating NULL character]

D23 Given **int x[][4] = {{1, 2}, {3, 4}, {5, 6}, {7, 8}}**, the value of ***x** is *__address of the start of the array x__* (ex. **0x7ffca5e5dcb0**).

D24 Given **int x[][4] = {{1, 2}, {3, 4}, {5, 6}, {7, 8}}**, the value of (***x == &x[0][0]**) is **true**.

D25 Given **int x[][4] = {{1, 2}, {3, 4}, {5, 6}, {7, 8}}**, the value of ***x[2]** is **5**.

D26 Given the declaration **int* i2**, the value of **i2** is **null**.

D27 Given the following code segment, the number of elements of array pointed to by x is **6**.

```
int** x = calloc(3, sizeof(int *));
x[0] = calloc(1, sizeof(int));
x[1] = calloc(2, sizeof(int));
x[2] = calloc(3, sizeof(int));
```

[x points to a ragged array, with 1 element in the first row, 2 elements in the second row, and 3 elements in the third row]

D28 Given the declaration `int* i3 = calloc(3, sizeof(int))`, the value of `i3` is *__address of start of an array of 3 integers__*.

D29 Given the declaration `int* i3 = calloc(3, sizeof(int))`, the values of the elements of the array of 3 integers referenced by `i3` are __0s__.

IOIOIOIOIOIOIOIOIOIOIOIOIOIOIOIOIOIOIOIOIOIOIOIOIOIOIOIOIOI

Essay-type Questions

D1 Given the following code segment, give the statement to assign to **x**, the array element with value 28 using **ap**.

```
int x, a[] = {2, 17, 25, 4, 16, 28, 6, 12};
int* ap = a;
```

Answer: `x = ap[5]; OR x = *(ap+5);`

D2 What is the output of the following code segment?

```
int i=3, a[5] = {2, 17, 25, 4, 16};
printf("%d %d\n", *(a-(i-5)), a[i-2]);
```

Output: **25 17**

D3 What is the output of the following code segment?

```
int a[5] = {2, 17, 25, 4, 16};
printf("%d %d\n", *(a-40), a[70]);
```

C does not check for array indices out of bounds. It prints some values which are not valid array element values.

D4 What is the output of the following code segment?

```
char *ps, str[15] = "Test String";
printf ("%s\n", str);
ps = &str[5];
```

191

```
printf ("%s\n", ps);
```

Output:
```
Test String
String
```

D5   What is the output of the following code segment?

```
char str[] = "PERUSING";
char *ps = str;
printf("%s\n", str);
printf("%s\n", ps+3);
printf("%s\n", str + 4);
```

Output:
```
PERUSING
USING
SING
```

D6   What is the output of the following code segment for inputs (a) contra, (b) contract, and (c) contraction? Explain the outcomes.

```
char a[5], b[5];
scanf("%s", a);
printf("a: %s\n", a);
printf("b: %s\n", b);
```

```
contra
a: contra
b: a
```

```
contract
a: contract
b: act
```

```
contraction
a: contraction
b: action
stack smashing detected
```

D7   What is the output of the following code segment?

```
int x[] = {1, 2, 3, 4, 5};
int *y = x;
for (int i = 0; i < 5; i++)
```

```
printf("%d ", y[i]);
```

The program outputs **1 2 3 4 5**. Note that when 'y' is an integer pointer, and is initialized to 'x', which can be treated as the address of the first element of the array. Thus, 'y' is now pointing to the array.

D8   What is the output of the following code segment?

```
int arr[2][3] = {{10, 15, 20}, {25, 30, 35}};
printf ("arr[0][0]: %d\n", **arr);
printf ("arr[0][2]: %d\n", *(*arr+2));
printf ("arr[1][0]: %d\n", *(*arr+3));
```

```
arr[0][0]: 10
arr[0][2]: 20
arr[1][0]: 25
```

The 2D array name **arr** can be considered as a pointer to pointer to **int**. Based on this, ***(*arr+2)** refers to the array element which is third from the beginning, which is **arr[0][2]**, with value 20. Similarly, ***(*arr+3)** refers to the fourth element from the beginning, which is **arr[1][0]**, with value 25. This illustrates that a 2-dimensional array is stored in row-major order.

D9   What does the following do? What will be the array contents when the input is {2, 9, 6, 4, 5, 1, 11, 3}?

```
void arr_fn1 (int arr[], int size){
  for (int i=1; i<size; i++)
    arr[i] += arr[i-1];
}
```

The function computes the prefix sum of a given integer array. Array. For the input {2, 9, 6, 4, 5, 1, 11, 3}, the array contents after the function call would be: {2 11 17 21 26 27 38 41}.

D10 What is the output of the following program? What will be the output for the input arr: {22, 19, 16, 24, 25, 17, 14, 12, 9, 15, 19}

```
#include <stdio.h>
#include <stdlib.h>
#define SAME 0
#define INCR 1
#define DECR 2
```

```
int tonicity (int arr[], int size){
    int mode=SAME, nchange=-1, prev = arr[0];
    for (int i=1; i<size; i++){
        if ((arr[i] < prev && mode != DECR) ||
(arr[i] > prev && mode != INCR)) {
            nchange++ ;
            mode = (arr[i] < prev) ? DECR : INCR;
        }
        prev = arr[i];
    }
    return nchange+1;
}
int main ()
{
    int arr[] = {2, 5, 6, 4, 12, 15, 17, 12, 25,
26, 23};
    int t = tonicity(arr, 11);

    printf ("Tonicity: %d\n", t);
}
```

Output: **Tonicity: 6**

For arr: {22, 19, 16, 24, 25, 17, 14, 12, 9, 15, 19}
Output: **Tonicity: 4**

The function determines the number of changes in the 'monotonicity' of the numbers in the given array. For example, if all the numbers are increasing or decreasing, the value returned is 1 (monotonic); if the values increase (decrease) and decrease (increase), the value returned is 2 (bitonic); etc.

D11   What is the effect of the following function? What will be the output for the call **print_permutations ("ant", 0)**?

```
#include <string.h>
#define STR_SIZE 80
void print_permutations (char* str, int k){
    char str1[STR_SIZE];

    strcpy (str1, str);
    if (k == strlen (str)-1)
        puts(str1);
    else {
        for (int i=k; i<strlen (str); i++) {
```

```
        char ch = str1[i];
        str1[i] = str1[k];
        str1[k] = ch;
        print_permutations (str1, k+1);
      }
    }
}
```

This function prints all the permutations of a given string. For the input string of "ant", it prints (each word in a separate line): **ant atn nat nta tan tna**

IOIOIOIOIOIOIOIOIOIOIOIOIOIOIOIOIOIOIOIOIOIOIOIOIOIOIOIOIOIOI

E. Structures, Unions, Enumerated Types

True/False Questions

E1   Members of a 'struct' can be of different datatypes. _**True**_

E2   Members of a 'struct' share storage. _**False**_
[Storage is allocated for every member of a 'struct' separately]

E3   Storage for the members of a 'struct' may not be allocated contiguously. _**False**_
[The members of a struct are allocated contiguously]

E4   A 'struct' cannot have another 'struct' as a member. _**False**_
[A struct can be a member of another struct, except itself]

E5   A 'struct' can have itself as a member. _**False**_

E6   A 'struct' can have a pointer to itself as a member. _**True**_

E7   A 'struct' cannot have a 'union' as a member. _**False**_
[A 'union' can be a member of a 'struct']

E8   A 'struct' can have an 'enum' as a member. _**True**_

E9   A 'struct' cannot have an array as a member. _**False**_

E10   Structs can have function definitons. _**False**_
[Function definitions are not allowed in structs. A function pointer can be a member of a struct]

E11   The names of members (fields) of a struct must be distinct. _**True**_

E12   Members of a 'struct' cannot be qualified with `const`. _**False**_

E13   Defining a 'struct' and declaring a variable of its type cannot be done at the same time. _**False**_

E14 Two different 'struct' definitions, even with identical member names and types are considered different. ***True***

E15 Members of a 'struct' cannot be initialized with values at the time of struct definition. ***True***

E16 Members of a 'struct' variable cannot be initialized with values at the time of declaration. ***False***

E17 Two 'structs' cannot be compared for equality by a single operator. ***True***

E18 Two variables of the same struct type can be directly assigned to one another. ***True***

E19 It is not possible to have pointers to individual members (fields) of a 'struct'. ***False***

E20 The declaration of a 'struct' within a block is not visible outside of the block. ***True***

E21 The definition of a 'struct' will not allocate any memory. ***True***

E22 The **sizeof** operator cannot be used with structures. ***False***

E23 The **sizeof** operator can be used with 'struct' members. ***True***

E24 The members of a 'union' share storage. ***True***

E25 The members of a 'union' can be of different datatypes. ***True***

E26 A 'union' cannot contain itself as a member. ***True***

E27 A union may contain a pointer to an instance of itself. ***True***

E28 A union may not contain a 'struct' as a member. ***False***

E29 A union holds atmost one component (member) at a time. ***True***

E30 Two components (members) of a union may have the same name. ***False***

E31 The **sizeof** operator cannot be used with unions. ***False***

E32 The datatype of enumeration constants could be any one of the integer types. *True*

E33 The members of a 'enum' type cannot be explicitly assigned values. *False*

E34 The members of a 'enum' type must have unique values. *False*
[It is valid for more than one member to have the same value]

E35 The values assigned to members of a 'enum' type are integers. *True*

E36 The value assigned to a member of a 'enum' type cannot be a negative integer. *False*

E37 The members (enumeration constants) of a 'enum' type, can be explicitly assigned only increasing values. *False*
[`enum box {b1=1, b2=5, b3= -2, b4=3}` is a valid declaration]

E38 The values of the members (enumeration constants) of a 'enum' type must be distinct. *False*
[`enum display {lcd=1, led=2, oled=2, plasma}` is a valid declaration]

E39 An enumeration constant cannot be used in place of an integer expression. *False*

IOIOIOIOIOIOIOIOIOIOIOIOIOIOIOIOIOIOIOIOIOIOIOIOIOIOIOIOIOI

Fill-in the-blanks Questions

E1 The name used between the keyword **struct** and the opening brace ({) is known as the *tag*.

E2 The storage allocated for a variable of a 'struct' containing members requiring 20 bytes, 4 bytes, 2 bytes, 8 bytes is **34 bytes**.

E3 Given that **DATE** is a 'struct' with member 'year' of type 'int', and d1 is a variable of type **DATE**, then the statement to set the 'year' of d1 to 1976 is **d1.year = 1976;**

E4   Given that **DATE** is a 'struct' with member 'month' of type 'int', then for **d1->month = 9;** to be syntactically correct, the declarartion of **d1** should be <u>**DATE *d1;**</u>

E5   Given that **DATE** is a 'struct' with member 'month' of type 'int', and the declaration **DATE d2,*dp**, then, to set the 'month' value of **d2** to 4 using **dp->month = 4**, **dp** should be initialized using the statement <u>**dp = &d2;**</u>

E6   Given that **DATE** is a 'struct' with member 'date' of type 'int', and **dp** is a pointer to a variable **d3** of type **DATE**, then the statement to set the 'date' of **d3** to 27 is <u>**d3->date = 27;**</u>

E7   Given that **DATE** is a 'struct' with member 'date' of type 'int', and **dp** is a pointer to a variable **d4** of type **DATE**, then the statement to set the 'date' of **d4** to 19 without using the **->** operator is <u>**(*d4).date = 19;**</u>

E8   The storage allocated for a variable of a 'union' containing members requiring 20 bytes, 4 bytes, 2 bytes, 8 bytes is <u>**20 *bytes***</u>.

E9   Given **enum device {phone, smart_phone, tablet, laptop, pc};** the value of **phone** is <u>0</u>.

E10   Given **enum device {phone, smart_phone, tablet, laptop, pc};** the value of **laptop** is <u>3</u>.

E11   Given **enum device {phone, smart_phone=5, tablet, laptop, pc=10};** the value of **laptop** is <u>7</u>.

E12   Given **enum device {phone=1, smart_phone, tablet, laptop=2, pc};** the value of **pc** is <u>3</u>.

IOIOIOIOIOIOIOIOIOIOIOIOIOIOIOIOIOIOIOIOIOIOIOIOIOIOIOIOIOIOIOIOI

Essay-type Questions

E1   Given the following 'struct' and the variable **book_list**
```
typedef struct book_str {
  char title[80];
```

```
        char authors[80];
        char publisher[30];
        int year, ISBN;
        float price;
} Book;

Book book_list[12];
```

How much storage is allocated to **book_list** assuming 1 byte for character, 4 bytes each for integer and floating point number?

A variable of type 'Book' requires 80+80+30+2*4+4 = 202 bytes. Thus **book_list** requires 202 * 12 = 2424 bytes.

E2   What is the statement to assign 11.95 to the 'price' of the 6th book in **book_list** ? (Note that the arrays are 0-indexed)

```
book_list[5].price = 11.95;
```

E3   What is the statement to assign **"Horizon"** to the 'publisher' field of the 3rd book in **book_list** ?

```
strcpy(book_list[2].publisher, "Horizon");
```

E4   What is the statement to print the book title and the price in the same line for the 10th book in **book_list** ?

```
printf("%s %.2f\n", book_list[9].title,
book_list[9].price);
```

E5   Given **BOOK b1, b2, *pb1;** what are two possible statements to assign to the 'price' member of 'b2', the value of 'price' of 'b1' using 'pb1' ?

```
b2.price = pb1->price;
b2.price = (*pb1).price;
```

E6   What is the output of the following code segment?

```
typedef struct time{
    int hr, min;
} TIME;
TIME t1, t2 = {10, 20};
printf ("%2d:%2d\n", t1.hr, t1.min);
```

```
printf ("%2d:%2d\n", t2.hr, t2.min);
```

-2110348416:32765 ('Garbage' values due to uninitialized members of **t1**)
10:20 (Values of initialized members of **t2**)

E7   Given the following declarations,
```
typedef struct date_str {
  int hour, min, sec;
} DATE;
DATE d1, *dp1;
d1.hour = 5; d1.min = 36; d1.sec = 24;
dp1 = &d1;
```

What is the error in the following statement? What is the fix?
```
DATE d2;
d2.hour = *dp1.hour;
```

The '.' (direct selection) operator has higher precedence than the '*' (indirection) operator. Since **dp1** is a pointer to 'struct' DATE, **dp1.hour** is not correct for a pointer. The 'hour' member of **d1** can be accessed via **dp1** using **dp1 -> hour** or **(*dp1).hour**.

E8   What is the output of the following program?
```
typedef struct test_str {
    char c;
    int a;
    float x;
} Test;

void print_test_str(Test t){
    printf ("%c %d %.2f\n", t.c, t.a, t.x);
}
int main()
{
  Test t1, t2, t3;
  char *cp; int* ip; float* fp;
  t1.c = 'x'; t1.a = 5; fp = &(t1.x);
  *fp = 12.34;
  t2.c = 'Q'; t2.x = 6.29; ip = &(t2.a);
  *ip = 24;
  t3.a = 17; t3.x = 3.14; cp = &(t3.c);
  *cp = 'M';
  print_test_str(t1);
  print_test_str(t2);
  print_test_str(t3);
```

```
    return 0;
}
```

Output:
```
x 5 12.34
Q 24 6.29
M 17 3.14
```

Use the following 'struct' definition for E9 – E11.

```
typedef struct date_str {
  int day, month, year;
} DATE;
```

E9   Write a function **get_date1** which takes no argument, and
      returns a variable of struct DATE, with fields initialized using
      values input via the keyboard by the user.

```
DATE get_date1 (){
  DATE d;

  printf ("Type the date [m d y]: ");
  scanf ("%d %d %d", &d.month, &d.day, &d.year);

  return (d);
}
```

E10   Write a function **get_date2** which takes as argument a pointer
      to a struct of type DATE, and initializes the fields using values input
      via the keyboard by the user.

```
void get_date2 (DATE *dp){
  printf ("Type the date [m d y]: ");
  scanf ("%d %d %d", &dp->month, &dp->day, &dp-
>year);
}
```

E11   Write a function **print_date** which takes as argument a struct of
      type DATE, and prints in the format: <month name> day, year. For
      example, if a variable of type DATE with values 8/22/1989 were
      given as argument, it should print out "August 22, 1989".

```
void print_date (DATE d){
  char *mnames[] = {"", "January", "February",
"March", "April", "May", "June", "July", "August",
"September", "October", "November", "December"};
```

```
    printf ("%s %d, %d\n", mnames[d.month], d.day,
    d.year);
    }
```

E12 What is the output of the following code segment?

```
typedef union mult_type
{
  char c1;
  int i1;
  float f1;
  double d1;
} MULTTYPE;

MULTTYPE mt1;

printf("c1: %lu, i1: %lu, f1: %lu, d1: %lu\n",
sizeof(char), sizeof(int), sizeof(float), sizeof
(double));

printf("Space for mt1 is: %lu\n", sizeof(mt1));
```

Output :
```
c1: 1, i1: 4, f1: 4, d1: 8
Space for mt1 is: 8
```

The following definitions are used for problems E13 – E17.
```
typedef struct {
  float monthly_sal;
} SAL_TYPE1;

typedef struct {
  float commission, weekly_sal;
} SAL_TYPE2;

typedef struct {
  float hr_rate, num_hrs;
} SAL_TYPE3;

typedef struct date {
  int month, day, year;
} DATE;

typedef struct {
  char name[30], dept[20];
  int id;
  DATE join_date;
  short sal_type;
  union {
```

```
        SAL_TYPE1 salary1;
        SAL_TYPE2 salary2;
        SAL_TYPE3 salary3;
      } salary;
    } EMP_REC;


    main ()
    {
      EMP_REC emprec;
      DATE date = {11, 3, 93};
    }
```

E13 Give the declaration for an array **emp_list** of **NUM_EMPS** records of type **EMP_REC**.

```
EMP_REC emp_list[NUM_EMPS];
```

E14 Give the statement to initialize the 'dept' field of element at index 5 of emp_list to "Marketing".

```
strcpy(emp_list[5].dept, "Marketing");
```

E15 Give the statements to initialize the 'commission' to 15 and 'weekly_sal' to 1,150 of element at index 7 of emp_list.

```
emp_list[7].salary.salary2.commission = 15.0;
emp_list[7]. salary.salary2.weekly_sal = 1150.0;
```

E16 Give the statements to initialize the 'join_date' field of the element at index 4 of emp_list to 4/23/1992.

```
emp_list[4].join_date.month = 4;
emp_list[4].join_date.day = 23;
emp_list[4].join_date.year = 1992;
```

E17 Give the declaration and initializer to declare a variable **er1** of type **EMP_REC** which is initialized at declaration to the field values: 'name': "Adam Adams"; 'dept': "Sales"; 'id': 341; 'join_date': 5/22/1978; 'sal_type': 2; (salary2): 'commision': 12.5; 'weekly_sal': 995.0.

```
EMP_REC er1 = {"Adam Adams", "Sales", 341, {5, 22,
1978}, 2, {.salary2={12.5, 995.0}}};
```

Consider the following declaration for E18 – E24.

```
typedef union {
  char a[15];
  int n;
  float x;
} U;
```

E18 What is the output of the following code segment?
```
U u1;
strcpy(u1.a,"Programming");
u1.n = 25;
u1.x = 22.50;
printf("Union u1: %s %d %f\n",u1.a,u1.n,u1.x);
```

Output:
```
Union u1:   1102315520  22.500000
```
Note that 'u1' is a variable of union type – storage for the largest member is allocated, which in this case is 15 bytes for the character array 'a', and is shared by the union members. The the bitstring in a union variable corresponds to type and format of the data of the most recent assignment. In this case, the most recent assignment to 'u1' is 22.5 for the floating point member. When all members are printed out, the bitstring corresponding to the floating point number 22.5 is interpreted. Thus other than u1.x, the other values will not make sense.

E19 What is the output of the following code segment?
```
U u1;
strcpy(u1.a,"Programming");
u1.x = 22.50;
u1.n = 25;
printf("Union u1: %s %d %f\n",u1.a,u1.n,u1.x);
```

Output:
```
Union u1:   25 0.000000
```
Since the last assignment was for the integer field 'n', only that value is properly displayed.

E20 What is the output of the following code segment?
```
U u1 = {101};
printf("Union u1: %s %d %f\n",u1.a,u1.n,u1.x);
```

Output:
```
Union u1: e 101 0.000000
```
Since the initialization at declaration was an integer, only the member 'n' will be properly displayed.

E21　What is the output of the following code segment?
```
U u1 = {"Test string"};
printf("Union u1: %s %d %f\n",u1.a,u1.n,u1.x);
```

Output:
```
Union u1: Test string 1953719636
7713521210690815006409223254835 2.000000
```
Since the initialization at declaration was a string, only the member 'a' will be properly displayed.

E22　What is the output of the following code segment?
```
U u1 = {"Test string", 101, 12.3};
printf("Union u1: %s %d %f\n",u1.a,u1.n,u1.x);
```

Output: The compiler will warn about "excess elements in union initializer".

E23　What is the output of the following code segment?
```
U u1 = {.a = "Test string", .n=101, .x=12.3};
printf("Union u1: %s %d %f\n",u1.a,u1.n,u1.x);
```

Output: The compiler will warn about "excess elements in union initializer", and may print out something which may not be correct.

E24　What is the output of the following code segment?
```
U u1 = {.n=101, .x=12.3, .a = "Test string"};
printf("Union u1: %s %d %f\n",u1.a,u1.n,u1.x);
```

Output:
```
Union u1: Test string 1953719636
7713521210690815006409223254835 2.000000
```

Since the string was the last to be initialized, only the member 'a' displays correctly.

IOIOIOIOIOIOIOIOIOIOIOIOIOIOIOIOIOIOIOIOIOIOIOIOIOIOIOIOIOIOIOI

F. Functions

True/False Questions

F1   A C program can have more than one **main()** function. *False*

F2   **main()** is never invoked by any other function. *True*

F3   **main()** can call itself. *True*

F4   There can be more than one function with the same name in a program. *False*

F5   A local variable and a formal parameter in a function cannot have the same name. *True*

F6   A local variable in a function cannot have the same name as a global variable. *False*
[A local variable in a function can have the same name as a global variable, in which case it is said to shadow the global variable, i.e., the global variable will not be visible in the function]

F7   In a function declaration, the formal parameters need not have names. *True*
[int fun1 (int, double, double); is a valid function declaration, where the types of parameters are mandatory. The function definition must have the names and types of formal parameters]

F8   The number of arguments passed to a function call must exactly match the number of parameters in the function definition. *False*
[Some arguments could be omitted if there are default parameters]

F9   Any mismatch of the type of argument and the corresponding type of formal parameter will always result in error. *False*
[The argument expressions are converted to the types of formal parameters. If the conversion is possible and allowed, there is no error]

F10   A function definition must have at least one parameter. *False*

F11   In a function call, if a default value is used for an argument, the subsequent arguments must have default values. *True*

F12   A struct can be passed as argument to a function. ***True***

F13   A struct cannot be returned from a function. ***False***

F14   When the formal parameter is passed by value, the actual parameter (argument) must be a constant value. ***False***
[When the formal parameter is passed by value, the argument can be any valid expression evaluating to a value of the parameter datatype]

F15   When the formal parameter is passed by reference, the actual parameter (argument) can be an expression. ***False***
[When the formal parameter is passed by reference, the argument must be a value, in memory, of the parameter datatype]

F16   Pointer to a 'union' cannot be returned from a function. ***False***

F17   Pointer to a 'struct' can be returned from a function. ***True***

F18   C supports both pass-by-value and pass-by-reference for primitive types. ***True***

F19   C supports only pass-by-reference for structs. ***False***
[C supports both pass-by-value and pass-by-reference for structs]

F20   The first statement to be executed always is the first executable statement in `main()`. ***True***

F21   Call-by-value is more efficient than Call-by-reference. ***False***
[In call-by-value, the values of the arguments are copied into the variables of the function parameters, whereas in call-by-reference, the addresses of the arguments are passed and there is no explicit copying of values]

F22   An inline function is expanded at runtime. ***False***
[An inline function is expanded at compile time so that the statements are ready for execution at runtime]

F23   An inline function can have loops. ***False***

F24   An inline function cannot have static variables. ***True***

F25   A recursive function cannot be an inline function. ***True***

F26   Default parameters can be listed anywhere in the parameter list of a function declaration/definition. ***False***

[The default parameters must be listed after all the non-default parameters]

F27 A constant parameter with the 'const' keyword cannot be a parameter of a function. *False*

F28 In C the parameter passing for arrays is call-by-value. *False*
[Arrays are always passed-by-reference, since the copying arrays is inefficient]

F29 In pass-by-value, it is possible for the called subprogram to change the values of the actual parameters of the calling subprogram. *False*
[In pass-by-value, only copies of values of actual parameters (arguments) are used within the called subprogram, and the actual values are unchanged]

F30 Individual 'structs' are passed by reference if they contain arrays. *False*
[Individual structs are always passed by value, even if they contain arrays]

F31 A function cannot contain more than one **return** statement. *False*
[A function may contain more than one return statement, but only one will ever be executed by any given function call]

F32 A function can return multiple results back to the calling subprogram. *False*
[The syntax of functions do not allow multiple return values in most languages. However, multiple values can be returned somewhat indirectly by passing references to return values to the subprogram]

F33 In C, a function definition can have further nested function definitions. *False*

F34 In C, the local variables of functions are always stack dynamic variables. *False*
[Local variables declared with the keyword **static** are not stack dynamic]

F35 In C, the local variables of functions are always stack dynamic variables, *by default*. *True*

F36 In C, the lifetimes of local variables declared with **static** keyword extend beyond the time the function is active. *True*

F37 In a recursive call of a subprogram, there are multiple instances of its activation record. *True*

F38 C supports both functions and procedures. ___False___
[All subprograms are functions. A procedure without a return value is defined as a function returning a 'void' type]

F39 In C, a function defined in a file cannot be called in another function in a different file. ___False___

F40 A function must be defined before it can be called. ___False___
[A function must be 'declared' before it can be called. However, the function 'definition' may or may not appear before it is called]

F41 In C, function names can be passed as arguments. ___False___
[C allows only pointers to functions to be passed as parameters. Note that a function call can be used as argument, and it is different from just using the function name]

F42 In C, pointers to functions can be passed as arguments. ___True___

F43 The argument in a function call must have the same name as the corresponding formal parameter in the function definition. ___False___

F44 A function's declaration and definition must be in the same file. ___False___

F45 The order of evaluation of a function's arguments is from left to right. ___False___
[C does not guarantee any particular order of evaluation of a function's arguments]

F46 An expression cannot be used as an argument to a function. ___False___
[An expression returning the proper datatype can be used as a function argument]

F47 A function call cannot be used as an argument to a function. ___False___
[A function call returning the proper datatype expected in place of the argument can be an argument to a function]

F48 All the arguments of a function are evaluated before control transfers to the called function. ___True___

F49 For a one dimensional array used as an argument in a function call, specifying the dimension is optional. ___True___

F50 For a multi-dimensional array used as an argument in a function call, specifying all dimensions is optional. ___False___

[For a multi-dimensional array argument in a function call, all dimensions except the first must be provided]

IOIOIOIOIOIOIOIOIOIOIOIOIOIOIOIOIOIOIOIOIOIOIOIOIOIOIOIOIOIOI

Fill-in the-blanks Questions

F1   The number of parameters and their data types of a function are together known as the ***signature***.

F2   The function that is invoked first when a program starts is **main()**.

F3   The function that is the last to finish in a program (under normal circumstance) is **main()**.

F4   The function that is not callable by any other function is **main()**.

F5   The default return type of a function is **int**.

F6   The default parameter passing mechanism for primitive types is ***call-by-value***.

F7   The default parameter passing mechanism for arrays is ***call-by-reference***.

F8   A 'struct' passed as argument to a function uses pass by ***value***.

F9   C does not allow ***arrays*** and ***functions*** as return types in functions.

F10 A function whose statements are executed, but without causing a 'jump/return' (save/restore of activation record) is known as ***inline*** function.

F11 A function, say A, calling itself, is known as ***direct recursion***.

F12 A function A, calling function B, which in turn calls A, is known as ***indirect recursion***.

F13 All C programs must have a function named **main** where the execution starts.

F14   The 'special' function that cannot be called from any other function is the **main ()**.

F15   The deault parameter passing for 'structs' is ***pass by value***.

IOIOIOIOIOIOIOIOIOIOIOIOIOIOIOIOIOIOIOIOIOIOIOIOIOIOIOIOI

Essay-type Questions

F1   What does the following function compute for $n \geq 0$?

```c
int fun1 (int m, int n)
{
  if (n == 0)
    return m;
  else
    return (1 + fun1 (m, n-1));
}
```

This function computes the sum of *n* and *m*.

F2   What does the following function compute for $n \geq 0$?

```c
int fun1 (int n, int m)
{
   if (m == 0 || n == 0)
      return 0;
   if (n == 1)
      return m;
   else
      return (m + fun1 (n-1, m));
}
```

This function computes the product of *n* and *m*.

F3   What does the following function compute for $n > 0$?

```c
int fun1 (int n)
{
  if (n == 1)
```

```
      return 1;
      return n + fun1(n-1);
}
```

This function computes the sum of the first *n* positive numbers.

F4   What does the following function compute for $n \geq 0$?

```
int fun1 (int n)
{
  if (n < 10)
    return 1;
  return (1 + fun1 (n/10));
}
```

It computes the number of the digits of *n*

F5   What does the following function compute for $n \geq 0$?

```
int fun1 (int num)
{
  if (num < 10)
    return (num);
  return (num % 10 + fun1 (num / 10));
}
```

This computes the sum of the digits of *num*.

F6   What does the following function compute (given that MAX returns the larger of its two arguments)?

```
int fun1 (int num)
{
  if (num < 10)
    return (num);
  return MAX(num % 10, fun1 (num / 10));
}
```

This computes the maximum–valued digit in *num*.

F7   What does the following function compute?

```
int fun1(int num){
    static int sum=0,rem;
    if(num > 0){
        rem = num%10;
```

```
        sum = sum*10+rem;
        reverse_dgts(num/10);
    }
    return sum;
}
```

This function computes the number whose value is the one with digits of 'num' in reverse order.

F8   What does the following function compute?

```
int fun1 (int n)
{
    if ((n == 0) || (n == 1))
        return 1;
    return (1 + fun1 (n / 2));
}
```

This function computes the number of bits in the binary representation of *n*.

F9   What does the following function compute?

```
int fun1 (int n)
{
    if (n == 0)
        return 0;
    else if (n % 2 == 0) // n is Even
        return fun1(n/2);
    else
        return 1 + fun1(n/2); // integer division
}
```

This computes the number of 1's in the Binary representation of *n*.

F10   What does the following function compute, for $n \geq 0$?

```
int fun1 (int n)
{
    if (n == 0 || n == 1)
        return 1;
    return (n * fun1 (n-1));
}
```

This function computes the factorial of *n*.

F11   What does the following function compute?

```
int fun1 (int n)
{
  if (n == 1) || (n == 2)
     return 1;
  return (fun1(n-1) + fun2(n-2));
}
```

It computes the nth Fibonacci number.

F12   What does the following function compute?

```
int fun1 (int n){
  if (n == 0)
     return 1;
  else
     return fun1(n-1) + fun1(n-1);
}
```

This function computes 2^n.

F13   What does the following function compute?

```
int fun1 (int n)
{
  if (n == 0)
     return 1;
  else
     return 2 * fun1(n-1);
}
```

This function computes 2^n.

F14   What does the following function compute?

```
int fun1 (int n, int m)
{
   if (n == 0)
      return 0;
   if (m == 0)
      return 1;
   if (n == 1)
      return 1;
   else
```

```
        return (n * fun1 (n, m-1));
    }
```

This function computes n^m.

F15 What does the following function compute?

```
int fun1 (int n, int m) {
    if (m == 0 || m == n)
        return 1;
    return fun1(n-1, m-1) + fun1(n-1, m);
}
```

This function computes the Binomial coefficient $\binom{n}{m}$

F16 What does the following function compute (given that MAX returns the larger of its two arguments)?

```
int fun1 (int A[], int L, int R)
{
    if (L == R)
        return (A[L]);

    return MAX(A[L], fun1(A, L+1, R));
}
```

This function returns the maximum value in the array given as input. If A is an array of N elements, then the function call would be `fun1(A, 0, N-1)`.

F17 What does the following function compute?

```
int fun1 (int A[], int L, int R)
{
    if (L == R)
        return (A[L]);

    int M = (L + R) / 2;
    return MAX(fun1(A,L,M), fun1(A,M+1,R));
}
```

This function returns the maximum value in the array given as input. If A is an array of N elements, then the function call would be `fun1(A, 0, N-1)`.

F18   What does the following function compute?

```
int fun1 (int A[], int L, int R)
{
  if (L == R)
    return A[L];

  return A[R] + fun1(A,L,R-1);
}
```

This function returns the sum of the elements of the input array. If
A is an array of N elements, then the function call would be fun1(A,
0, N-1).

F19   What does the following function compute?

```
int fun1 (int A[], int L, int R)
{
  if (L == R)
    return A[L];

  int M = (L + R) / 2;
  return fun1(A,L,M) + fun1(A,M+1,R);
}
```

This function returns the sum of the elements of the input array. If
A is an array of N elements, then the function call would be fun1(A,
0, N-1).

F20   What is the output of the following function?

```
void fun1 (int N)
{
  if (N/2 == 0) {
    if (N == 0)
      putchar('0');
    else
      putchar('1');
    return;
  }
  fun1 (N / 2);
  putchar((N % 2)+ '0');
}
```

This function prints the binary equivalent of the input N.

F21 What is the output of the following function?

```
void fun1 (int N){
  if (N == 1){
    printf("1 ");
    return;
  }
  fun1(N-1);
  printf("%d ", N);
}
```

It prints 1 2 3 4 … N, for a given argument N.

F22 What is the output of the following program?
```
void fun1 (int A[], int L, int R){
  if (L == R){
    printf("%d ", A[L]);
    return;
  }
  fun1(A, L+1, R);
  printf("%d ", A[L]);
}
int main()
{
  int arr[]= {3, 4, 7, 2, 9, 1, 8, 5, 6};
  fun1 (arr, 0, 8);
}
```

6 5 8 1 9 2 7 4 3
The function 'fun1' is called recursively. When the array length is 1, it prints the array element. Otherwise, it recursively calls with the array argument which extends from the element next to the leftmost in the current call to the rightmost element, followed by printing the leftmost element in the current call. It thus prints the array in the reverse order.

F23 What does the following function compute?

```
#define FALSE 0
#define TRUE 1

unsigned fun1 (char str[], int L, int R])
{
  if (L >= R)
    return TRUE;
  if (str[L] != str[R])
```

```
        return (FALSE);
      return (fun1(str, L+1, R-1]);
}
```

The function is called with an array of characters, and the left and right bounds as arguments. For example, if **str** is declared as **char str[N]**, where *N* is an integer constant, the function call is **fun1 (str[],0,N-1)**. It returns 'true' if **str** is a palindrome, 'false', otherwise.

F24 What is the output of the following program?
```
void fun(int *p, int *q) {
  p = q;
  *p = 7;
}

int main() {
  int i = 3, j = 5;
  fun(&i, &j);
  printf("i=%d j=%d\n", i, j);
  return 0;
}
```

Output: **i=3 j=7**

F25 What is the output of the following program?
```
void fn1 (int a, int* b)
{
  int *x, y;

  x = &a;
  *x += *b;
  *b += *x;
  x = b;
  b = &y;
  *b = 5;
  *x += y;
}
main ()
{
  int n, m;

  n = 10; m = 20;
  fn1 (n, &m);
  printf ("n=%d m=%d\n", n, m);
  fn1 (n, &m);
  printf ("n=%d m=%d\n", n, m);
```

```
```

```
n=10 m=55
n=10 m=125
```

F26 What is the output of the following program segment?

```
int i, num, fac=1, inc=1;
for (i=1; i<=6; i++) {
  num = 4*fac;
  inc++;
  fac += inc;
  printf("%d\n", num);
}
```

Output:
```
4
12
24
40
60
84
```

F27 What is the output of the following program segment?

```
int a = 156, b = 273;
printf ("a=%d, b=%d\n", a, b);
a = a ^ b;
b = a ^ b;
a = a ^ b;
printf ("a=%d, b=%d\n", a, b);
```

Output:
```
a=156, b=273
a=273, b=156
```

F28 What is the output of the following program segment?

```
char s1[] = "a""z";
char s2[] = "\"\"";
char s3[] = "\\""\\";

printf ("s1: %s\n", s1);
printf ("s2: %s\n", s2);
printf ("s3: %s\n", s3);
```

```
s1: az
s2: ""
s3: \\
```

F29 What is the output of the following program segment?
```
char c1, c2;
float n1, n2;
c1 = 'a'; c2 = c1+16;
printf ("c1: %c   c2: %c\n", c1, c2);
c1 = 127; c2 = c1+5;
printf ("c1: %d   c2: %d\n", c1, c2);

n1 = 26.13283476;
n2 = 728.8382108348;
printf ("n1: %f n2: %f\n", n1, n2);
printf ("n1: %6.2f n2: %6.2f\n", n1, n2);
```

Output:
```
c1: a   c2: q
c1: 127   c2: -124
n1: 26.132835 n2: 728. 838196
n1:   26.13 n2: 728.84
```

F30 What is the output of the following program?

```
fn2 (int x, int* y, int z, int *w)
{
  x += *y + *w;
  *y += x + z;
  z = x + *y;
  *w = *y + z;
  printf ("%d %d %d %d\n", x, *y, z, *w);
}

main ()
{
  int a=3, b=5, c=4, d=6;
  printf ("%d %d %d %d\n", a, b, c, d);
  fn2 (a, &b, c, &d);
  printf ("%d %d %d %d\n", a, b, c, d);
}
```

Output:
```
3   5   4   6
```

```
14   23   37   60
3    23   4    60
```

F31   What is the output of the following program?

```
int fn1 (int a, int *b)
{
  int *x, y;

  x = &y;
  *b += 5;
  a += 3;
  *x = a;
  return (y);
}

void fn2 (int *x, int y)
{
  int a, *b;

  a = 5;
  b = &a;
  *b += 3;
  *x = fn1(y, b);
  printf ("%d\n", *x);
  y = fn1(a, x);
  printf ("%d\n", y);
}

int main ()
{
  int n, m;

  n = 10; m = 20;
  fn2 (&n, m);
  printf ("n=%d m=%d\n", n, m);
}
```

Output:
```
23
16
n=28 m=20
```

F32   What is the output of the following program?

```
int fn1 (int a, int b)
{
  int x;
```

```
    a += b;
    b += a;
    x = a + b;
    return (x);
}

void fn2 (int a, int *b)
{
    int *x, y;

    x = b;  y = a;
    *x += y;  y += *x;
    printf ("fn2: (*x)=%d y=%d\n", *x, y);
}

void fn3 (int *a, int b)
{
    int x, *y;

    x = *a;  y = &b;
    *a += *y; b += x;
    printf ("fn3: x=%d (*y)=%d\n", x, *y);
}

int main()
{
    int n = 5, m = 12, p;

    p = fn1 (n, m);
    printf ("n=%d m=%d p=%d\n", n, m, p);
    fn2 (n, &m);
    printf ("n=%d m=%d\n", n, m);
    fn3 (&n, m);
    printf ("n=%d m=%d\n", n, m);
}
```

Output:
```
n=5 m=12 p=46
fn2: (*x)=17 y=22
n=5 m=17
fn3: x=5 (*y)=22
n=22 m=17
```

F33   What is the output of the following program?
```
void fun(int x, int y){
    x += x;
    y += y;
```

```
    printf("Values in fun: %d %d\n", x, y);
}
int main(){
    int list[2] = {1, 3};
    fun(list[0], list[1]);
    printf("Values   in   main:   %d   %d\n",   list[0],
list[1]);
}
```

Output:
```
Values in fun: 2 6
Values in main: 1 3
```

F34   What is the output of the following code?

```
int fun1 (int x){
    int a;
    x = x * 2;
    a = x + 3;
    x = a - 5;
    printf("fun1: x = %d a = %d\n", x, a);
    return a;
}

int main (){
    int a = 5, b;
    b = fun1 (a);
    a = fun1 (b);
    printf("main: a = %d b = %d\n", a, b);
    return 0;
}
```

Output:
```
fun1: x = 8 a = 13
fun1: x = 24 a = 29
main: a = 29 b = 13
```

F35   What is the output of the following code?

```
int fun1 (int x, int y){
    int a;
    x = y * 2;
    y = x * 3;
    a = y - x;
    printf("fun1: x = %d y = %d a = %d\n", x,y,a);
    return a;
}
int main (){
```

```
    int a = 5, b = 4, c, d;
    c = fun1 (a, b);
    d = fun1 (b, a);
    printf("main: a = %d b = %d c = %d d = %d\n", a, b,
c, d);
    return 0;
}
```

Output:
```
fun1: x = 8 y = 24 a = 16
fun1: x = 10 y = 30 a = 20
main: a = 5 b = 4 c = 16 d = 20
```

F36   What is the output of the following program?

```
void fn1 ()
{
  int i=0;
  i++;
  printf ("fn1: i=%d, ", i);
}

void fn2 ()
{
  static int i=0;
  i++;
  printf ("fn2: i=%d\n", i);
}

int main()
{
  int i;

  for (i=1; i<=3; i++){
    printf ("[Call %d] ", i);
    fn1 ();
    fn2 ();
  }
}
```

Output:
```
[Call 1] fn1: i=1, fn2: i=1
[Call 2] fn1: i=1, fn2: i=2
[Call 3] fn1: i=1, fn2: i=3
```

F37   What is the output of the following code?
```
int fun1(int* x, int c)
```

```
{
    c--;
    if (c == 0) return 1;
    (*x)++;
    return fun1(x, c) * (*x);
}
int main()
{
    int a = 4;
    printf ("%d\n", fun1(&a, a));
    return 0;
}
```

343. In this program as one parametere is passed by value and other is passed by reference so after 4 calls when c == 0 is true, then the value of x = 7 and as x is passed by reference so all the changes will be reflected back in all the previous calls. Therefore, the answer 1*7*7*7 = 343.

F38 What is the output of the following code?

```
int fun1 (int a)
{
    return 2*a+3;
}
void fun2 (int a, int b)
{
    a += 2*b;
    printf ("fun2: a = %d\n", a);
}
int main()
{
    int x = 7, y = 5;
    fun2 (x, fun1(y));
    return 0;
}
```

Output: **fun2: a = 33**
Note that **fun1 (5)** returns 2*5+3 = 13, and in the call to **fun2 (7, fun1(5))**, **a += 2*b** evaluates to 7 + 2*(13) = 33.

F39 What is the output of the following code?
```
int* fun1()
{
    static int x = 10;
    x += 5;
    return &x;
}
int main()
```

```
{
    printf("%d\n", *fun1());
    printf("%d\n", *fun1());
    return 0;
}
```

Output:
```
15
20
```

The static local variable 'x' is initialized once to 10. After the first call to 'fun1', the value of x will be 15, whose address is retuned, and in the 'main', it is dereferenced and printed. The value of 'x' will be retained between successive calls to 'fun1'. After the second call to 'fun1', the value of x will be 20.

F40   What is the output of the following code?

```
void fun (){
    static int i = 2;
    while (i-- > 0){
        printf ("%d ", i);
        fun();
    }
}
int main(){
    fun();
    return 0;
}
```

Output: 1 0
Note that since the variable 'i' is static, it is initialized to 2 just once, and subsequent calls will access this storage location, and the decrement will be reflected in subsequent calls. Therefore, the recursion terminates.

F41   What is the output of the code of the previous problem if the **static** keyword of 'i' is removed?

Output: 1 1 1 1 1 ... ... It is an infnine loop.
Note that in each recursive call of 'fun', the variable gets initialized to 2.

F42   What is the output of the following code?
```
int main()
{
    void fun();
    fun();
```

```
    (*fun) ();
  }
  void fun() {
    printf("In fun()\n");
  }
```

Output:
```
In fun()
In fun()
```

Note that **void fun();** is the function declaration. **fun()** and **(*fun) ()** are equivalent, since **fun**, the function name is also equivalent to pointer to the function.

F43   What is the output of the following code?
```
void fun1(){
  printf ("fun1 called.\n");
  return;
}
void fun2(){
  printf ("fun2 called.\n");
  return;
}
void fun3(void (*fun)()){
  fun();
  return;
}
int main(){
  fun3(fun1);
  fun3(fun2);
  return(0);
}
```

```
fun1 called.
fun2 called.
```

Note that the parameter to fun3 is a function pointer, and fun3 is called with arguments fun1 and fun2.

F44   What is the output of the following code?

```
int fun1(int a){
  return 3*a;
}
int fun2(int (*fun)(), int a){
  return fun(a);
}

int main(){
  int i;
```

```
    i = fun2(fun1, 5);
    printf ("i = %d\n", i);
    return(0);
}
```

```
i = 15
```

Note that the parameters to fun2 is a pointer to a function fun, and an 'int' a, and it returns the result of calling fun with argument a. fun2 is called with arguments fun1 and 5, whose result is 15.

F45   What is the output of the following code?
```
int fun1(int a){
    return 3*a;
}
float fun2(int (*fun)(), int a){
  return 2.35 + fun(a);
}
int main(){
  int i=5; float z;
  z = fun2(fun1, i);
  printf ("z = %.2f\n", z);
  return(0);
}
```

Output: `z = 17.35`

IOIOIOIOIOIOIOIOIOIOIOIOIOIOIOIOIOIOIOIOIOIOIOIOIOIOIOIOIOI

G. Dynamic Storage Management

True/False Questions

G1   The **malloc** function will always be able to allocate storage. *False*
[**malloc** fails to allocate storage if the program has used up all memory available to it]

G2   The **malloc** function returns an address. *True*
[The returned address is the start of the storage allocated]

G3   The **malloc** function returns a pointer to a specific type. *False*
[The **malloc** function returns a **void** pointer]

G4   Consecutive calls to **malloc** are guaranteed to allocate storage contiguously. *False*

G5   Dereferencing a pointer whose memory has been deallocated causes runtime error. *False*
[It does not cause any runtime error. However, it could cause unpredictable program behavior which may be difficult to debug]

G6   The size of storage to be allocated by **malloc** must be specified at compile time. *False*
[The size could be specified at runtime. Thus the storage allocated by **malloc** is referred to as synamic memory]

G7   The pointer returned by **realloc()** will always be the same as the original pointer. *False*
[if **realloc()** is used to increase a memory block and there is not enough available memory at the end of the existing block, a large enough block of memory is found at another memory location, and the pointer returned by **realloc()** could be different]

G8   Memory allocated using the **malloc** operator must be explicitly released when it is no longer needed. *True*

G9   The memory allocation using the **malloc** operator is done in the stack area of memory. *False*
[The memory allocation using the 'malloc' operator is done in the heap area of memory]

G10 The memory allocation using the **calloc** operator is done in the data area of memory. *False*
[The memory allocation using the 'calloc' operator is done in the heap area of memory]

G11 The statement **free(ptr)**, when the **ptr** is NULL, causes an error. *False*
[Deleting a null pointer has no effect]

G12 Given **p1** is a pointer to memory allocated using 'malloc' operator, **free(p1)** would release memory allocated by 'malloc' and also that for **p1**. *False*
[The **free(p1)** releases only memory allocated by 'malloc']

G13 The **free(ptr)** function does not delete the pointer variable **ptr**. *True*
[The 'free' operation deletes only the memory area (object) pointed to by the pointer variable]

G14 The **free()** function can be used to release storage allocated to any variable. *False*
[The free() function can be used to delete only the dynamic storage allocated using 'malloc', 'calloc', or 'realloc']

G15 **malloc** does not clear the memory that it allocates. *True*

G16 **calloc** clears (zeros out) the memory before returning. *True*

G17 The **realloc()** function reallocates memory previously allocated using **malloc** or **calloc**. *True*

G18 The **realloc()** function can only increase the memory allocation, but not decrease it. *False*
[The realloc() function can be used for both increasing and decreasing the dynamic storage]

G19 The **realloc()** function leaves the existing data unchanged up to the smaller of the old and new size. *True*

G20 The **realloc()** function always makes a new allocation. *False*
[A new allocation is made if the requested size is greater than the existing size]

G21 The **realloc()** function cannot be called with a **NULL** pointer. *False*

[If **realloc** is called with the **NULL** pointer, it behaves like **malloc**]

G22 The **realloc()** function cannot be called with a zero size. *False*
[If **realloc** is called with zero size, then the existing storage is deallocated]

G23 After dynamic memory is freed up using **free(ptr)**, the pointer **ptr** is set to NULL. *False*
[Even after **free(ptr)**, the pointer **ptr** still contains the address of the location it was pointing to]

IOIOIOIOIOIOIOIOIOIOIOIOIOIOIOIOIOIOIOIOIOIOIOIOIOIOIOIOIOI

Fill-in the-blanks Questions

G1 The function used to allocate a block of storage is **malloc()**.

G2 If the **malloc** function fails to allocate memory, it returns **NULL**.

G3 The type returned by **malloc** function is **void ***.

G4 The **malloc** function call required to allocate storage for 10 unsigned integers is **malloc (10*sizeof(unsigned));**

G5 The **malloc** function call required to allocate storage for 25 chaacters is **malloc (25*sizeof(char));**

G6 The type returned by **calloc** function is **void ***.

G7 The function used to release (deallocate) a block of storage is **free()**.

G8 The function used to increase or decrease the size of dynamically allocated storage is **realloc()**.

G9 Objects created dynamically using the 'malloc' function are allocated in the *heap* area of memory.

G10 The functions used for dynamic allocation of memory in the heap area are **malloc** and **malloc**.

G11   The function used to release the memory allocated by the 'malloc' and 'calloc' operators is **free**.

G12   The functions **malloc**, **calloc** and **free** manage storage in the *heap* area of memory.

IOIOIOIOIOIOIOIOIOIOIOIOIOIOIOIOIOIOIOIOIOIOIOIOIOIOIOI

Essay-type Questions

G1   What is the argument expected by a malloc function?

The argument for a function statement is an integer which is the number of bytes of storage to be allocated.

G2   What is the return value and type of a malloc statement?

The return value of a malloc function is a pointer to (address of) the start of the storage which has been allocated. The return type is (void *) which must be cast to the type of data being stored in the allocated memory.

G3   What are the arguments and return value/type of the calloc function?

The calloc's takes two arguments – (i) the number of objects, and (ii) the size of each object. It returns (void *) pointer to the start of the allocated memory.

G4   What is a dangling pointer?

After dynamic memory is freed up using **free(ptr)**, the pointer **ptr** will still be pointing to the start of the location of memory which was allocated earlier, but has since been freed. In this situation, the **ptr** is known as dangling pointer.

G5   What is memory leak?

When a pointer to dynamically allocated memory is assigned the another address (to point to another location), without freeing the storage that it is currently pointing to, the earlier reference to the storage will be lost. This situation is known as memory leak.

G6 What is the effect of the following statement?
```
int* ip = malloc(10*sizeof(int));
```

It causes an error since the **(void *)** returned by malloc has not been cast to **(int *)**, before assigning to **ip**.

G7 What is the effect of the following statement?
```
char* cp = (char *)malloc(25*sizeof(char));
```

It allocates storage for 25 characters, and returns **(void *)** pointer to the start of the allocated storage, which is then cast to **(char *)** and assigned to **cp**.

G8 What is the effect of the following statement?
```
int* ptr = (int *)calloc(len, sizeof(int));
```

It allocates consecutive storage for **len** number of integers, and returns a pointer to the start of the allocated storage, which is then cast to **(int *)** and assigned to **ptr**.

G9 Give the equivalence of **ptr = calloc(m, n);** to the combination of **malloc** and **memset**.

```
ptr = malloc(m*n);
memset(ptr, 0, m*n);
```

malloc(m*n) allocates storage for **m*n** bytes, and the start of the allocated memory is assigned to **ptr**. **memset** sets each of the **m*n** bytes starting at **ptr** to 0.

G10 What is the output of the following program? Describe the salient steps of the program.
```
#include <stdio.h>
#include <stdlib.h>
int main(void) {
  int* iptr1 = NULL;
  int* iptr2 = NULL;
  iptr1 = (int*) malloc (sizeof(int));
  iptr2 = (int*) malloc (sizeof(int));
  printf ("Type two integers: ");
  scanf("%d", iptr1);
```

```
    scanf("%d", iptr2);
    printf("iptr1  deref.  =  %d,  iptr2  deref.  =  %d\n",
*iptr1, *iptr2);
    printf("iptr1  content  =  %p,  iptr2  content  =  %p\n",
iptr1, iptr2);
    free(iptr1);
    free(iptr2);
    return 0;
}
```

Output:
```
iptr1 deref. = 53, iptr2 deref. = 68
iptr1 content = 0x11ad010, iptr2 content = 0x11ad030
```

Two integer pointers **iptr1** and **iptr2** are declared. The **malloc** calls allocate storages for two integers whose addresses are assigned to **iptr1** and **iptr2**. Two integer values are read from keyboard (standard input) and stored in the locations pointed to by **iptr1** and **iptr2**. The integers, as well as their locations (addesses) are then printed. The **free** statements release the storages allocated my the **malloc**'s.

G11 What is the output of the following code segment? Describe the behavior.
```
int *p;
p = (int*) calloc(10, sizeof(int));
printf ("%p\n", p);
free(p);
printf ("%p\n", p);
```

The output of the **printf** will be the contents of the pointer 'p', which will be the starting address of the memory allocated by **calloc** . Both the **printf** will output the same address both after **calloc** and after **free**, which demonstrates that the pointer to dynamically allocated storage will continue to point to the location even after the memory has been freed.

IOIOIOIOIOIOIOIOIOIOIOIOIOIOIOIOIOIOIOIOIOIOIOIOIOIOI

H. Input / Output and Library Functions

True/False Questions

H1 **stdin**, **stdout**, and **stderr** are binary streams. *False*
[**stdin**, **stdout**, and **stderr** are text streams]

H2 The number of expressions following the format string must be exactly same as the number of format specifiers in the string of **printf**. *True*

H3 The expressions following the format specifiers in **scanf** need to be memory addresses of where the scanned data is to be stored. *True*

H4 **printf** cannot handle a 'struct' argument. *True*

H5 Structs and unions can be directly read by **scanf**. *False*

H6 Given **str** is a character string, **printf("%s", &str)** results in error. *True*
[**str** is also a pointer to the start of the string. Therefore, the '&' address operator is not required]

H7 Given **str** is a character string, **printf("%s", str)** outputs a newline character after printing **str**. *False*

H8 Given **str** is a character string, **printf("%s", &str[0])** prints **str**. *True*
[**&str[0]** is a pointer to the start of the string. Therefore, **str** is printed]

H9 Given **str** is a character string, **puts(str)** outputs a newline character after printing **str**. *True*

H10 **printf** cannot handle structured types (arrays, structs, unions). *True*

H11 **fprintf** outputs formatted data in variables into an output stream. *True*

H12 **fprintf** cannot output formatted data in variables on standard output (monitor). *False*

H13 **sprintf** outputs formatted data in variables into memory (buffer). *True*

H14 **sprintf** can also output formatted data in variables on standard output (monitor). *False*

H15 **scanf** can only be used for reading primitive types and character strings. *True*

H16 The **scanf** statement to read into an integer variable **num**, is **scanf("%d", num);** *False*
[**scanf** expects the address of the variable where data has to be read into. Thus, it should be **&num**]

H17 **getchar()** reads characters from the keyboard after the 'Enter' key has been pressed. *False*

H18 **scanf** reads in a string of characters up to the first newline character. *False*
[**scanf** reads up to a space, tab, or newline character]

H19 **scanf** appends the encountered a newline character to the end of the character string stored. *False*

H20 **scanf** appends a null character to the end of the character string stored. *True*

H21 **scanf** has only side-effect, and no return value. *False*
[**scanf** returns the number of fields that were successfuly read and stored]

H22 **fscanf** can read from keyboard (stdin) also. *True*

H23 **sscanf** can read from keyboard (stdin) also. *False*

H24 The **gets** function continues to read strings of characters even after encounting space ot tab characters. *True*

H25 A limit on the number of characters read by **gets** can be specified. *False*

H26 **fputs** writes a string to a file, but not on the terminal. ***False***
[**fputs(str, stdout)** outputs the contents of **str** on the terminal]

H27 A NULL return value of **fgets** always indicates error. ***False***
[**fgets** returns NULL on error or when end of file is normally reached]

H28 A limit on the maximum number of characters read using **fgets** can be specified. ***True***

H29 **fgets** can be used to read from a file but not from the keyboard. ***False***
[Using **stdin** in place of file pointer, **fgets** can read from the keyboard]

H30 After encounting a newline character, **fgets** stops reading and stores the newline character. ***True***

H31 **fprintf** is always returns a posiive number. ***False***
[The return value of **fprintf** is the number of characters successfully printed. It returns a negative number in case of error]

H32 When **fopen** is used in **"r"** mode, the file must be existing. ***True***

H33 When **fopen** is used in **"r"** mode, the file cannot be written into. ***True***

H34 When **fopen** is used in **"w"** mode, the file must be existing. ***False***

H35 When **fopen** is used in **"w"** mode, the existing contents of a preexisting file with the given name is erased. ***True***

H36 When **fopen** is used in **"a"** mode, the file must be existing. ***False***
[If the file does not exist, a file with the name will be created]

H37 When **fopen** is used in **"a"** mode, the existing contents of a preexisting file with the given name is erased. ***False***

H38 When **fopen** is used in **"a"** mode, writing into the file can be done anywhere. ***False***
[The wriring can only be done starting from the end of the existing file, or from the beginning of a new file]

H39 When **fopen** is used in **"r+"** mode, it expects a preexisting file. ***True***

H40 When **fopen** is used in "**r+**" mode, the file can be written into. *True*

H41 When **fopen** is used in "**w+**" mode, it expects a preexisting file. *False*
[If the file is not preexisting, a new file with the name is created]

H42 When **fopen** is used in "**w+**" mode, reading from the file is not allowed. *False*
[Both reading and writing are allowed in "**w+**" mode]

H43 When **fopen** is used in "**a+**" mode, it expects a preexisting file. *False*
[If the file is not preexisting, a new file with the name is created]

H44 When **fopen** is used in "**a+**" mode, both reading and writing are allowed. *True*

H45 When **fopen** is used in "**a+**" mode, reading and writing are allowed anywhere in the file. *False*

H46 When **fopen** is used in "**a+**" mode, reading/writing can be done anywhere in the file. *False*
[The wriring can only be done starting from the end of the existing file, or from the beginning of a new file]

H47 There are library functions for converting strings of lower/upper case characters fron one to the other. *False*

H48 The value of **tolower(toupper(ch))** is the same as **tolower(ch)** for any character. *True*

H49 The value of **tolower(tolower(ch))** is the same as **tolower(ch)** for any character. *True*

H50 The functions **tolower** and **toupper** have no effect on character 'ch' for which **isalpha(ch)** is true. *True*

IOIOIOIOIOIOIOIOIOIOIOIOIOIOIOIOIOIOIOIOIOIOIOIOIOIOIOIOIOIOI

Fill-in the-blanks Questions

H1   The three text streams which are predefined when a C program begins execution are **stdin**, **stdout**, and **stderr**.

For H2 – H8: Given **char str[] = "SAMPLE STRING";**

H2   The output of **printf("%s", str)** is **SAMPLE STRING**.

H3   The output of **printf("%s", &str[0])** is **SAMPLE STRING**.

H4   The output of **printf("%s", &str[1])** is **AMPLE STRING**.

H5   The **printf** statement to print **RING** (part of **str**) is **printf("%s", &str[9])**.

H6   The **printf** statement to print **M** (3rd letter of **str**) is **printf("%c", str[2])**.

H7   The output of **puts(str)** is **SAMPLE STRING**.

H8   The **puts** statement to print **STRING** (part of **str**) is **puts(&str[7])**.

H9   The **gets** function reads a string of characters from ***standard input (keyboard)***.

H10   When fscanf encounters the end of the file before the desired number of items are be scanned in, it returns ***EOF*** (End Of File).

H11   The file I/O function which flushes buffers from RAM out to disk is **fclose**.

H12   The function which returns a character at a time, read from the **stdin** stream is **getchar**.

H13   Functions to read a character at a time from a given input stream are **getc** and **fgetc**.

H14   The function which outputs a character at a time onto the **stdout** stream is **putchar**.

H15 Functions which output a character at a time to a given output stream are **putc** and **fputc**.

H16 The function which puts back a character read from an input stream is **ungetc**.

H17 The function which reads characters into a character array from standard input is **gets**.

H18 The function which prints from a character array to standard output (screen) is **puts**.

H19 The library function to output a character at a time onto standard output (screen) is **putc**.

H20 The library function to output a character string (buffer of characters) at a time to an output stream is **fputs**.

H21 The function to output/transfer formatted data from variables to standard output (monitor) only is **printf**.

H22 The function to read/transfer formatted data from only standard input (keyboard) into variables is **scanf**.

H23 The function to output/transfer formatted data from variables to an output stream is **fprintf**.

H24 The function to read/transfer formatted data from an input stream into variables is **fscanf**.

H25 The function to output/transfer formatted data from variables to memory (buffer) is **sprintf**.

H26 The function to read/transfer formatted data from memory (buffer) into variables is **sscanf**.

H27 When **fopen** is unable to open a requested file it returns **NULL**.

H28 The fopen modes where the stream pointer is placed at the beginning of the file are **r, r+, w, w+**.

H29 The fopen modes where the stream pointer is placed at the end of the file are **a, a+**.

H30   The function to check end-of-file in an input stream is **feof**.

H31   The function to check for the error bit in a stream is **ferror**.

H32   The function to clear error bit in a stream is **clearerr**.

H33   The function to get the file descriptor associated with a given file is **fileno**.

H34   The function to reset a file to the beginning is **rewind**.

H35   The function to directly jump to a certain position in a file is **feek**.

H36   The function which gives the position (for reading/writing) in a file is **ftell**.

H37   The argument of **feek** to specify the offset relative to the file beginning is **SEEK_SET**.

H38   The argument of **feek** to specify the offset relative to current position is **SEEK_CUR**.

H39   The argument of **feek** to specify the offset relative to current position is **SEEK_END**.

H40   The function to read from a binary file is **fread**.

H41   The function to write to a binary file is **fwrite**.

Library Functions

H42   Function to check whether a character is alphabetic is **isalpha()**.

H43   Function to check whether a character is alphanumeric is **isalnum()**.

H44   Function to check whether a character is a digit is **isdigit()**.

H45   Function to check whether a character is a space or tab is **isblank()**.

H46 Function to check whether a character is tab or a control code is `iscntrl()`.

H47 Function to check whether a character is tab or space or whitespace control code is `isspace()`.

H48 Function to check whether a character is printable is `isprint()`.

H49 Function to check whether a character is punctuation mark is `ispunct()`.

H50 Function to check whether a character is hexadecimal is `isxdigit()`.

H51 The value of `islower(toupper(c))` for any alphabetic character is *false*.

H52 The value of `iscntrl(c) && isalnum(c)` for any character 'c' is *false*.

H53 When `isalnum(c) && isalpha(c) && isupper(c)` is 'true', the value of 'c' is between '**A**' and '**Z**'.

H54 When `isalnum(c) && isdigit(c)` is 'true', the value of 'c' is between '**0**' and '**9**'.

H55 The value of `abs(3 - 5 - abs (2 - 9))` is 9.

H56 The value of `fabs(2.3 - 4.5 + fabs(3.2-7.1))` is 1.7

H57 The value of `round(1.49)` is 1.

H58 The value of `round(1.5)` is 2.

H59 The value of `rint(1.49)` is 1.

H60 The value of `rint(1.5)` is 2.

H61 The value of `ceil(1.01)` is 2.0.

H62 The value of `ceil(1.99)` is 2.0.

H63 The value of `floor(1.99)` is 1.0.

H64 The value of **floor(1.01)** is **1.0**.

H65 The statement to compute $e^{2.3}$ (where e is the base of the natural logarithm) is **exp(2.3)**.

H66 The statement to compute $\log_e 5.7$ is **log(5.7)**.

H67 The statement to compute $\log_{10} 7.3$ is **log10(7.3)**.

H68 The statement to compute $\sqrt{4.5}$ is **sqrt(4.5)**.

H69 The statement to compute $3.2^{4.5}$ is **pow (3.2, 4.5)**.

H70 The value of **pow(9, 1/2)** is **1.0**.
     [Note that 1/2 is 0, and $9^{\frac{1}{2}} = 9^0 = 1.0$]

H71 The value of **pow(9, 1.0/2)** is **3.0**.

H72 The function to initialize the pseudo-random-number generator is **srand**.

H73 **rand()** returns a random number (integer) between **0** and **RAND_MAX**.
     [**RAND_MAX** is a constant defined in **<stdlib.h>**]

H74 The statement to generate a random number between 1 and 100 (inclusive) is **rand() % 100 + 1**.

H75 The statement to generate a random number between −273 and 200 (inclusive) is **rand() % 474 - 273**.

H76 The statement to generate a random number between 0 and 1 is **(float) rand() / RAND_MAX**.

H77 The statement to generate random integers 0 or 1 is **rand() % 2**.

H78 The statement to generate random integers in the range 18 to 65 is **rand() % 48 + 18**

H79 To obtain a random integer between values **a** and **b**, a possible statement would be **a + rand() % (b−a+1)**

H80 The function used to parse a string of numeric characters into a number of type int is **atoi**.

H81 The function used to parse a string of numeric characters into a number of type double is **atof**.

H82 The function used to parse a string of numeric characters into a number of type long int is **atol**.

H83 Given **str** is a character array of size 20, and **str** contains the string "**Test String**", the value of **strlen(str)** is **11**.
[Returns the string length (not counting the null byte), not the array size]

H84 Given **str1** contains the string "**Test** ", **str2** contains the string "**String**", the value of **strcat(str1, str2)** is "**Test String**".

H85 Given **str1** contains the string "**Test** ", **str2** contains the string "**String**", the value of **strncat(str1, str2, 3)** is "**Test Str**".

H86 Given **str1** contains the string "**Test** ", **str2** contains the string "**String**", the value of **strlen(strcpy(str2, str1)** is **5**.

H87 The value of **strcmp("Sang", "Sing")** is **−1**.

H88 The value of **strcmp("sing", "Sing")** is **1**.

H89 For any valid character string str, The value of **strcmp(str,str)** is **0**.

H90 The value of **strncmp("Singular", "Single", 4)** is **0**.

H91 Given **str = "BICYCLING"**, **char* s1=strchr(str, 'C');** the output of **printf("%s\n", s1)** is **CYCLING**.

H92 Given **str = "BICYCLING"**, **char* s1=strrchr(str, 'C');** the output of **printf("%s\n", s1)** is **CLING**.

H93 Given `str = "INSIDER"`, `char* s1=strstr(str, "SIDE");` the output of `printf("%s\n", s1)` is <u>SIDER</u>.

IOIOIOIOIOIOIOIOIOIOIOIOIOIOIOIOIOIOIOIOIOIOIOIOIOIOIOIOIOIOIOI

Essay-type Questions

H1   What is the behavior of the following program?

```
int main ()
{
  FILE *infile;
  char c, fname[80];

  printf ("Type the file name: ");
  scanf ("%s", fname);

  if ((infile = fopen (fname, "r")) == NULL){
    printf ("Can't open file\n");
    exit (1);
  }

  while ((c=getc (infile)) != EOF)
    putchar (c);
}
```

This program reads characters one by one, from a given input text file obtained as user input, and writes the characters on to the screen. If the file does not exist, it gives an error. Thus, it essentially prints the contents of a file on the screen.

H2   What is the behavior of the following program?

```
int main (int argc, char* argv)
{
  FILE *infile, *outfile;
  char c;

  if (argc != 3) {
    fprintf (stderr, "Number of args should be
two.\n");
    exit (1);
```

```
    }
    if ((infile = fopen (argv[1], "r")) == NULL) {
       fprintf (stderr, "Can't read file %s\n",
argv[1]);
       exit (2);
    }
    if ((outfile = fopen (argv[2], "w")) == NULL) {
       fprintf (stderr, "can't write to file %s\n",
argv[2]);
       exit (3);
    }

    while ((c=getc (infile)) != EOF)
       putc (c, outfile);
}
```

This program takes two filenames as part of command line input. It reads characters from the input text file and writes them on to the output text file. It gives suitable errors if the file open operation fails. Thus, it essentially copies the contents of one text file to another.

H3   What is the behavior of the following program?

```
#define BUFSIZE 80

main ()
{
   FILE *infile;
   char fname[80], buf[BUFSIZE];

   printf ("Type the file name: ");
   scanf ("%s", fname);

   if ((infile = fopen (fname, "r")) == NULL) {
      printf ("Can't open file\n");
      exit (1);
   }

   while (fgets (buf, BUFSIZE, infile) != NULL)
      fputs(buf, stdout);
}
```

This program reads characters into a buffer, from a given input text file obtained as user input, and writes the contents of the buffer on to the screen. Thus, it essentially prints the contents of a file on the screen in 'buffer mode'.

H4   Write statement to open an existing file named "sales_07.dat" for reading only.

```
FILE *fp = fopen ("sales_07.dat", "r");
```

H5   Write statement to open an existing file named "sales_09.dat" for reading and writing.

```
FILE *fp = fopen ("sales_09.dat", "r+");
```

H6   Write statement to create a new file named "sales_07.dat" for wriring into it. An already existing file may be overwriiten

```
FILE *fp = fopen ("sales_07.dat", "w");
```

H7   Write statement to create file named "sales_09.dat" for writing and reading. An already existing file may be overwriiten.

```
FILE *fp = fopen ("sales_09.dat", "w+");
```

H8   Write statement to open a file named "sales_07.dat" for appending (only writing after the end of existing file). If the file does not exist, it should create it.

```
FILE *fp = fopen ("sales_07.dat", "a");
```

H9   Write statement to open a file named "sales_09.dat" for reading and writing after the end of existing file. If the file does not exist, it should create it,

```
FILE *fp = fopen ("sales_09.dat", "a+");
```

H10   Write statements to create a file named "emp_records_01.dat" with a file pointer named "empf", and write to the file "num_recs" records, each record of type "EMPREC", the data given in an array pointed to by "emp_recs".

```
FILE * empf = fopen ("emp_records_01.dat", "w");
fwrite ((void *) emp_recs, sizeof (EMPREC),
num_recs, empf);
```

H11   Write   statements   to   open   an   existing   file   named "emp_records_03.dat" with a file pointer named "empf", and read from the file "num_recs" records, each of type "EMPREC", into an array pointed to by "emp_recs".

```
FILE * empf = fopen ("emp_records_01.dat", "r");
fread ((void *) emp_recs, sizeof (EMPREC),
num_recs, empf);
```

H12 Write statement to position the file pointer named "fp" to the byte number "byte_num" from the start of file.

```
fseek (fp, (long)byte_num, SEEK_SET);
```

H13 Write statement to position the file pointer named "fp" to the byte number "byte_num" from the current position in the file.

```
fseek (fp, (long)byte_num, SEEK_CUR);
```

H14 Write statement to position the file pointer named "fp" to the byte number "byte_num" backwards from the current position.

```
fseek (fp, (long)-byte_num, SEEK_CUR);
```

H15 Write statement to position the file pointer named "fp" to the end of file.

```
fseek (fp, 0L, SEEK_END);
```

H16 Write statement to position the file pointer named "fp" to the byte number "byte_num" before the end of file.

```
fseek (fp, (long)-byte_num, SEEK_END);
```

IOIOIOIOIOIOIOIOIOIOIOIOIOIOIOIOIOIOIOIOIOIOIOIOIOIOIOIOIOIOI

I. Programming Problems

I1   Write the code segment to determine if a given 'year' is leap year or not, and return a Boolean value accordingly. Note that a year is leap year if it is divisible by 4 or if it is a century boundaries, it must be divisible by 400. For example, 1976 is a leap year, 1982 is not a leap year, 1900 is not a leap year, and 2000 is a leap year.

```
leapYear = ((year % 400 == 0) || (year % 100 != 0
&& year % 4 == 0));
```

I2   Write a 'for-loop' for printing the 'N' numbers of the sequence given below for a given N.
1 2 5 10 17 26 .. ..

```
int i, num=1, inc=1;
for (i=1; i<=N; i++) {
  printf ("%d\n", num);
  num += inc;
  inc += 2;
}
```

I3   Write the code segment for printing the numbers of the sequence given below as long as the numbers are less than or equal to a given positive integer 'N'.
1 2 5 10 17 26 .. ..

```
int i, num=1, inc=1;
while (num <= N) {
  printf ("%d\n", num);
  num += inc;
  inc += 2;
}
```

I3   Write a function which takes an array of integers and its size as arguments, and determines and returns the number of times the maximum element occurs in the array, using only one pass through the array.

```
int max_count (int A[], int size, int* maxval){
  int maxcnt = 1, max = A[0];
  for (int i = 1; i < size; i++){
   if (A[i] > max){
```

```
      max = A[i];
      maxcnt = 1;
    }
    else if (A[i] == max)
      maxcnt++;
  }
  *maxval = max;
  return (maxcnt);
}
```

The driver main program to test the function is given below.

```
int main()
{
  int arr[] = {2, 5, 12, 5, 4, 3, 5, 12, 12, 9, 5,
5, 12, 7};
  int max_value, *maxp;
  maxp = &max_value;
  int mc = max_count (arr, 14, maxp);
  printf ("Maximum value of %d, occurs %d times\n",
max_value, mc);
}
```

I4   Write the statements to assign to variable 'max3' the maximum of
       three numbers in variables a, b, and c.

A possible way is shown below.
```
if (a > b){
    if (a > c)
      max3 = a;
    else
      max = c;
  }
  else if (b > c)
    max3 = b;
  else
    max3 = c;
```

Another way would be:
```
if (a > b && a > c)
  max3 = a;
else if (b > a && b > c)
  max3 = b;
else
  max3 = c;
```

Another way would be:

```
max3 = c > (a > b ? a : b) ? c : ((a > b) ?
a : b);
```

I5   An interval (*b*, *e*) is a pair of real numbers (*b*: begin, *e*: end).
Intervals (2.7, 5.3) and (4.8, 12.2) overlap, (3.4, 6.6) and (6.6, 7.3)
do not overlap, and (2.7, 5.3) and (7.1, 9.5) do not overlap. Declare
a struct **Interval** with fields **begin** and **end**. Write a function
overlap which takes two intervals as arguments, and returns the
extent of overlap (0 if no overlap).

```
#define MIN(x,y)  ((x)<(y)?(x):(y))
#define MAX(x,y)  ((x)>(y)?(x):(y))

typedef struct interval_str {
  float begin, end;
} Interval;

float interval_overlap(Interval i1, Interval
i2){
  float leftmost = MIN(i1.begin, i2.begin);
  float rightmost = MAX(i1.end, i2.end);
  float extent_i1 = i1.end - i1.begin;
  float extent_i2 = i2.end - i2.begin;
  if (rightmost - leftmost >= extent_i1 +
extent_i2)
      return 0;
  else
      return MIN(i1.end, i2.end) -
MAX(i1.begin, i2.begin);
}
```

I6   An interval (*b*, *e*) is a pair of real numbers (*b*: begin, *e*: end). Write
a function **interval_pos** which takes two intervals as
arguments, and returns the relative positions of the two intervals: 1.
The intervals do not overlap; 2. The intervals just touch (end of one
interval equals the beginning of the other); 3. The intervals overlap;
4. One interval completely contains the other.

1. No Overlap (Disjoint)   2. No Overlap   3. Overlap   4. Containment
(End of 1 = Begin of 2)

```
#define MIN(x,y)  ((x)<(y)?(x):(y))
#define MAX(x,y)  ((x)>(y)?(x):(y))
#define NO_OVERLAP 1
#define ABUTMENT 2
#define OVERLAP 3
#define CONTAINMENT 4

typedef struct interval_str {
  float begin, end;
} Interval;

int interval_pos(Interval i1, Interval i2){
  float leftmost = MIN(i1.begin, i2.begin);
  float rightmost = MAX(i1.end, i2.end);
  float extent_i1 = i1.end - i1.begin;
  float extent_i2 = i2.end - i2.begin;
  float extent_i1i2 = rightmost - leftmost;
  if (extent_i1i2 > extent_i1 + extent_i2)
    return NO_OVERLAP;
  else if (extent_i1i2 == extent_i1 +
extent_i2)
    return ABUTMENT;
  else if ((extent_i1i2 == extent_i1) ||
(extent_i1i2 == extent_i2))
    return CONTAINMENT;
  else
    return OVERLAP;
}
```

I7   Write a function which takes two arguments: (1) a 'struct' representing a circle containing fields (a) 'center' which is a 'struct' of type 'point' consisting of two real numbers, and (b) 'radius' which is a real number, and (2) a 'point', and returns an integer: 1. If the point is on the circle (circumference); 2. If the point is inside the circle; 3. If the point is outside the circle.

```
#define ON_CIRCLE 1
#define INSIDE_CIRCLE 2
#define OUTSIDE_CIRCLE 3
#define SQR(x)  ((x)*(x))

typedef struct point_str {
  float x, y;
} POINT;
```

```
typedef struct circle_str {
  POINT Center;
  float Radius;
} CIRCLE;

int point_in_circle(CIRCLE c, POINT p){
  float dist = sqrt(SQR(c.Center.x - p.x) +
SQR(c.Center.y - p.y));
  if (dist < c.Radius)
    return INSIDE_CIRCLE;
  else if (dist > c.Radius)
    return OUTSIDE_CIRCLE;
  else
    return ON_CIRCLE;
}
```

I8   Write a function which takes as arguments three real numbers representing the sides of a triangle, and determines and returns true or false, based on whether it is a valid triangle or not. **Note:** In a valid triangle, the sum of the lengths of any two sides is greater than the length of the third side. For example, if the given side lengths are 10.7, 5.6, and 2.9, it should return false.

```
unsigned isValidTriangle (double a, double b,
double c){
  return (a >= b + c || b >= a + c || c >= a + b);
}
```

I9   Write a program, without using the 'pow' library function, to print all the odd powers of 3 less than or equal to a given N, obtained as user input. (ex. It should print 3 27 243 ... as long as the odd power of 3 is $\leq N$)

```
main ()
{
  int n, oddpow3 = 3;
  printf("Typein the value of N: ");
  scanf("%d", &n);
  while (oddpow3 <= n) {
    printf("%d ", oddpow3);
    oddpow3 *= 9;
  }
}
```

I10   Write a program which prints the following sequence up to a given
      length. The length of the sequence is read from the keyboard.
      Sequence: 1 2 4 7 11 16 22 29 ....
      The program should prompt: "Type the sequence length: ". If 5 is
      typed in, then the output should be: "1 2 4 7 11".

```c
int main () {
  int i, j, n;
  i = 1; j = 1;
  printf("Type the sequence length: ");
  scanf("%d", &n);
  for ( ; n > 0; n--){
    printf("%d ", j);
    j = j + i;
    i++ ;
  }
  return 0;
}
```

I11   Write a program that calculates and prints the sequence, as shown
      below.

```
        9
       89
      789
     6789
      ::
      ::
123456789
```

```c
int main () {
  int n, nd, ndgts, num;
  for (ndgts = 1; ndgts <= 9; ndgts++ ){
    nd = ndgts;
    n = 10 - nd;
    num = 0;
    while (nd > 0) {
      num = num*10 + n;
      n++;
      nd--;
    }
    printf("%d\n", num);
  }
}
```

255

I12   Write a program to determine the least number of coins using quarters, dimes, nickels, pennies to be given as change.

```c
int main() {
    int amt, quarters, dimes, nickels, pennies;
    char str[10];
    do {
        printf ("Type the change amount[1-99]: ");
        scanf("%d", &amt);
    } while (amt < 1 || amt > 99);

    quarters = amt/25;
    amt %= 25;
    dimes = amt/10;
    amt %= 10;
    nickels = amt/5;
    pennies = amt % 5;

    printf("The change is: ");
    if (quarters > 0)
      printf("%d Quarter(s), ", quarters);
    if (dimes > 0)
      printf("%d Dime(s), ", dimes);
    if (nickels > 0)
      printf("%d Nickel(s), ", nickels);
    if (pennies > 0)
      printf("%d Pennies", pennies);
    printf("\n");
}
```

I13   Write a program which reads the number of seconds elapsed since the clock has 'struck 12' and prints the number of hours, minutes and seconds. For example, if the number is **371,** it should print **0:6:11**; for **36522**, it should print **10:8:42**

```c
int main () {
    int nsecs, hr, min, sec;
    printf("Type in the number of seconds: ");
    scanf("%d", &nsecs);
    hr = nsecs / 3600;
    nsecs = nsecs % 3600;
    min = nsecs / 60;
    sec = nsecs % 60;
    printf("%d:%d:%d\n", hr, min, sec);
    return 0;
}
```

I14   Write a function which takes an integer argument and returns the
number of digits in the number. Use main() as a driver to test it.

```
int num_digits (int num){
  num = abs(num);
  int ndigits = 0;
  do {
    num /= 10;
    ndigits++;
  } while (num != 0);
  return ndigits;
}

int main ()
{
  int num, nd;

  printf ("Key-in the number: ");
  scanf ("%d", &num);
  nd = num_digits (num);

  printf ("The number of digits in %d is
%d\n", num, nd);
}
```

I15   Write a function which takes an integer argument and returns the
sum of digits in the number. Use main() as a driver to test it.

```
int sum_of_digits (int num){
  num = abs(num);
  int sum_digits = 0;
  while (num > 0) {
    sum_digits += num % 10;
    num /= 10;
  }
  return sum_digits;
}

int main ()
{
  int num, sumd;

  printf ("Key-in the number: ");
  scanf ("%d", &num);
```

```
    sumd = sum_of_digits (num);

    printf ("The sum of digits of %d is %d\n",
num, sumd);
}
```

I16 Write a function which takes an integer as argument and returns 'true' if it has any of the digits repeated, 'false', otherwise. Assume the input to be within the valid range of integers.
Example: for 3538291, it should return 'true'; for 7384961, it should return 'false'.

```
#define FALSE 0
#define TRUE 1
unsigned digit_repeat (int num){
  int d, n = num;
  if (num / 10 == 0)// single digit number
    return FALSE;
  while (num / 10 != 0){
    d = num % 10;
    num = num / 10;
    n = num;
    while (n != 0){
      if (d == n % 10)
      return TRUE;
      n = n / 10;
    }
  }
  return FALSE;
}
```

I17 Write a function which takes a number 'n' and a digit 'd' as arguments and determines and returns the number of occurrences of the digit in the number.
Ex. Input: (536714, 3), Output: 1; Input: (2354392, 3), Output: 2;
Input: (2352, 6), Output: 0

```
int dgt_occur (int n, int d){
  int dcnt = 0;
  do {
    if (n % 10 == d)
    dcnt++ ;
    n = n / 10;
  } while (n != 0);
```

```
   return dcnt;
}
```

I18 Write a function which takes two integers 'num' and 'pos' as arguments, and returns the digit at position 'pos' of the number 'num'. Note that pos = 1 denotes the unit's position. For example, Input: (6753, 3), Output: 7; Input: (372519, 4), Output: 2. Use main() as a driver to test it.

```
int num_digits (int num){
   num = abs(num);
   int ndigits = 0;
   do {
     num /= 10;
     ndigits++;
   } while (num != 0);
   return ndigits;
}
int dgt_at_pos (int num, int pos)
{
   int dgt;

   while (pos > 0) {
     dgt = num % 10;
     num /= 10;
     pos-- ;
   }
   return (dgt);
}

main ()
{
   int num, pos, ndgts;

   do {
     printf ("Key-in the number and digit position: ");
     scanf ("%d %d", &num, &pos);
     ndgts = num_digits (num);
     if (pos < 1 || pos > ndgts)
       printf ("The digit position must be between [1-%d].\n", ndgts);
   } while (pos < 1 || pos > ndgts);
```

```
    printf ("The digit at position %d in %d is
%d\n",
        pos, num, dgt_at_pos(num, pos));
}
```

I19 Write a function which takes an integer as argument and returns an integer with the digits reversed. For example, if the input is 536327, the output is 723635.

```
int reverse_dgts(int num){
  int sum = 0,rem;
  while (num > 0){
    rem = num%10;
    sum = sum*10+rem;
    num = num/10;
  }
   return sum;
}

int main ()
{
  int num;
  printf("Type in a number: ");
  scanf("%d", &num);
  printf("Input number: %d\n", num);
  num = reverse_dgts (num);
  printf("Number with digits reversed: %d\n",
num);
}
```

I20 Given an integer, adding the digits of the number yields another integer. Repeating this process results in a single digit number. Write a function which takes an integer argument, and returns the number of 'stages' required to obtain the single digit number. For example, if the number is 798, after one stage, the number obtained is 7+9+8 = 24. After the second stage, the number is 2+4 = 6. Thus, two stages are required. A typical output is given below.

```
Type in a number: 7383926
Stage: 1 Stage sum: 38
Stage: 2 Stage sum: 11
Stage: 3 Stage sum: 2
The number of stages: 3
```

```
int num_stages (unsigned int num){
  int stage_num = 0, sum_digits, stage_sum =
num;
  while (stage_sum > 9){
    sum_digits = 0;
    num = stage_sum;
    stage_num++;
    while (num > 0) {
      sum_digits += num % 10;
      num /= 10;
    }
    stage_sum = sum_digits;
    printf ("Stage: %d Stage sum: %d\n",
stage_num, stage_sum);
  }
  return stage_num;
}

int main ()
{
  unsigned int num, nstages;

  printf ("Type in a number: ");
  scanf ("%d", &num);
  nstages = num_stages (num);

  printf ("The number of stages: %d\n",
nstages);
}
```

I21 The overview of Russian Peasant multiplication to find the product P of two integers N and M, is as follows:
```
1) Initialize product: P to 0.
2) While N is greater than 0 do
   a) If N is odd, add M to P
   b) Double M and halve N
3) Return P
```

Write a function which takes two integers as arguments, and computes and returns their product using the Russian Peasant multiplication scheme. Use main() as a driver to test it.

```
int fast_mult (int N, int M)
{
  int P = 0, mask = 1;

  if (N == 0)
    return 0;
  while ( N > 0) {
    if (N & mask)
      P += M;
    N >>= 1; // Right-shift equiv. to / by 2
    M <<= 1; // Left-shift equiv. to * by 2
  }
  return (P);
}

int main ()
{
  int i, j, k;

  printf ("Type the two numbers to be
multiplied: ");
  scanf ("%d %d", &i, &j);
  k = fast_mult (i, j);
  printf ("The product of %d and %d is
%d\n", i, j, k);
}
```

I22 Write a function which reads an integer limit and determines and prints out all 'Armstrong numbers' within the limit. An Armstrong number is one which equals the sum of the cubes of its digits. A sample output is shown below.

```
Enter limit: 1000
1 153 370 371 407

int main () {
  int q, r, s, lim;
  printf("Enter limit: ");
  scanf("%d", &lim);
  for (int i = 1; i <= lim; i++) {
    q = i; s = 0;
    while (q != 0) {
      r = q % 10;
      q = q / 10;
      s += r*r*r;
```

```
      }
      if (s == i)
        printf("%d ", i);
   }
}
```

I23 Write a function to calculate and print all the well-ordered numbers of a given number of digits. It should take as input the number of digits, and return the number of well-ordered numbers of that many digits. A well-ordered number is one whose digits strictly increase from left to right. A sample output is given below.

```
Type the number of digits [1-9]: 2
12 13 14 15 16 17 18 19 23 24
25 26 27 28 29 34 35 36 37 38
39 45 46 47 48 49 56 57 58 59
67 68 69 78 79 89
Number of well ordered numbers of 2 digits =
36
```

```
#define FALSE 0
#define TRUE 1
int wellOrdered(int nDigits) {
  int n, nd, num, loLim, hiLim=1, cnt=0,
curDigit, prevDigit, wellOrder;

  for (n = nDigits; n > 0; n--)
    hiLim *= 10;

    loLim = hiLim / 10;
    for (n = loLim; n < hiLim; n++) {
      num = n;
      wellOrder = TRUE;
      prevDigit = num % 10;
      num /= 10;
      while (num != 0) {
        curDigit = num % 10;
        if (curDigit >= prevDigit) {
          wellOrder = FALSE;
          break;
        }
        prevDigit = curDigit;
        num /= 10;
      }
      if (wellOrder) {
        cnt++ ;
```

```
            printf("%d ", n);
            if (cnt % 10 == 0)
               putchar('\n');
        }
    }
    putchar('\n');
    return (cnt);
}

int main (){
    int nDigits, cnt;
    printf("Type the number of digits [1-9]: ");
    scanf("%d", &nDigits);
    cnt = wellOrdered (nDigits);
    printf("Number of well ordered numbers of %d
digits is %d\n", nDigits, cnt);
}
```

I24   Write a recursive function for fast power computation of a^N using the facts that:

- when $N = 0$, then the result is 1.
- when N is even, the result is $(a^{N/2})^2$.
- when N is odd, the result is $(a^{(N-1)/2})^2 * a$.

Assume the availablity of a function $SQR(x)$ which computes x^2. 'a' and 'N' are obtained as user input. Use the 'main()' as the driver function.

```
#define SQR(a) a*a
int FAST_POWER (int a, int N){
   if (a == 0)
      return 0;
   if (N == 0)
      return 1;
   else if (N % 2 == 0) // N is Even
      return SQR (FAST_POWER (a, N/2));
   else
      return SQR(FAST_POWER(a,(N-1)/2))*a;
}
int main (){
   int x, N, p;
   printf("Type in the values of base and
exponent: ");
   scanf("%d %d", &x, &N);
   p = FAST_POWER (x, N);
```

```
printf("%d raised to power %d is %d\n", x,
N, p);
}
```

I25 Write a recursive function which checks for the presence of digit '*d*' in a given number '*N*', and returns a Boolean value accordingly. '*d*' and '*N*' are obtained as user input. Use the 'main()' as the driver function.

```
bool fun1 (int N, int d){
  if (N == 0)
    return false;
  if (N % 10 == d)
    return true;
  return (fun1(N/10, d));
}

int main(){
  int N, d;
  printf("Type a number and a digit: ");
  scanf("%d %d", &N, &d);
  if (fun1(N,d))
    printf ("digit %d is present in %d\n", d,
N);
  else
    printf ("digit %d is not present in %d\n",
d, N);
}
```

I26 Write a recursive function which computes, and prints out the number of different partitions of a given integer. Partition of an integer is the number of distinct ways of representing it as a sum of natural numbers.

```
int num_partitions (int m, int n)
{
  if (m == 1)
    return (1);
  else if (n == 1)
    return (1);
  else if (m < n)
    return (num_partitions (m, m));
  else if (m == n)
    return (1 + num_partitions (m, m-1));
  else
```

265

```
      return (num_partitions (m, n-1) +
num_partitions (m-n, n));
   }

   main ()
   {
     int num, numpart, i;

     printf ("Type an integer: ");
     scanf ("%d", &num);

     for (i=1; i<=num; i++) {
       numpart = num_partitions (num, i);
       printf ("No. of partitions of %d, each
summand no > than %d = %d\n",
             num, i, numpart);
     }
   }
```

I27 Write a program that computes and prints the square root 'r' of a
     number 'x' using Newton's method, and the number of iterations
     required. Compare it with the value given by the library function.
     An example output is given below.

```
Type the number: 57
Square root of 57.000000 using Newton's method is
7.549835
The number of iterations required was 6
Square root computed by library function =
7.549834
```

Newton's method: Start with r = 1. If 'r' is an approximation to the
square root of 'x', then a better approximation to the square root is
given by: $(x/r + r)/2$. This is iterated till the error converges (*i.e.*
keep itearating until error becomes less than a small number ε, say
0.001.

```
#include <stdio.h>
#include <math.h>
int main() {
  double x, r = 1.0, err;
  int iter = 0;
  printf("Type the number: ");
  scanf("%lf", &x);

  do {
    iter++;
```

```
    r = (x/r + r)/2.0;
    err = r*r - x;
    if (err < 0.0)
       err = -err;
} while (err > 0.001);

  printf("Square root of %lf using Newton's
method is: %lf\n", x, r);
  printf("The number of iterations required was:
%d\n", iter);
  printf("Square root computed by sqrt function
is: %lf\n", sqrt(x));
}
```

I28   Write a function which takes as argument a number *N* (integer), and returns the sum of the sequence: 1/2 + 2/3 + 3/4 + ... + *N*/(*N*+1). Note that the sequence sum is a real number. For example, if *N* = 100, it should output 95.8027.

```
double seriesSum (int n) {
  int i;
  double sum = 0;
  for (i = 1; i <= n; i++) {
    sum += (double)i / (i + 1);
  }
  return sum;
}
```

I29   Write a program to determine the value of *N* (sequence length) when the sum of the sequence: 1/2 + 2/3 + 3/4 + ... + *N*/(*N*+1) exceeds a given value which is read from the keyboard. Assume that the entered sequence sum is > 0.

```
#include <stdio.h>
int main() {
  int n=1;
  double seqsum, sum = 0;
  printf("Type the sequence sum: ");
  scanf("%lf", &seqsum);
  while (sum <= seqsum){
    sum += (double)n / (n + 1);
    n++;
  }
  printf("The value of N when sequence sum
exceeds %lf is %d\n", seqsum, (n-1));
}
```

I30 Write a program to read a number N (integer) from the terminal, and compute π using the first N terms of the approximation given below.

$$\pi = 4\left(1 - \frac{1}{3} + \frac{1}{5} - \frac{1}{7} + \frac{1}{9} - \frac{1}{11} + \cdots + \frac{(-1)^{N+1}}{2N-1}\right)$$

```
#include <stdio.h>
int main() {
    int i, seqLen;
    double Pi, den=1, term, sum = 0;
    printf("Type in the sequence length: ");
    scanf("%d", &seqLen);

    for (i = 1; i <= seqLen; i++) {
        term = 1.0/den;
        if (i % 2 == 0) // even value of i
            term = -term;
        sum += term;
        den += 2;
    }
    Pi = 4.0 * sum;
    printf("The value of π using %d terms is
%lf\n", seqLen, Pi);
}
```

I31 Write a program to read a number N (integer) from the terminal, and compute e, the base of the natural logarithm, using the first N terms of the approximation given below.

$$e = 1 + \frac{1}{1!} + \frac{1}{2!} + \frac{1}{3!} + \cdots + + \frac{1}{N!}$$

```
#include <stdio.h>
int main() {
    int i, seqLen;
    double conste = 1, den=1;
    printf("Type in the sequence length: ");
    scanf("%d", &seqLen);

    for (i = 2; i <= seqLen; i++) {
        conste += 1.0/den;
        den *= i;
    }
    printf("The value of e using %d terms is
%lf\n", seqLen, conste);
}
```

I32 Write a program prints the first "N" numbers of the *Padovan* series. "N" is read from the keyboard. The *Padovan* series is 1,1,1,2,2,3,4,5,7,9,12,16,21,28,37,...   Each number is obtained by skipping the previous one and adding the two before that. Have the program also print the ratio of two successive *Padovan* numbers.

```
#include <stdio.h>
#include <stdlib.h>
int main() {
  int i, seqLen, prev1=1, prev2=1, prev3=1,
num;
  do {
     printf("Enter the Padovan sequence
length [>=1]: ");
     scanf("%d", &seqLen);
  } while (seqLen < 1);

  for (i=1; i<=3 && i<=seqLen; i++)
     printf("1 1.0\n");

  if (seqLen <= 3)
     exit(0);

  seqLen -= 3;
  for (; seqLen > 0; seqLen--) {
     num = prev2 + prev3;
     prev3 = prev2;
     prev2 = prev1;
     prev1 = num;

     printf("%d %.2f\n", num,
(float)prev1/(float)prev2);
  }
}
```

I33 Write a program to compute the amounts after compounding of interest quarterly, monthly, and daily, over a range of years.

A sample output is given below.

```
Type in the principal: 10000
Type in the Interest rate (%): 6.5
Type in the term range (ex. 5 10): 6 12
Yield on 10000.0 at 6.5%
```

		Quarterly	Monthly	Daily
6	Years	14,723.58	14,754.27	14,769.30
7	Years	15,704.19	15,742.39	15,761.10
8	Years	16,750.12	16,796.69	16,819.50
9	Years	17,865.70	17,921.60	17,948.97
10	Years	19,055.59	19,121.84	19,154.30
11	Years	20,324.72	20,402.46	20,440.57
12	Years	21,678.38	21,768.85	21,813.21

```
#include <stdio.h>
#include <math.h>
int main() {
  double amtQty, amtMonthly, amtDaily,
principal, intRate;
  int term1, term2;
  printf("Type in the principal: ");
  scanf("%lf", &principal);
  printf("Type in the Interest rate (%%): ");
  scanf("%lf", &intRate);
  printf("Type in the term range (ex. 5, 10): ");
  scanf("%d %d", &term1, &term2);
  printf("Yield on %.2lf at %.2lf%%\n",
principal, intRate);
  printf(" Compounded    Quarterly    Monthly
Daily\n");
  for (; term1 <= term2; term1++){
    amtQty = principal*pow(1.0 + (intRate
/(100*4)), 4*term1);
    amtMonthly = principal*pow(1.0
+(intRate/(100*12)), 12*term1);
    amtDaily = principal*pow(1.0
+(intRate/(100*365)), 365*term1);
    printf ("%2d %s %12.2f %12.2f %12.2f\n",
term1, "Years", amtQty, amtMonthly, amtDaily);
  }
}
```

I34   The formula for the future value of an Annuity is given below:

$$A = \frac{R\left[\left(1 + \frac{r}{n}\right)^{nt} - 1\right]}{\frac{r}{n}}$$

Where A is the future value of the annuity, R is the regular periodic payment, r is the annual interest rate, n is the number of payments made per year, t is the term of the annuity in years.

Write a program which reads the values of A, r, and printout a
table which gives the monthly payment required to reach the target
with the given interest rate over 5, 10, 15, 20, 25, and 30 years. A
sample output is given below.

```
Type in the target amount: 35000
Type in the interest rate (%): 7.5

Years    Monthly Payment
-----------------------
    5       482.58
   10       196.71
   15       105.70
   20        63.21
   25        39.90
   30        25.98
```

```
int main() {
  int year;
  double targetAmt, intRate, numr, denr;
  printf("Type in the target amount: ");
  scanf("%lf", &targetAmt);
  printf("Type in the interest rate (%%): ");
  scanf("%lf", &intRate);
  printf("Years    Monthly Payment\n");
  printf("-----------------------\n");
  for (year = 5; year <= 30; year += 5) {
    numr = targetAmt * (intRate/100)/12;
    denr = pow((1 + (intRate/100)/12), 12*year) -
1;
    printf ("%5d %10.2f\n", year, numr/denr);
  }
}
```

I35 Write a function which takes as input an Integer N, and prints out N
down to 1 in the first row, (N – 1) down to 1 in the second row, etc.,
and 1 in the last row. For example, if the input value of N is 5, the
output should be:

```
5 4 3 2 1
4 3 2 1
3 2 1
2 1
1
```

```
#include <stdio.h>
void printNumTri (int num){
  int j;
  for (; num >= 1; num--) {
    for (j = num; j >= 1; j--)
      printf("%d ", j);
    putchar('\n');
  }
}
int main() {
  int num;
  printf("Type in the number: ");
  scanf("%d", &num);
  printNumTri (num);
}
```

I36 Write a program which determines the 'day number', given the date. For example, given Dec 18, 1973, it should determine that it is the 352nd day.

```
#include <stdio.h>
#include <stdlib.h>
#include <string.h>

int leap_year (year)
int year;
{
  return ((year % 400 == 0) || (year % 100
!= 0 && year % 4 == 0));
}

int daynum (int month, int day, int year)
{
  int days_in_month[12] = {31, 28, 31, 30,
31, 30, 31, 31, 30, 31, 30, 31};
  int i, ndays = 0;

  if (leap_year (year))
    days_in_month[1] += 1;

  for (i=0; i<month-1; i++)
    ndays += days_in_month[i];

  ndays += day;
```

```
    return (ndays);
}

main ()
{
  int day_num, month, day, year;
  char suffix[2];

  printf ("Type in the date [mm dd yy]: ");
  scanf ("%d %d %d", &month, &day, &year);

  day_num = daynum (month, day, year);

  if (day_num >= 11 && day_num <= 13)
    strcpy (suffix, "th");
  else {
    switch (day_num % 10)
      {
      case 1: strcpy (suffix, "st");
        break;
      case 2: strcpy (suffix, "nd");
        break;
      case 3: strcpy (suffix, "rd");
        break;
      default: strcpy (suffix, "th");
        break;
      }
  }
  printf ("%d/%d/%d is the %d%s day\n",
month, day, year, day_num, suffix);
}
```

I37 Write a program to determine the 'date', given the 'year' and 'day number'. For example, given year as 1973 and day number as 352, the program should print the corresponding date as Dec 18.

```
#include <stdio.h>
#include <stdlib.h>
#include <string.h>


int leap_year (year)
int year;
```

```c
{
  return ((year % 400 == 0) || (year % 100
!= 0 && year % 4 == 0));
}

void find_date (int year, int daynum)
{
  char *mnames[12] = {"Jan", "Feb", "Mar",
"Apr", "May", "Jun", "Jul", "Aug", "Sep",
"Oct", "Nov", "Dec"};
  int days_in_month[12] = {31, 28, 31, 30,
31, 30, 31, 31, 30, 31, 30, 31};
  int date, month=1, ndays=0;

  if (leap_year (year))
    days_in_month[1] += 1;

  while (ndays+days_in_month[month-1] <
daynum) {
    ndays += days_in_month[month-1];
    month++ ;
  }

  date = daynum - ndays;
  printf ("The date is %s %d\n",
mnames[month-1], date);

}

int main ()
{
  int daynum, year, uplim;

  do {
    printf ("Type in the year [YYYY] and day
number: ");
    scanf ("%d %d", &year, &daynum);

    uplim = (leap_year (year)) ? 366 : 365;
  } while (daynum <= 0 || daynum > uplim);

  find_date (year, daynum);
}
```

I38 Write a program to print the Gray code of a given number of bits. The number of bits is specified via user input.

```
#include <stdio.h>
#include <stdlib.h>
#include <string.h>

#define INT_LEN 32

void print_bits (num, k)
int num, k;
{
  int i, mask;
  int bits[32];

  mask = 0x00000001;

  for (i=0; i<32; i++) {
    bits[i] = mask & num >> i;
  }
  for (i=k-1; i >=0; i--)
    printf ("%d", bits[i]);
  printf ("\n");
}

int exp_2 (k)
int k;
{
  int i, n = 1;

  n = n << k;
  return (n);
}

int pow_of_2 (num)
int num;
{
  int i, mask, power, one_seen;

  if (num <= 0)
    exit (1);

  one_seen = 0; mask = 1;
```

```
      for (i=0; i<INT_LEN; i++, num >>= 1) {
        if (num & mask == 1) {
          if (! one_seen) {
            one_seen = 1; power = i;
          }
          else
            return (-1);
        }
      }
      return (power);
    }

int main ()
{
  int i, k, mask, num;

  printf ("This prints the Gray code of a
given number of bits.\n");
  printf ("Type the number of bits: ");
  scanf ("%d", &k);
  if (k < 0)
    exit (1);

  num = 0;
  print_bits (num, k);

  for (i=1; i<exp_2(k); i++) {
    mask = 1;
    if (i % 2 == 0) { /* even number */
      while (! (i & mask) != 0)
        mask = mask << 1;
    }
    num = num ^ mask;

    print_bits (num, k);
  }
  printf ("\n");
}
```

I39 Give a code segment to initialize an integer variable **x** to a given power N of 2 (*i.e.* $x = 2^N$).

```
x = 1;
while (N--)
```

```
x <<= 1;
```

I40 Give a code segment to store in a signed integer variable **x**, the largest positive number which is a power of 2.

```
x = INT_MIN; x = x^(x>>1)
```

Note that in an 'int' which requires 4 bytes, the bits 0 to 30 (right-to-left) are used for the number, and bit 31 (leftmost) is used for the sign. The highest power of 2 will have '1' in bit 30, and all other bits '0's. The following code segment illustrates the above concepts.

```
int x = INT_MIN, y = INT_MAX, z = 1;
printf("%d\n", x);
printf("%d\n", y);
printf("%.01f\n", pow(2,30));
printf("%d\n", x^(x>>1));
printf("%d\n", z<<30);
```

Output:
```
-2147483648
2147483647
1073741824
1073741824
1073741824
```

I41 Suppose an integer variable **x** contains the lowest integer value (**INT_MIN**). Write one statement which will store the maximum integer value (**INT_MAX**) in **x** without direct assignment of **INT_MAX**, but using bit operations.

```
x = ~x;
```

In general, the lowest and highest integer values of a signed integer of N bits are -2^{N-1} are $2^{N-1} - 1$. For a 32 bit integer, the bit pattern for the lowest valued integer will have a '1' in bit position 31 (leftmost), and 0's in bits 30 – 0 [**1000...0**], and the bit pattern for the highest valued integer will have a '0' in bit position 31, and '1' in bits 30 – 0 [**0111...1**]. Thus bit operation(s) to turn **x = 1000...0** to **0111...1** are required, which is done by the bit complement (**~**) operator.

I42 Write a function which takes an integer as argument, and returns the the number of 1's in it.

```
int count1s (int x){
  int num1s = 0;
  for (int i=0; i<sizeof(int)*8-1; i++){
    if (x & 1)
      num1s++;
    x >>= 1;
  }
  return num1s;
}
```

Driver for testing:
```
int main()
{
  int x;
  printf ("Type in a number: ");
  scanf ("%d", &x);
  int n1s = count1s(x);
  printf ("Number of 1's: %d\n", n1s);
  return 0;
}
```

I43 Write a function which takes an integer as argument, and returns the the number of 0's in it.

```
int count0s (int x){
  int num0s = 0;
  for (int i=0; i<sizeof(int)*8-1; i++){
    if (~x & 1)
      num0s++;
    x >>= 1;
  }
  return num0s;
}
```

I44 Write a function which takes a positive integer as argument, and returns the exponent if it is a power of 2, and returns −1, otherwise.

```
#define FALSE 0
#define TRUE 1

int check_pow_2 (int num){
  int one_seen = FALSE, mask = 1, exp;
  for (int i = 0; i < sizeof(int)*8-1; i++){
    if (num & mask){
      if (one_seen)
```

```
            return -1;
         else {
            one_seen = TRUE;
            exp = i;
         }
      }
      mask <<= 1;
   }
   return exp;
}
```

Driver for testing:
```
int main ()
{
   int num, exp;

   printf ("Type a number: ");
   scanf ("%d", &num);
   if (num <= 0)
      exit (1);

   exp = check_pow_2 (num);
   if (exp == -1)
      printf ("%d is not a power of 2.\n", num);
   else
      printf ("%d is 2 raised to %d.\n", num,
exp);
}
```

I45 Give a code segment to check if bit number 6 of an unsigned integer variable **x** is a 1 or 0, and sets a string variable **status** to "Error" or "Okay", accordingly. (Note that the rightmost bit is bit 0)

```
unsigned flag = 1;
status = (x & flag << 6) ? "Error" : "Okay";
```

I46 Write a program which generates a random integer between 1 and 1,000 and have the user guess the number. Based on the input, it should notify the user whether the guess was lower/higher than the generated number. There should be a maximum of 10 guesses allowed.

```
#include <stdio.h>
#include <stdlib.h>
#include <time.h>
int main() {
   const int guessMax = 10;
```

```
  int guess, guessCnt=0;
  printf("This generates a random number between
1 and 1000.\n");
  printf("You are allowed %d guesses.\n",
guessMax);
  printf("It tells you whether your ");
  printf("guess is more or less than the
generated number.\n");
  srand(time(NULL));
  int num = rand()%1000 + 1;
  while (guessCnt < guessMax) {
    printf("Type your guess: ");
    scanf("%d", &guess);
    guessCnt++;
    if (guess == num) {
      printf("Yes! The number is %d\n", num);
      printf("You guessed in %d trials\n",
guessCnt);
      return 0;
    }
    else if (guess < num)
      printf("Your guess is low. ");
    else
      printf("Your guess is high. ");
  }
  printf("You have exceeded the limit on
guesses.\n");
  printf("The number was %d\n", num);
}
```

I47 Write a function which takes as argument two numbers (rows and columns), and prints a rectangle of '*'s.

```
void printRectangle (int nRows, int nCols){
  for (int i = 1; i <= nRows; i++) {
    for (int j = 1; j <= nCols; j++)
      putchar('*');
    putchar('\n');
  }
}
```

I48 Write a function which takes an integer argument which specifies the height of a triangle and prints it using '*'s and spaces. Examples:

```
height 1:        *
```

```
                     *
height 2:           ***


                     *
height 3:           ***
                   *****

void printTriStars (int height){
  for(int i = 1; i <= height; i++){
    for(int j = 1; j <= height-i; j++)
      putchar(' ');
    for(int j = 1; j <= 2*(i-1)+1; j++)
      putchar('*');;
    putchar('\n');
  }
}
```

I49   Write a program to read a number (integer) *N* from the terminal, and
      print an arrow of '*'s of a given height.

```
height 1:    *

                *
height 2:    **
                *

                *
height 3:    **
             ***
             **
                *
```

```
#include <stdio.h>
void printUpTriangle (int height){
  for (int i = 1; i <= height; i++){
    for (int j = 1; j <= i; j++)
      putchar('*');
    putchar('\n');
  }
}
void printDownTriangle (int height){
  for (int i = 1; i <= height; i++){
    for (int j = 1; j <= height-i+1; j++)
      putchar('*');
    putchar('\n');
```

```
    }
  }
  void printArrow (int height){
    printUpTriangle (height);
    printDownTriangle (height-1);
  }
```

I50 Write a function which takes two integer arguments (rows and columns), and prints a "hollow" rectangle of '*'s. (The boundary consists of single '*'s)

```
void hollowRectangle(int rows, int cols) {
  if (rows <= 2 || cols <= 2) {
    for (int i = 1; i <= rows; i++) {
      for (int j = 1; j <= cols; j++)
        putchar('*');
      putchar('\n');
    }
    return;
  }
  for (int j = 1; j <= cols; j++)
    putchar('*');
  putchar('\n');
  for (int i = 2; i <= rows-1; i++) {
    putchar('*');
    for (int j = 2; j <= cols-1; j++)
      putchar(' ');
    putchar('*'); putchar('\n');
  }
  for (int j = 1; j <= cols; j++)
    putchar('*');
  putchar('\n');
}
```

I51 Write a function which takes an integer argument N indicating the number of nested boxes, and prints N nested boxes. The output for values 1, 2 and 3 are given below.

```
                              +----+
               +--+           |+--+|
      ++       |++|           ||++||
      ++       |++|           ||++||
               +--+           |+--+|
                              +----+
void nestedBoxes (int n)
{
  int i, j, k, l;
```

```
for (i=1; i<=2*n; i++) {
  k = (i<=n) ? (i-1) : (2*n-i);
  l = 2*n-2*k-2;

  for (j=1; j<=k; j++)
    putchar ('|');

  putchar ('+');

  for (j=1; j<=l; j++)
    putchar ('-');

  putchar ('+');

  for (j=1; j<=k; j++)
    putchar ('|');

  putchar ('\n');
  }
}
```

This can be tested by calling the function within a main driver function.

I52   Write a function to print an "X" shape of '*'s of a given height.

```
h=1            *


               * *
h=2             *
               * *


             *     *
              * *
h=3            *
              * *
             *     *
```

i	preGap	formula	midGap	formula
1	0	(i–1),	5	(2h–1–2i),
2	1	i ≤ h	3	i < h
3	2		1	
4	3		0	
5	2	(2h–1–i),	1	2(i – h) – 1,
6	1	i > h	3	i > h
7	0		5	

```
void printX(int height) {
  int i, j, preGap, midGap=0;
  for (i = 1; i <= 2*height-1; i++){
    preGap = (i <= height)? (i-1) : (2*height-1-
i);
    midGap = (i < height) ? (2*height-1-2*i) :
2*(i-height)-1;
    for (j = 1; j <= preGap; j++)
      putchar(' ');
    putchar('*');
    for (j = 1; j <= midGap; j++)
      putchar(' ');
    if (i != height){
      putchar('*');
      putchar('\n');
    }
    else
      putchar('\n');
  }
}
```

I53 Write a function to print an "Z" shape of '*'s of a given height.

```
            **
h=2         **

            *  *
h=3          *
            *  *
```

```
                ****
                 *
h=4              *
                ****
```

```c
void printZ (int height){
  int i, j;

  if (height < 2)
    return;
  for (j = 1; j <= height; j++) // topmost line
    putchar('*');
  putchar('\n');
  for (i = 2; i <= height-1; i++){
    for (j = 1; j <= height-i; j++)
      putchar(' ');
    putchar('*'); putchar('\n');
  }
  for (j = 1; j <= height; j++) // last line
    putchar('*');
  putchar('\n');
}
```

I54   Write a function to print an "N" shape of '*'s of a given height.

```
h=2              **
                 **


                 *  *
h=3              ***
                 *  *


                 *    *
h=4              ** *
                 *  **
                 *    *
```

```c
void printN (int height){
  int i, j, sp1, sp2;
  if (height < 2)
    return;
  putchar('*');
  for (j = 2; j <= height-1; j++)
    putchar(' ');
```

```
  putchar('*'); putchar('\n');
  for (i = 2; i <= height-1; i++){
    sp1 = (i-2); sp2 = height-1-i;
    putchar('*');
    for (j = 1; j <= sp1; j++)
      putchar(' ');
    putchar('*');
    for (j = 1; j <= sp2; j++)
      putchar(' ');
    putchar('*'); putchar('\n');
  }
  putchar('*');
  for (j = 2; j <= height-1; j++)
    putchar(' ');
  putchar('*'); putchar('\n');
}
```

I55 Write a function to print an "M" shape of '*'s of a given height.

h=2
```
* *
***
```

h=3
```
 *   *
** **
 * * *
```

h=4
```
 *     *
**     **
 * * * *
 *  *  *
```

```
void printM (int height){
  int i, j, sp1, sp2, sp3;
  if (height < 2)
    return;
// first row
  putchar('*');
  for (j = 1; j <= 2*height-3; j++)
    putchar(' ');
  putchar('*'); putchar('\n');
// rows other than first and last
  for (i = 2; i <= height-1; i++){
    sp1 = sp3 = i-2; sp2 = 2*height-1-2*i;
    putchar('*');
    for (j = 1; j <= sp1; j++)
      putchar(' ');
```

```
        putchar('*');
        for (j = 1; j <= sp2; j++)
          putchar(' ');
        putchar('*');
        for (j = 1; j <= sp3; j++)
          putchar(' ');
        putchar('*'); putchar('\n');
    }
    // last row
    putchar('*');
      for (j = 1; j <= height-2; j++)
        putchar(' ');
    putchar('*');
      for (j = 1; j <= height-2; j++)
        putchar(' ');
      putchar('*'); putchar('\n');
}
```

I56   Write a function to print an "V" shape of '*'s of a given height.

```
h=1             *


h=2             * *
                 *


                *     *
h=3              * *
                  *


                *       *
h=4              *     *
                  * *
                   *
```

```
void printV (int height){
  int i, j, sp1, sp2;
  for (i = 1; i <= height-1; i++){
    sp1=(i-1); sp2=(2*height-1-2*i);
    for (j = 1; j <= sp1; j++)
      putchar(' ');
    putchar('*');
    for (j = 1; j <= sp2; j++)
      putchar(' ');
    putchar('*'); putchar('\n');
  }
```

```
    for (j = 1; j <= height-1; j++)
      putchar(' ');
    putchar('*'); putchar('\n');
}
```

I57 Write a function to print an "K" shape of '*'s of a given height.

h=1   **

             * *
h=2   **
             * *

             *   *
             * *
h=3   **
             * *
             *   *

```
void printK (int height){
  int i, j, spaces=0;
  for (i = 1; i <= 2*height-1; i++){
    spaces = (i <= height)? (height-i) : (i-height);
    putchar('*');
    for (j = 1; j <= spaces; j++)
      putchar(' ');
    putchar('*'); putchar('\n');
  }
}
```

I58 Write functions to (i) print time in HH:MM format, (ii) add two 'times', (iii) subtract two 'times', where 'times' are struct variables. The 'time' struct has two integer members representing hours and minutes. Test them in the main program.

```
typedef struct Time_str {
  unsigned int Hour;
  unsigned int Min;
} Time;
void printTime (Time time){
  if (time.Hour < 10)
    putchar('0');
  printf ("%d:", time.Hour);
  if (time.Min < 10)
```

```
      putchar('0');
    printf ("%d\n", time.Min);
}
Time addTime (Time t1, Time t2){
    Time tSum;
    int min, carry = 0;
    min = t1.Min + t2.Min;
    if (min > 59){
      min = min - 60;
      carry = 1;
    }
    tSum.Min = min;
    tSum.Hour = t1.Hour + t2.Hour + carry;
    return tSum;
}
Time subTime (Time t1, Time t2){
    Time tDiff;
    if (t1.Min < t2.Min){
      tDiff.Hour = t1.Hour - t2.Hour - 1;
      tDiff.Min = t1.Min + 60 - t2.Min;
    }
    else {
      tDiff.Hour = t1.Hour - t2.Hour;
      tDiff.Min = t1.Min - t2.Min;
    }
    return tDiff;
}
int main() {
    Time t1, t2, t3, t4;
    printf ("Type in the hours minutes for t1:
");
    scanf ("%d %d", &t1.Hour, &t1.Min);
    printf ("Type in the hours minutes for t2:
");
    scanf ("%d %d", &t2.Hour, &t2.Min);
    t3 = addTime(t1, t2);
    t4 = subTime(t2, t1);
    printTime(t1);
    printTime(t2);
    printTime(t3);
    printTime(t4);
}
```

I59   Write a function which takes as arguments (i) an array of integers, (ii) the number of elements of the array, (iii) a given number (say, target), and returns the index of the array element which is 'closest' to the target.

```
int find_closest( int arr[], int size, int
target )
{
  int j, diff;
  int min_diff, min_diff_indx;

  min_diff = arr[0] - target;
  if (min_diff < 0 )
     min_diff = - min_diff;
  min_diff_indx = 0;

  for ( j=1; j < size; j++ )
  {
    diff = arr[j] - target;
    if ( diff < 0 ) diff = -diff;

    if ( diff < min_diff )
    {
      min_diff = diff;
      min_diff_indx = j;
    }
  }
  return min_diff_indx;
}
```

I60   Write a function which takes (i) an array of integers, (ii) the array size, and (iii) an integer item, and determines and returns the 'rank' of the given item in the array. In an array of N elements, the smallest element has a rank of 1, the next smallest has a rank of 2, ... and the largest element has a rank of N. If the item is not found, it returns a rank of 0.

```
int rank (int a[], int size, int item)
{
  int i, rank=0, found=FALSE;

  for (i=0; i<size; i++) {
    if (a[i] < item)
```

```
        rank++ ;
      else if (a[i] == item)
        found = TRUE;
    }

    if (found)
      rank++ ;
    else
      rank = 0;

    return (rank);
}
```

I61 Write a program which determines the first common element, if any, in three sorted lists and prints that element and the indices of the three arrays where it occurs. Otherwise, it prints a "Not Found" message. (For simplicity you may assume that elements in each array are distinct. You may use arrays initialized at declaration)

```
int main() {
  int A[] = {2, 5, 6, 10, 14, 17, 23};
  int B[] = {1, 4, 8, 9, 11, 12, 13, 14, 19, 23};
  int C[] = {3, 7, 14, 20, 24};
  int lenA = sizeof(A)/sizeof(int);
  int lenB = sizeof(B)/sizeof(int);
  int lenC = sizeof(C)/sizeof(int);
  int i=0, j=0, k=0;

  while (i < lenA && j < lenB && k < lenC) {
    if ((A[i] == B[j]) && (B[j] == C[k])){
      printf("%d %d %d %d", A[i], i, j, k);
      exit(1);
    }
    if (A[i] <= B[j] && A[i] <= C[k])
      i++;
    else if (B[j] <= A[i] && B[j] <= C[k])
      j++;
    else if (C[k] <= A[i] && C[k] <= B[j])
      k++;
  }
  printf("Not Found\n");
}
```

I62 Write a program to check if a given point is (a) inside, (b) on a border, or (c) outside of a given rectangle.

```c
int main() {
  double lowerLeftX, lowerLeftY, width,
height, Px, Py;
  printf("Type in the lower left corner point
(x,y): ");
  scanf("%lf %lf", &lowerLeftX, &lowerLeftY);
  printf("Type in the width and height: ");
  scanf("%lf %lf", &width, &height);
  printf("Type in the point coordinates (x,y):
");
  scanf("%lf %lf", &Px, &Py);
  unsigned inside = (Px > lowerLeftX && Px <
lowerLeftX+width && Py > lowerLeftY && Py <
lowerLeftY+height);
  unsigned outside = (Px < lowerLeftX || Px >
lowerLeftX+width || Py < lowerLeftY || Py >
lowerLeftY+height);
  if (inside)
    printf ("Point (%.2lf, %.2lf) is inside\n",
Px, Py);
  else if (outside)
    printf ("Point (%.2lf, %.2lf) is outside\n",
Px, Py);
  else if (Px == lowerLeftX && Py >= lowerLeftY
&& Py <= lowerLeftY + height)
    printf ("Point (%.2lf, %.2lf) is on the left
border\n", Px, Py);
  else if (Px == lowerLeftX + width && Py >=
lowerLeftY && Py <= lowerLeftY + height)
    printf ("Point (%.2lf, %.2lf) is on the right
border\n", Px, Py);
  else if (Py == lowerLeftY && Px >= lowerLeftX
&& Px <= lowerLeftX + width)
    printf ("Point (%.2lf, %.2lf) is on the
bottom border\n", Px, Py);
  else if (Py == lowerLeftY + height && Px >=
lowerLeftX && Px <= lowerLeftX + width)
    printf ("Point (%.2lf, %.2lf) is on the top
border\n", Px, Py);
}
```

I63   Write a program to compute the solutions of the quadratic equation $ax^2 + bx + c$, given a, b, and c.

```c
#include<math.h>
int main(){
  double a, b, c, det;
```

```
    printf("Type in the coefficients (a,b,c): ");
    scanf("%lf %lf %lf", &a, &b, &c);
    det = b*b - 4*a*c;
    if (det < 0)
      printf("The roots are complex\n");
    else if (det == 0)
      printf("The roots are equal, and is %.2lf\n",
-b/(2*a));
    else {
      double term = sqrt(det)/2*a;
      printf("The roots are: %.2lf, %.2lf\n", -b +
term, -b - term);
    }
}
```

I64   Write a function which maintains a sorted list of K largest integer values in an array. The function takes as input (a) a sorted array of K integers, (b) the array length, and (c) a key Q, and places Q in the appropriate position. For example, suppose the array is {3, 5, 11, 15, 23}. If the input Q is 2, nothing changes in the array. If Q is 11, nothing changes in the array, If Q is 25, the array becomes {5, 11, 15, 23, 25}. If Q is 19, the array becomes {5, 11, 15, 19, 23}.

```
void KLargest(int KL[], int size, int Q)
{
   if (Q < KL[0])
     return;
   int i=0;
   while (Q > KL[i] && i < size)
     i++;
   if (i < size && KL[i] == Q)
     return;
   i--;
   for (int j = 1; j <= i; j++)
     KL[j-1] = KL[j];
   KL[i] = Q;
}
void print_arr(int arr[], int size)
{
   for (int i=0; i<size; i++)
     printf ("%d ", arr[i]);
   putchar('\n');
}
int main()
{
```

```
    int arr[] = {5, 9, 11, 12, 15, 19, 22, 25};
    int key;
    printf ("Typein an integer: ");
    scanf ("%d", &key);
    print_arr(arr, 8);
    KLargest(arr, 8, key);
    print_arr(arr, 8);
}
```

I65 Write a program to simulate the tossing of a fair coin for different number of tosses, which is read from the keyboard. A sample output is shown below:

```
Enter the no. of trials: 1000
Number of Tails: 496
Number of Heads: 504
```

```
#include <stdio.h>
#include <stdlib.h>
#include <time.h>
enum Face
{
    HEAD, TAIL
};
enum Face tossCoin (){
    return (rand() % 2 == 0 ? TAIL : HEAD);
}

int main ()
{
    int numTrials, tailCnt=0, headCnt=0;
    printf("Enter the no. of trials: ");
    scanf("%d", &numTrials);
    srand (time(NULL)); /* init. random seed */
    for (int i=1; i<=numTrials; i++){
      enum Face faceUp = tossCoin ();
      if (faceUp == TAIL)
        tailCnt++;
      else
        headCnt++;
    }
    printf("Number of Tails: %d\n", tailCnt);
    printf("Number of Heads: %d\n", headCnt);
}
```

I66 Write a program to simulate the tossing of a fair coin for different number of tosses, N: 100, 1,000, 10,000, 100,000. Display the number of outcomes of exactly 3 and exactly 5 consecutive heads coming up.

```
#include <stdio.h>
#include <stdlib.h>
#include <time.h>
enum Face
{
    HEAD, TAIL
};
enum Face tossCoin (){
    return (rand() % 2 == 0 ? TAIL : HEAD);
}

int main ()
{
  int numTrials;
  int headCnt=0, tailCnt=0, consecHeadCnt=0;
  int head3ConsecCnt=0, head5ConsecCnt=0;
  printf("Enter the no. of trials: ");
  scanf("%d", &numTrials);
  srand (time(NULL)); /* init. random seed */
  for (int i=1; i<=numTrials; i++){
    enum Face faceUp = tossCoin ();
    if (faceUp == TAIL){
    tailCnt++;
    if (consecHeadCnt == 3)
      head3ConsecCnt++;
    else if (consecHeadCnt == 5)
      head5ConsecCnt++;
    consecHeadCnt = 0;
    }
    else {
      headCnt++;
      consecHeadCnt++;
    }
  }
  printf("Number of Trials: %d\n", numTrials);
  printf("Number of Tails: %d\n", tailCnt);
  printf("Number of Heads: %d\n", headCnt);
  printf("Number of 3 consecutive heads: %d\n",
head3ConsecCnt);
  printf("Number of 5 consecutive heads: %d\n",
head5ConsecCnt);
}
```

I67 Write a program to simulate the tossing of a fair coin and determine the minimum number of trials required for exactly 3 consecutive heads coming up. Also determine the number of tails and heads. Have the program to run a certain number of runs as specified by an input. A sample output for 2 runs is shown below.

```
Enter the no. of runs: 2
Run number: 1
T T T H H T T H H H H T H T H T T H H H H T H H H T
Number of Trials: 26
Number of Tails: 11
Number of Heads: 15
Run number: 2
H T H H H T
Number of Trials: 6
Number of Tails: 2
Number of Heads: 4
```

```c
#include <stdio.h>
#include <stdlib.h>
#include <time.h>
#define FALSE 0
#define TRUE 1
enum Face
{
    HEAD, TAIL
};
enum Face tossCoin (){
    return (rand() % 2 == 0 ? TAIL : HEAD);
}
int main() {
  int numRuns;
  printf("Enter the no. of runs: ");
  scanf("%d", &numRuns);
srand (time(NULL)); /* init. random seed */
for (int i=1; i<=numRuns; i++){
    int headCnt=0, tailCnt=0, numTrials=0;
    int consecHeadCnt=0;
    unsigned head3Consec = FALSE;
    printf("Run number: %d\n", i);
    while (head3Consec != TRUE){
      enum Face faceUp = tossCoin ();
      numTrials++;
      if (faceUp == TAIL)
        printf("T ");
      else
```

```
      printf("H ");
    if (faceUp == TAIL){
      tailCnt++;
      if (consecHeadCnt == 3)
        head3Consec = TRUE;
      consecHeadCnt = 0;
    }
    else {
      headCnt++;
      consecHeadCnt++;
    }
  }// endwhile
  printf("\nNumber of trials until exactly 3
consecutive heads coming up: %d\n", numTrials);
  printf("Number of Tails: %d\n", tailCnt);
  printf("Number of Heads: %d\n", headCnt);
}// endfor
}
```

I68 Write a program to simulate the roll of a fair die, and to count the number of times each of the faces comes up in a given number of trials. The number of trials is given as user input. A sample output is shown below.

```
Enter the no. of trials: 10000
Number of trials = 10000
Face   No. of times
1        1635
2        1714
3        1680
4        1653
5        1675
6        1643
```

```
#include <stdio.h>
#include <stdlib.h>
#include <time.h>
#define NUM_FACES 6
int roll_die (){
   return rand()%NUM_FACES + 1;
}
int main() {
  int face_up, num_trials;
  int face_cnt[] = {0, 0, 0, 0, 0, 0};
  printf("Enter the no. of trials: ");
  scanf("%d", &num_trials);
```

```
      srand (time(NULL)); /* init. random seed */
      for (int i = 1; i <= num_trials; i++){
        face_up = roll_die ();
        face_cnt[face_up-1]++;
      }
      printf("Number of trials = %d\n", num_trials);
      printf("Face  No. of times\n");
      for (int i = 0; i < NUM_FACES; i++)
        printf("%d        %d\n", i+1, face_cnt[i]);
    }
```

I69 Simulate and determine the number of throws of a single die until all faces have come up. A sample output is shown below. Note that the theoretical expected number of throws is $6/6 + 6/5 + 6/4 + 6/3 + 6/2 + 6/1 \approx 14.7$

Sample output:
```
2 5 2 1 3 4 2 3 4 4 2 4 3 5 6
Number of trials required for all faces to come
up was 15
```

```
#include <stdio.h>
#include <stdlib.h>
#include <time.h>
#define NUM_FACES 6
#define FALSE 0
#define TRUE 1
int roll_die (){
    return rand()%NUM_FACES + 1;
}
int main() {
  unsigned face_cameup[] = {FALSE, FALSE, FALSE,
FALSE, FALSE, FALSE};
  unsigned all_faces_up = FALSE;
  int face_up, num_trials = 0;
  srand (time(NULL)); /* init. random seed */
  while (all_faces_up == FALSE){
    all_faces_up = TRUE;
    face_up = roll_die ();
    num_trials++;
    face_cameup[face_up-1] = TRUE;
    printf("%d ", face_up);
    for (int i = 0; i < NUM_FACES; i++)
        all_faces_up = all_faces_up &&
face_cameup[i];
  } // while
```

```
    printf("\nNumber of trials required for all
faces to come up was %d\n", num_trials);
}
```

I70   Write a function which takes an array of integers and its length as
       arguments and checks if it has duplicates. It and returns true or false
       based on whether the array has duplicates or not.

```
#define FALSE 0
#define TRUE 1
unsigned checkDupl (int arr[], int len){
    for (int i=0; i<len-1; i++){
        for (int j=i; j<len; j++){
            if (arr[i] == arr[j+1])
                return TRUE;
        }
    }
    return FALSE;
}
```

I71   Write a function which takes an array of integers and its length as
       arguments, and prints out the elements such that repeating
       (duplicate) elements are printed just once. For example, if the input
       is: 5 2 7 2 4 7 8 12 3 2 3 2 9 2 4, the output should
       be: 5 2 7 4 8 12 3 9

```
#define FALSE 0
#define TRUE 1
void print_distinct(int arr[], int len){
    for (int i=0; i<len; i++) {
        bool isDistinct = TRUE;
        for (int j=0; j<i; j++) {
            if(arr[i] == arr[j]) {
                isDistinct = FALSE;
                break;
            }
        }
        if(isDistinct)
            printf("%d ", arr[i]);
    }
}
```

172   Write a function which takes an array of integers and its length as arguments, and prints out only the unique (non-repeating) and returns a count of the unique elements. For example, if the input is:
5 2 7 2 4 7 8 12 3 2 3 2 9 2 4 the output should be:
5 8 12 9 and the return value should be 4.

```c
#define TRUE 1
#define FALSE 9

int count_unique (int a[], int size)
{
  int i, j, count=0, dupl_found;

  for (i=0; i<size; i++) {
    dupl_found = FALSE;
    for (j=0; j<size; j++) {
      if ((i != j) && (a[i] == a[j])) {
      dupl_found = TRUE;
      break;
      }
    }
    if (dupl_found == FALSE) {
      count++ ;
      printf ("%d ", a[i]);
    }
  }
  return (count);
}

void print_array (int a[], int size)
{
  int i;

  for (i=0; i<size; i++)
    printf ("%2d   ", a[i]);
  printf ("\n");
}

void rand_init2_array (int a[], int size, int
intrvl)
{
  int i;

  for (i=0; i<size; i++)
    a[i] = rand() % intrvl+1;
}

int main ()
```

```
{
    int a[20], unique_cnt;
    rand_init2_array (a, 20, 15);

    print_array (a, 20);

    unique_cnt = count_unique (a, 20);
    printf ("\nNo. of unique elements = %d\n",
unique_cnt);
}
```

I73 Write a function which takes a sorted array and its length as arguments, and prints the starting index of the most occurring number, the number, and the number of occurrences. If all the elements are distinct, then it does not print anything.

```
void find_most_occur(int arr[], int len) {
    int cnt=1;
    int mode = arr[0], num_mode=1, mode_index=0;
    for (int i=1; i<len; i++) {
        if(arr[i] != arr[i-1]){
            if (cnt > num_mode){
                mode = arr[i-1];
                num_mode = cnt;
                mode_index = i-cnt;
            }
            cnt = 1;
        }
        else
        cnt++;
    }
    if (num_mode > 1) {
        printf("Most occurring number: %d\n", mode);
        printf("Starting index: %d\n", mode_index);
        printf("Number of occurrences: %d\n",
num_mode);
    }
}
```

I74 Write a program to determine and print out the elements of an array of integers that are repeated, along with the indices of the first occurrence and the repetitions. For example, if the input array is:
17, 7, 18, 2, 3, 18, 18, 16, 3, 18, 17, 4, 10, 19, 3, 11, 10, 8, 16, 8

the output should be:

```
17 at [0] repeated at indices:  10
18 at [2] repeated at indices:  5 6 9
3 at [4] repeated at indices:  8 14
16 at [7] repeated at indices:  18
10 at [12] repeated at indices:  16
8 at [17] repeated at indices:  19
```

```c
#include <stdio.h>
#include <stdlib.h>
#define FALSE 0
#define TRUE 1
void check_dupl(int numlist[], int len) {
  unsigned* dupl = calloc(len, sizeof(unsigned));
  for (int i = 0; i < len; i++)
    dupl[i] = FALSE;
  printf("Original list:\n");
  for (int i = 0; i < len; i++)
    printf("%d ", numlist[i]);
  putchar('\n');
  for (int i=0; i < len-1; i++){
    unsigned firstSeen = TRUE;
    for (int j = i+1; j < len; j++){
      if (numlist[i] == numlist[j]){
        if (dupl[i] == FALSE && firstSeen ==
TRUE) {
            printf("\n%d at [%d] repeated at
indices: ", numlist[i], i);
        firstSeen = FALSE;
        }
        if (dupl[j] == FALSE){
          printf("%d ", j);
          dupl[j] = TRUE;
        } // inner if
      } // outer if
    } // inner for
  } // outer for
}
```

The sample **main()** used as 'driver function' is given below.

```c
int main()
{
    int arr[] = {17, 7, 18, 2, 3, 18, 18, 16, 3,
18, 17, 4, 10, 19, 3, 11, 10, 8, 16, 8};
    check_dupl(arr, 20);
}
```

I75   Write a function which takes an array and its length as arguments, and prints a 'histogram' based on values in the array. It. A sample output for array of {5, 3, 2, 7, 4} is shown below.

```
    *
    *
 *  *
 *  **
** **
*****
*****
```

```
void printHist (int arr[], int len){
  int max=arr[0];
  for (int i=1; i<len; i++){
    if (arr[i] > max)
      max = arr[i];
  }
  for (int h=max; h>=1; h--){
    for (int i=0; i<len; i++){
      if (arr[i] < h)
        putchar(' ');
      else
        putchar('*');
    }
    putchar('\n');
  }
}
```

I76   Write a function to partition an array into ODD and EVEN integers. After partition, the array will have all odd elements followed by all even elements. It takes an array as an argument and partitions it in-place.

```
void partitionOddEven (int arr[], int len){
  int i = 0, j = len-1;
  while (i < j){
    while (arr[i] % 2 != 0 && i<j)
      i++;
    while (arr[j] % 2 == 0 && j>i)
      j--;
    int temp=arr[i];arr[i]=arr[j];arr[j]=temp;
    i++; j--;
  }
}
```

}

I77 Write a function to print common elements in two sorted arrays, each having distinct values.

```
void printCommonElements (int arr1[], int
len1, int arr2[], int len2){
  int i = 0, j = 0;
  printf("Common elements:");
  while (i < len1 && j < len2){
    if (arr1[i] < arr2[j])
      i++;
    else if (arr1[i] > arr2[j])
      j++;
    else {// arr1[i] equals arr2[j]
      printf("%d ", arr1[i]);
      i++; j++;
    }
  }
}
```

I78 Write a function which takes (i) an array 'a' of integers, (ii) the size of the array, and (iii) an array 'permu_arr' which specifies a permutation of the indices, and permutes the data in array 'a' in-place, based on the specified permutation.

```
void permute_arr (int a[], int size, int
permu_arr[]){
  int i;
  int *temp;

  temp = (int *)calloc (size, sizeof(int));

  for (i=0; i<size; i++)
    temp[i] = a[permu_arr[i]];

  for (i=0; i<size; i++)
    a[i] = temp[i];

  free (temp);
}
```

I79 Write a program to simulate the fall of marbles in a Galton board. Show the outcome graphically. Shown below is a 3-level Galton board.

```
    o
   o o
  o o o
 | | | | |
 | | | | |
 +-+-+-+-+
```

```c
#include <stdio.h>

double drand48();
double erand48(unsigned short []);

#define SCRN_CTR 40
#define LEVELS   10

void draw_pegs (int nlvls)
{
  int i, n;

  for (n=1; n<=nlvls; n++) {
    for (i=0; i<(SCRN_CTR-n); i++)
      putchar (' ');
    for (i=1; i<=n; i++)
      printf ("o ");
    printf ("\n");
  }
}

void draw_bins (int nlvls)
{
  int i;

  for (i=0; i<(SCRN_CTR-nlvls-2); i++)
    putchar (' ');
  for (i=1; i<=nlvls+2; i++)
    printf ("| ");
  printf ("\n");

  for (i=0; i<(SCRN_CTR-nlvls-2); i++)
    putchar (' ');
  for (i=1; i<=nlvls+2; i++)
```

```
      printf ("| ");
    printf ("\n");

    for (i=0; i<(SCRN_CTR-nlvls-2); i++)
      putchar (' ');
    for (i=1; i<nlvls+2; i++)
      printf ("+-");
    printf ("+\n");
}

void draw_histogram (int count[], int nbins)
{
  int n, max = -1, total=0, freq;
  char c;

  for (n=0; n<nbins; n++) {
    total += count[n];
    if (count[n] > max)
      max = count[n];
  }

  for (n=0; n<nbins; n++)
    count[n] = count[n] * 100 / total;

  for (freq=max*100/total; freq>0; freq--) {
    for (n=0; n<nbins; n++) {
      c = (count[n] >= freq) ? '*' : ' ';
      putchar (c);
    }
    putchar ('\n');
  }
}

void simulate_marble_drop (int nmarbles, int
count[], int nlvls)
{
  int l, n, x;
  double r;
  unsigned short rsubi[3];

  for (n=1; n<=nmarbles; n++) {
    x = 0;
    for (l=1; l<=nlvls; l++) {
      r = erand48 (rsubi);
```

```
        if (r <= 0.5)
    x-- ;
        else
    x++ ;
      }
      count[(nlvls+x)/2]++ ;
    }
}

int main ()
{
  int i, nmarbles;
  int count[LEVELS+1] = {0};

  printf ("Type the number of marbles in the
simulation: ");
  scanf ("%d", &nmarbles);

  simulate_marble_drop (nmarbles, count,
LEVELS);

  draw_pegs (LEVELS);
  draw_bins (LEVELS);
  draw_histogram (count, LEVELS+1);
}
```

I80 Mathematically, a square matrix A is said to be symmetric if $A(i, j)$ = $A(j, i)$ for all valid i, j. Write a function which takes a 2D array and its size as arguments, and checks if the matrix is symmetric or not, and returns 'true' or 'false' accordingly.

```
#define FALSE 0
#define TRUE 1
unsigned isSymmetric (int** mat, int size){
  for (int row = 1; row < size; row++){
    for (int col = 0; col < row; col++)
      if (mat[row][col] != mat[col][row])
        return FALSE;
  }
  return TRUE;
}
```

181 Write a function which takes a square matrix and its size as arguments, and transposes the matrix. The transpose A^T of a matrix A is such that $A^T(i,j) = A(j,i)$.

```
void transpose(int** arr, int size){
  for (int r = 0; r < size; r++){
    for (int c = 0; c < r; c++){
      int temp = arr[r][c];
      arr[r][c] = arr[c][r];
      arr[c][r] = temp;
    }
  }
}
```

182 Write a function to initialize a square matrix to an Identity matrix, where all diagonal elements are 1's and all the remaining elements are 0's.

```
void init_id_matrix (int** arr, int size){
for (i=0; i<size; i++)
  for (j=0; j<size; j++)
    arr[i][j] = (i==j) ? 1 : 0;
}
```

183 Write a function which takes a square array and its size as arguments, and rotates it clock-wise by 90 degrees. The rotation is done in-place, without using any temporary array. Test this by using functions for creating a dynamic array of a given size (given as user input), initializing with random numbers, and printing the array.

```
int ** create_sq_array (int size){
  int **ap, i, j;
  ap = (int **) calloc (size, sizeof (int *));
  for (i=0; i<size; i++) {
    ap[i]=(int *) calloc (size, sizeof (int));
  }
  return (ap);
}

void rand_init_sq_array (int **a, int size){
  int i, j;

  for (i=0; i<size; i++)
```

```
   for (j=0; j<size; j++)
      a[i][j] = rand()%20+1;
}

void print_sq_array (int **a, int size){
   int i, j;

   for (i=0; i<size; i++) {
      for (j=0; j<size; j++)
         printf ("%3d", a[i][j]);
      printf ("\n");
   }
   printf ("\n");
}

void rotate_sq_array (int **a, int size){
   int i, j, k, n, temp;

   i = j = 0;

   for (n=size; n>=2; n-=2) {
      for (k=0; k<n-1; k++) {
         temp = a[i][j+k];
         a[i][j+k] = a[size-1-i-k][j];
         a[size-1-i-k][j] = a[size-1-i][size-1-
j-k];
         a[size-1-i][size-1-j-k] = a[i+k][size-
1-j];
         a[i+k][size-1-j] = temp;
      }
      i++; j++;
   }
}

int main ()
{
   int size, **a;

   printf ("Type the size of the array: ");
   scanf ("%d", &size);

   a = create_sq_array (size);
   rand_init_sq_array (a, size);
   print_sq_array (a, size);
```

```
    rotate_sq_array (a, size);
    printf ("Rotated array:\n");
    print_sq_array (a, size);
}
```

I84 Write a function which takes a string as argument, and checks if the
     string is a palindrome or not, and returns 'true' or 'false' accordingly.

```
#define FALSE 0
#define TRUE 1
bool isPalindrome(string str) {
  int i = 0, j = str.length() - 1;
  while (i < j) {
    if (str[i] != str[j])
      return FALSE;
    i++;
    j--;
  }
  return TRUE;
}
```

I85 Write a function which takes an integer 'N' (≥ 1) as argument, and
     generates the 'Pascal triangle' of height 'N', and returns it. 'Pascal
     triangle' is a triangular array of binomial coefficients. An example
     with N = 5 is shown below.

```
1
1 1
1 2 1
1 3 3 1
1 4 6 4 1
```

```
int** pascalTriangle(int N){
  int** pascal_tri = calloc(N, sizeof(int*));
  for (int i = 0; i < N; i++){
    pascal_tri[i] = calloc(i+1, sizeof(int));
    pascal_tri[i][0] = pascal_tri[i][i] = 1;
    for (int j = 1; j < i; j++)
      pascal_tri[i][j] = pascal_tri[i-1][j] +
pascal_tri[i-1][j-1];
  }
  return pascal_tri;
}
```

The sample **main()** used as 'driver function' is given below.

```
int main()
{
  int N = 5;
  int ** pas_tri = pascalTriangle(N);
   for (int i = 0; i < N; i++){
      for (int j = 0; j <= i; j++)
         printf("%d ", pas_tri[i][j]);
      putchar('\n');
   }
}
```

I86 Write a function which takes a 2D array as argument, and determines the minimum and maximum elements, and returns them in an array of two elements.

```
int* find_minmax (int** mat, int nrows, int
ncols)
{
  int* minmax = calloc(2, sizeof(int));
  minmax[0] = minmax[1] = mat[0][0];
  for (int row = 0; row < nrows; row++){
    for (int col = 0; col < ncols; col++){
      if (mat[row][col] < minmax[0])
        minmax[0] = mat[row][col];
      else if (mat[row][col] > minmax[1])
        minmax[1] = mat[row][col];
    }
  }
  return minmax;
}
```

The sample **main()** used as 'driver function' is given below.

```
void print_2d_array (int** arr, int size)
{
  for (int i=0; i<size; i++){
    for (int j=0; j<size; j++)
      printf("%2d ", arr[i][j]);
    putchar('\n');
  }
}

int main()
```

```
    {
      const int SIZE = 9;
      int** arr2d = calloc(SIZE, sizeof(int*));
      srand (time(NULL));
      for (int i=0; i<SIZE; i++){
        arr2d[i] = calloc(SIZE, sizeof(double));
        for (int j=0; j<SIZE; j++){
          arr2d[i][j] = 5 + rand()% 50;
        }
      }
      print_2d_array (arr2d, SIZE);
      int* mm = find_minmax (arr2d, 9, 9);
      printf ("min: %d, max: %d\n", mm[0], mm[1]);
    }
```

I87   An N x N unit matrix is a matrix of N rows and N columns where all the diagonal elements are '1's and all the remaining elements are '0's. Write a function which takes a 2D array of integers and its size as arguments, and returns 'true' or 'false' if the matrix corresponding to the 2D array is a unit matrix or not.

```
#define FALSE 0
#define TRUE 1
unsigned isUnitMatrix (int** mat, int size){

  for (int row = 0; row < size; row++){
    for (int col = 0; col < size; col++){
      if (row != col){
        if (mat[row][col] != 0)
          return FALSE;
      }
      else if (mat[row][col] != 1)
        return FALSE;
    }
  }
  return TRUE;
}
```

I88   Write a function which takes as arguments a 2D square array of integers and its size (number of rows), and returns 'true' if all the elements are distinct, and 'false', otherwise.

```
#define FALSE 0
#define TRUE 1
unsigned no_dupl (int** arr, int size){
```

```
int i, j, k, l, check_item;
for (i = 0; i < size; i++){
  for (j = 0; j < size; j++){
    check_item = arr[i][j];
    for (l = j+1; l < size; l++)
      if (check_item == arr[i][l])
        return FALSE;

    for (k = i+1; k < size; k++)
      for (l = 0; l < size; l++)
        if (check_item == arr[k][l])
          return FALSE;
  }
}
return TRUE;
}
```

The sample **main()** used as 'driver function' is given below. The function can be tested for various other values in the array.

```
int main()
{
  const int N = 3;
  int** arr = calloc(N, sizeof(int*));

  for (int i = 0; i < N; i++){
    arr[i] = calloc(N, sizeof(int));
    for (int j = 0; j < N; j++) {
      arr[i][j] = (i+3)*2 + (j+5)*3; //some init
      printf("%d ", arr[i][j]);
    }
    putchar('\n');
  }
  if (no_dupl (arr, N))
    printf ("All elements are distinct\n");
  else
    printf ("There are some duplicates\n");
  return 0;
}
```

I89 A Magic Square is N x N matrix of integers such that the sum of every row, column, and diagonal is the same. Write a function which takes a 2D array as an argument and returns true/false depending on whether the array is a magic square or not.

```c
#define FALSE 0
#define TRUE 1
unsigned isMagicSquare (int** mSquare, int
size){
  int sum1=0, sum2;

  //check if all elements are distinct
  if (! no_dupl (mSquare, size))
    return FALSE;

  //get sum of 1st row
  for (int col = 0; col < size; col++)
    sum1 += mSquare[0][col];
  // check rows
  for (int row = 1; row < size; row++){
    sum2 = 0;
    for (int col = 0; col < size; col++)
      sum2 += mSquare[row][col];
    if (sum2 != sum1)
      return FALSE;
  }

  // check columns
  for (int col = 0; col < size; col++){
    sum2 = 0;
    for (int row = 0; row < size; row++)
      sum2 += mSquare[row][col];
    if (sum2 != sum1)
      return FALSE;
  }

  // check TopLeft-to-BottomRight diagonal
  sum2 = 0;
  for (int i = 0; i < size; i++)
    sum2 += mSquare[i][i];
  if (sum2 != sum1)
    return FALSE;

  // check TopRight-BottemLeft diagonal
  sum2 = 0;
  for (int i = size-1; i >= 0; i--)
    sum2 += mSquare[i][i];
  if (sum2 != sum1)
    return FALSE;
```

```
    return TRUE;
}
```

I90   The pair-wise distances between 'N' cities are given in a triangular array, as shown below. Write a function which takes the 'distance' array and its size as inputs, and prints out the farthest pair of cities and their distance. An example of pair-wise distance of 10 cities, and the expected output is given below. (Note: The C's marked in red are not part of the array).

	C1	C2	C3	C4	C5	C6	C7	C8	C9
C10	202.26	164.96	134.24	181.28	205.76	77.31	10.87	103.76	240.65
C9	98.01	167.79	28.84	38.30	41.42	196.61	120.22	83.76	
C8	212.39	86.70	195.99	210.22	227.05	91.37	93.19		
C7	210.84	194.46	153.12	39.87	10.73	59.35			
C6	119.70	51.58	188.96	248.81	124.86				
C5	237.66	239.67	23.41	125.51					
C4	110.72	161.45	103.84						
C3	182.53	39.73							
C2	16.43								

Max distance is 248.81 between cities 6 and 4

```
void farthest_pair(double** distArray, int
size)
{
   int i, j, maxIndex1=0, maxIndex2=0;
   double maxDist = 0;
   for (i=0; i<size-1; i++){
     for (j=0; j<size-1-i; j++){
       if (distArray[i][j] > maxDist){
         maxDist = distArray[i][j];
         maxIndex1 = i; maxIndex2 = j;
       }
     }
   }
   printf("Largest distance is %.2f", maxDist);
   printf(" between cities %d and %d\n", size-
maxIndex1, maxIndex2+1);
}
```

The sample **main()** used as 'driver function' is given below.

```c
void print_dist_array (double** distArray, int size)
{
  for (int i=0; i<size; i++){
    for (int j=0; j<size-i; j++)
      printf(" %6.2f ", distArray[i][j]);
    putchar('\n');
  }
}

int main()
{
  const int SIZE = 9;
  double** distArray = calloc(SIZE, sizeof(double*));
  srand (time(NULL));
  for (int i=0; i<SIZE; i++){
    distArray[i] = calloc(SIZE-i, sizeof(double));
    for (int j=0; j<SIZE-i; j++){
      distArray[i][j] = 50 + (double)rand()/RAND_MAX*250;
    }
  }
  print_dist_array (distArray, SIZE);
  farthest_pair(distArray, SIZE);
}
```

IOIOIOIOIOIOIOIOIOIOIOIOIOIOIOIOIOIOIOIOIOIOIOIOIOIOIOIOIOIOIOI

Books on C Programming

- C Programming Language (2nd Edition). Brian W. Kernighan and Dennis M. Ritchie. Pearson, 1988. ISBN: 978-0131103627.

- C: A Reference Manual (5th Edition). Samuel Harbison and Guy Steele Jr. Pearson, 2002. ISBN : 978-0130895929.

- C Programming: A Modern Approach (2nd Edition). K. N. King. W. W. Norton & Company, 2008. ISBN: 978-0393979503.

- Programming in C (Developer's Library) (4th Edition). Stephen Kochan. Addison-Wesley Professional, 2014. ISBN: 978-0321776419.

- C in a Nutshell: The Definitive Reference (2nd Edition). Peter Prinz and Tony Crawford. O'Reilly Media, 2016. ISBN: 978-1491904756.

- Practical C Programming (Nutshell Handbooks) (3rd Edition). Steve Oualline. O'Reilly Media, 1997. ISBN: 978-1565923065.

- Understanding and Using C Pointers. Richard M Reese. O'Reilly Media, 2013. ISBN: 978-1449344184.

- 21st Century C: C Tips from the New School (2nd Edition). Ben Klemens. O'Reilly Media, 2014. ISBN: 978-1491903896

Other Related Quiz Books

	This is a quick assessment book / quiz book. It has a vast collection of over 1,100 questions on Data Structures. Questions have a wide range of difficulty levels and are designed to test a thorough understanding of the topical material. The coverage includes elementary and advanced data structures – Arrays (single/multidimensional); Linked lists (singly–linked, doubly–linked, circular); Stacks; Queues; Heaps; Hash tables; Binary trees; Binary search trees; Balanced trees (AVL trees, Red–Black trees, B–trees/B+ trees); Graphs.
	This is a quick assessment book / quiz book. It has a vast collection of over 900 questions, with answers on Algorithms. The book covers questions on standard (classical) algorithm design techniques; sorting and searching; graph traversals; minimum spanning trees; shortest path problems; maximum flow problems; elementary concepts in P and NP Classes. It also covers a few specialized areas – string processing; polynomial operations; numerical & matrix computations; computational geometry & computer graphics
	This is a quick assessment book / quiz book. It has a wide variety of over 1,600 questions, with answers on Operating Systems. The questions have a wide range of difficulty levels and are designed to test a thorough understanding of the topical material. The book covers questions on the operating systems structures, fundamentals of processes and threads, CPU scheduling, process synchronization, deadlocks, memory management, I/O subsystem, and mass storage (disk) structures.

Computer Security Quiz Book A Compendium of over 1,700 short questions with answers S.R. Subramanya	This is a quick assessment book / quiz book. It has a wide variety of over 1,700 questions, with answers on Computer Security. The questions have a wide range of difficulty levels and are designed to test a thorough understanding of the topical material. The book covers all the major topics in a typical first course in Computer Security – Cryptography, Authentication and Key Management, Software and Operating Systems Security, Malware, Attacks, Network Security, and Web Security.
Programming Languages and Compilers Quiz Book A Compendium of ~1,400 short questions with answers S.R. Subramanya	This is a quick assessment book / quiz book. It has wide variety of ~1,400 questions on Programming Languages and Compilers. It covers questions on: Bindings and Scopes, Data types, Expressions and Assignment statements, Subprograms and Parameter passing mechanisms, Abstract Data Types, Object- Oriented constructs, and Exception handling. The topics related to Compilers include programming language syntax and semantics, lexical analysis, parsing, and different parsing techniques.
 **Java Quiz Book** A Compendium of over 1,200 questions, with answers and programs S.R. Subramanya	This is a quick assessment book / quiz book. It has a vast collection of over 1,200 short questions, with answers and programs, on Java programming language. The topical coverage includes data types, control structures, arrays, classes, objects, and methods, inheritance and polymorphism, exception handling, and stream and text I/O

	This is a quick assessment book / quiz book. It has a vast collection of over 1,000 short questions, with answers and programs, on C++ programming language. The topical coverage includes data types, control structures, arrays, pointers and reference, classes and objects, inheritance and polymorphism, exception handling, and stream and text I/O.
	This is a quick assessment book / quiz book. It has a vast collection of over 1,500 short questions with answers. The topical coverage includes the various layers of the Internet (TCP/IP) protocol stack (going from the actual transmission of signals to the applications that users use) – physical layer, data link layer, network layer, transport layer, and application layer, network security, and Web security.
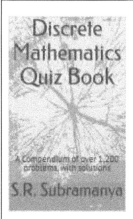	This is a self–assessment / quiz /exercise book. It has a vast collection of over 1,200 questions, with solutions, in Discrete Mathematics. Questions have a wide range of difficulty levels and are designed to test a thorough understanding of the topical material. The topical coverage includes: Logic and Proof methods, Sets, Functions, Relations, Properties of integers, Sequences, Induction and Recursion, Basic and advanced counting methods, Discrete probability, Graph theory, Modeling computation, and Boolean algebra.